TEACHING RESEARCH METHODS IN THE SOCIAL SCIENCES

Teaching Research Methods in the Social Sciences

Edited by

MARK GARNER
University of Aberdeen, UK

CLAIRE WAGNER
University of Pretoria, South Africa

BARBARA KAWULICH
University of West Georgia, USA

ASHGATE

Published by
Ashgate Publishing Limited
Wey Court East
Union Road
Farnham
Surrey, GU9 7PT
England

Ashgate Publishing Company
Suite 420
101 Cherry Street
Burlington
VT 05401-4405
USA

www.ashgate.com

British Library Cataloguing in Publication Data
Teaching research methods in the social sciences.
1. Social sciences--Research--Methodology--Study and teaching.
I. Garner, Mark. II. Wagner, Claire. III. Kawulich, Barbara.
300.7'2-dc22

Library of Congress Cataloging-in-Publication Data
Teaching research methods in the social sciences / edited by Mark Garner, Claire Wagner, and Barbara Kawulich.
    p. cm.
Includes bibliographical references and index.
ISBN 978-0-7546-7352-1 (hardback) -- ISBN 978-0-7546-7354-5 (pbk.)
1. Social sciences--Methodology--Study and teaching. 2. Social sciences--Research--Study and teaching. 3. Social sciences--Research--Methodology. I. Garner, Mark. II. Wagner, Claire. III. Kawulich, Barbara.

    H62.T286 2009
    001.4'2--dc22

2009009819

ISBN   978 0 7546 7352 1 (hbk)
ISBN   978 0 7546 7354 5 (pbk)
ISBN   978 0 7546 9147 1 (ebk)

Mixed Sources
Product group from well-managed forests and other controlled sources
www.fsc.org Cert no. SGS-COC-2482
© 1996 Forest Stewardship Council

Printed and bound in Great Britain by
TJ International Ltd, Padstow, Cornwall

Contents

List of Figures

List of Tables

Notes on Contributors

Grace Brown is a Lecturer in the School of Social Work and Social Policy at La Trobe University, Bendigo, Australia. She became interested in social work practice research as an active member of a practice-based research interest group, auspiced by the Australian Association of Social Workers. She has taught research methods in social work for the past seven years and is currently engaged in PhD research in the area of educating social workers for rural practice. She has presented several papers on her PhD topic and has also presented at international conferences about teaching research methods to social workers.

David W. Carroll is Professor of Psychology and Associate Dean of Academic Affairs at the University of Wisconsin-Superior. He received a BA in psychology and philosophy from the University of California at Davis and an MA and PhD in experimental and developmental psychology from Michigan State University. He teaches courses in the psychology of language, cognitive psychology and the history of psychology, and conducts research on the teaching of psychology and the linguistic analysis of written text.

Phil Francis Carspecken is Professor of Inquiry and Philosophy in the School of Education at Indiana University (Bloomington). His interests are in philosophy, social theory and methodological theory. He is the author of a number of books, including: *Critical Ethnography in Educational Research*; *Four Scenes for Posing the Question of Meaning*; and (with Xuehui Xie) *Philosophy, Learning and the Mathematics Curriculum*.

Virginia A. Dickson-Swift is a Lecturer in the Department of Public Health at La Trobe University, Bendigo, Australia. She specializes in qualitative methods and has been teaching research methods units to both undergraduate and postgraduate students undertaking a variety of health courses for the past five years. She is interested in RM curriculum design that incorporates mixed methodologies and has presented a range of papers at both national and international conferences.

Mark A. Earley is an Associate Professor of Educational Research and Statistics at Bowling Green State University in Bowling Green, Ohio, USA. He has taught doctoral level educational research methods courses covering quantitative, qualitative and mixed methods approaches, and a master's level introductory course. He has worked with over 50 students on their theses and dissertations. His scholarship in recent years explores reflective teaching and the teaching and learning of research methods, including guest editorship of a special issue of the *Journal of Research Practice* in which 11 graduate students reflected on their research experiences.

José Antonio Flores Farfán is a Linguistics Professor at the *Centro de Investigaciones y Estudios Superiores en Antropología Social* (CIESAS) in Mexico City. His areas of interest include sociolinguistics, especially language revitalization and planning. He has taught at the American Language Development Institute at the University of Arizona and at the University of Amsterdam. As part of his courses in Mexico, he has worked on teaching research methods to indigenous students, particularly exploring autobiographies as a means for a better understanding the processes associated with language shift and reversal. His numerous publications include multimedia materials for children in indigenous languages.

Mark Garner teaches a year-long research methods course at the University of Aberdeen, where he is convener of postgraduate programmes in linguistics. He has held similar positions elsewhere in Britain, Australia and Indonesia. In the mid-1990s, he received an Australian Government grant to produce a video on research methods; this aroused his interest in developing effective pedagogical approaches in the subject. Later he received a grant from an English university to investigate project work as a preliminary to methodological studies. He has published a number of books and articles on theory and method in applied linguistics.

Annabelle L. Grundy is a teacher of students who are deaf and hard of hearing at the Ernest C. Drury Senior School for the Deaf, Ontario, Canada. She specializes in the visual arts at the secondary level and teaches students using American sign language. Her interest in accessible research methods originates from her research experiences as someone who is hard of hearing. She has presented several papers and published articles about accessible research methods and accessible research methods education. She wrote her MEd thesis about the learning experiences of graduate students who work as research assistants on faculty-led research projects.

Erica L. James is a Senior Research Academic at the Centre for Health Research and Psycho-oncology, Cancer Council NSW and University of Newcastle, Australia. She leads the physical activity and nutrition stream at the centre and teaches research methods to undergraduate and postgraduate students in disciplines including health promotion, nursing, social work, pharmacy, education and business. In 2006, Erica was awarded an 'Excellence in Teaching Award' in recognition of her efforts in teaching postgraduate research methods. She has published a number of papers and book chapters on teaching research methods and epidemiology to students from health-related disciplines.

Barbara B. Kawulich is an Associate Professor in the Educational Leadership Department at University of West Georgia in Carrollton, Georgia. She teaches qualitative and action research, ethics and leadership to graduate students and multicultural diversity to undergraduates. Her research focus centres on qualitative methods and issues of interest to Muscogee (Creek) women. She has numerous chapters and articles published on these topics.

Sandra A. Kippen is now retired but currently holds the honorary position of Adjunct Senior Lecturer in the Division of Health Studies at La Trobe University, Australia. She specializes in historiography and sociology of health and illness, and has taught research methods at both undergraduate and postgraduate levels for the past 15 years. Her recent publications include reports on research projects, discussion on Indigenous education, teaching at higher education levels and ethics in research.

Brian T. Lam is an Assistant Professor in the Department of Social Work at the California State University, Long Beach, USA. He received his doctorate in social work from Columbia University in 2003. His current research interests focus on ethnic identity, community influences on psychological distress and behavioural proneness among minority adolescents. His teaching area is in direct social work practice and social work research. His articles appear in the *International Journal of Behavioral Development*; *International Journal of Intercultural Relations*; and *The American Journal of Orthopsychiatry.*

Shijuan Liu is currently a Research Fellow in the Kelley School of Business at Indiana University. She holds a PhD in instructional systems technology. Her interest in teaching RM originated from the excellent RM courses that she took when working on her doctorate at Indiana University. She has conducted a number of research projects and presented at many local, national and international conferences. Her work has appeared as book chapters and in refereed journals.

David J.F. Maree is a Full Professor in the Department of Psychology at the University of Pretoria, South Africa and a registered Research Psychologist. He coordinates the training for the MA degree that leads to professional registration as a research psychologist in South Africa. He teaches research methods to postgraduate students in psychology. His academic interests, culminating in conference proceedings and journal publications, include cognitive psychology, test development (especially Rasch modelling), research methods and statistical analysis.

Donna McAuliffe is a Senior Lecturer in the School of Human Services, Griffith University, Queensland, Australia. She specializes in professional ethics education in social work and human services which includes research ethics. She supervises research higher degree students and is engaged in practice-based research in the field using a range of research methodologies. She is also the National Ethics Group Convener for the Australian Association of Social Workers and a Research Ethics Adviser at Griffith University.

Michelle K. McGinn is an Associate Professor of Education at Brock University in St. Catharines, Canada, where she specializes in research methodology, especially qualitative research approaches. She is also a member of the Social Sciences and Humanities Research Ethics Special Working Committee (Canada), where she is engaged in research ethics policy development. She is interested in issues related to researcher development, research education, mentorship, collaboration and academic identity. She has numerous conference presentations and publications related to these topics, including recent work about research teams and the pleasures and pains associated with research.

Tuyen D. Nguyen is an Assistant Professor in the Human Services Department at California State University, Fullerton. He has experience teaching undergraduate and graduate courses and seminars. Academic subjects taught range from issues in research to human nature, development and assessment. He has served on 23 thesis and dissertation committees, with research topics ranging from PTSD among war veterans to children in foster care. He is the editor of *Domestic Violence in Asian American Communities* and *Many Paths, One Purpose: Career Paths for Social Work and Human Services Majors*. He is on the editorial boards of the *Journal of Emotional Abuse*; *The Qualitative Report*; and *Violence Against Women*.

João Batista Carvalho Nunes is Professor in the Faculty of Education and co-coordinator of the Master in Education at Ceará State University, Brazil. He specializes in educational technology and research and evaluation methods. He has been teaching research methods and computer-aided data analysis to postgraduate students in education. His current mixed methods research about free software and education has grants from the National Council for Scientific and Technological Development (CNPq) and the Ceará State Foundation of Support for Scientific and Technological Development (FUNCAP). He has scientific publications in books and conference proceedings about educational research and evaluation.

Chinedu Onochie Okeke is a Lecturer in the Department of Educational Foundations and Management, University of Swaziland. He specializes in sociology of education and qualitative research methods and has been teaching educational foundation courses to undergraduate and postgraduate students in the Department of Educational Foundations. His interest in qualitative research culminated in a PhD thesis, which triangulated various qualitative methods in a demonstration study aimed at making popular the qualitative research methods within the Nigerian research tradition. He has published some international papers on the conduct of research within the Nigerian research tradition, qualitative research and sociology of education.

Jan Pascal is a Lecturer and Researcher in both the School of Social Work and Social Policy and the School of Public Health at La Trobe University, Bendigo, Australia. She specializes in teaching social work and health care practice skills across a range of disciplines. She also teaches research methods at an undergraduate level, as well supervizing doctoral students. Her areas of expertise include methodological design, particularly phenomenology and exploring the lived experience of significant health issues. Her PhD presented a phenomenological interpretation of cancer survival, and she has presented and published several papers about cancer care.

Blaine F. Peden is a Professor in the Department of Psychology at the University of Wisconsin-Eau Claire. He completed a baccalaureate degree at Fresno State College and a doctoral degree at Indiana University. He has taught research methods since 1975. He performs collaborative research with undergraduates presented at professional conferences. Early interests and publications included topics in animal learning and behaviour. More recent interests and publications include teaching and learning about research methods, critical thinking, group matching, virtual research ethics, online courses, scientific writing, teaching with technology and the scholarship of teaching and learning.

Judith Preissle is the 2001 Distinguished Aderhold Professor in the College of Education at the University of Georgia (UGA). She studies the anthropology of education, gender, immigration, ethics and qualitative research design. She founded the qualitative research programme at UGA, now offering a graduate certificate. She coauthored *Ethnography and Qualitative Design in Educational Research* (1984; 1993) and coedited *The Handbook of Qualitative Research in Education* (1992) and her other work has appeared in numerous journals and anthologies. The second edition of her most recent book, *Educating Immigrant Students* (1998), coauthored with Xue Lan Rong, is in preparation for 2008.

Wolff-Michael Roth is Lansdowne (endowed) Professor of Applied Cognitive Science at the University of Victoria, Canada. His research programme is concerned with studying cognition, identity and emotion across the lifespan, especially in the context of mathematics and science. He edits *Mind, Culture, and Activity* and coedits *Cultural Studies of Science Education* and *FQS: Forum Qualitative Sozialforschung/Forum Qualitative Social Research*. Trained as a statistician, he now teaches qualitative research methods. His most recent methods books include the single-authored *Doing Teacher Research: A Handbook for Perplexed Practitioners* and, edited with K. Ercikan, *Generalizing from Educational Research: Beyond the Qualitative-Quantitative Opposition*.

Kathryn Roulston is an Associate Professor in the Qualitative Research Programme in the Department of Lifelong Education, Administration and Policy at the University of Georgia, Athens, USA. She teaches coursework in qualitative research methods to graduate students in education as well as other disciplines. Her research interests include qualitative interviewing, the study of ethnomethodological and conversation analytic approaches to the analysis of talk-in-interaction and topics related to music education. She has published articles on qualitative research methodology in *Qualitative Inquiry*, *Qualitative Research* and journals in education and has presented her research at national and international conferences on qualitative research.

Peter Sercombe holds a PhD in Sociolinguistics and currently teaches in Applied Linguistics at Newcastle University, UK. His academic interests include issues in qualitative research; Austronesian languages; cultural maintenance and adaptation; and the sociolinguistics of language use and language change. His publications include work on the Penan (hunter-gatherers of Borneo), he recently coedited the book *Beyond the Green Myth: Hunter-Gatherers of Borneo in the 21st Century* and acted as a consultant for the BBC's *Tribe* programme on the Eastern Penan. He is also an editor for *The Linguistics Journal*.

Pamela C. Snow is a Psychologist and Speech Pathologist with over 20 years experience in clinical practice, research and academia. She has taught research methods in a wide variety of undergraduate health disciplines and currently coordinates the Psychological Medicine component of Year 4 of the Monash University MBBS at a regional clinical school in Victoria, Australia. Her research is concerned with various aspects of risk in childhood and adolescence, and has been published in a range of international journals.

Terrell L. Strayhorn is Assistant Professor of Higher Education and Special Assistant to the Provost at the University of Tennessee, Knoxville, where he also teaches in the College of Arts and Sciences. He specializes in advanced quantitative data analysis and modelling techniques, and teaches research methods courses to graduate students in fields across the social sciences. His research interests centre on how college affects students and social/educational disparities that affect the success of historically underrepresented groups in higher education. He is the author of three books and over 60 chapters, articles, reviews and scholarly conference papers.

Peter Taylor is a Research Fellow and Leader of the Participation, Power and Social Change Team at the Institute of Development Studies, UK. With a PhD in agricultural education, he convenes the MA in Participation, Power and Social Change and is involved in several international initiatives on knowledge, learning and capacity for social change. He teaches courses on participatory research methods and has been engaged in a wide range of research and advisory work in Africa, South East and Central Asia. He is a member of the editorial boards of the *Community Development Journal* and *Participatory Learning and Action*.

Claire Wagner is a Senior Lecturer in the Department of Psychology at the University of Pretoria, South Africa. She specializes in research psychology and teaches research methods to undergraduate and postgraduate students in psychology as well as across the social sciences. Her interest in teaching RM culminated in a PhD that examined RM curricula and how they are constructed at universities in South Africa. She has presented a number of papers at international conferences about teaching RM and has published articles on RM teaching in psychology, RM teaching within higher education policy and the future of teaching RM.

Bernadette M. Ward is a Lecturer in the School of Public Health at La Trobe University, Bendigo, Australia. She has extensive experience in teaching research to both undergraduate and postgraduate students from a range of health-related disciplines. She has published in refereed journals on teaching research methods and in 2004, She was awarded an 'Excellence in Teaching Award' for online teaching.

Donna M. Zucker is an Associate Professor of Nursing at the University of Massachusetts Amherst, MA. She teaches community health and leadership to undergraduate nursing students. She also teaches the history of nursing and philosophy of science, and offers electives in chronic illness and case method to doctoral nursing students. She conducts research with vulnerable groups who are homeless, incarcerated and at high risk for communicable diseases. Her publications are concerned with research aspects of chronic illness symptoms, and the development of wellness strategies based on case study and other qualitative methods.

Introduction

Towards a Pedagogical Culture in Research Methods

Mark Garner, Claire Wagner and Barbara Kawulich

This book arose from a recognition on the part of the editors of our great ignorance about the teaching of research methods in the social sciences. Despite, between us, having taught the subject in some form or other over more than two decades at eight universities in six countries, we were aware of many questions about what and how we should teach it – and a disconcerting lack of anywhere to turn for answers. Aside from one or two immediate colleagues, we were working in isolation from what must be a very large number of fellow academics around the world who are engaged in the same educational endeavour. In the absence of a professional association or a body of literature devoted to research methods pedagogy, we decided to take the initiative by bringing together a collection of writings on the topic aimed at academics who teach research methods at the tertiary level, researchers, scholars and academic peers. The book is not intended for the textbook, practitioner or policymaker market. We created a web page and called for contributions. The enthusiastic response – we received well over 60 proposals as well as innumerable encouraging comments – showed that there are many others in the field who share our concerns. Clearly the time is right for a thorough examination of research methods education.

As far as methodology was concerned, earlier generations of research students (among whom we number ourselves and no doubt many of our fellow contributors) were generally flying in the dark. They were either told to follow a specified line of enquiry (or left to pick up methodological skills as and when they could) in the process of doing their research. Those who were fortunate had supervisors who initiated them into the research process through a sort of apprenticeship. Otherwise, they had to rely on what they could glean from books on methodology, research reports and *ad hoc* methodological seminars. The notion that research methods could or should be a subject in the curriculum (let alone a compulsory subject) was largely unknown.

The contemporary situation, in many parts of the world, is very different. Under pressure to increase enrolments and improve completion rates among research students, universities have begun stressing the importance of a sound training in how to conduct research. Research methodology, whether discipline-specific or generic, is now a component of most postgraduate, as well as a number of undergraduate, programmes. However, the status and function of these programmes vary widely. The research methods component may be anything from a short series of seminars or workshops to courses that run for a semester, a year or even over several years. Attendance may be optional or compulsory. Assessment differs too: simply attending may be enough to ensure a pass or the courses may include a full range of assignments that are graded on a par with all other programme components. Such variation may be inevitable and even desirable, but it should not be left to occur by default. It is one of many issues that research methods teachers need to consider evaluate and debate. We believe it is time to develop what might be termed a 'pedagogical culture' relating to research methods. By this we refer to the exchange of ideas within a climate of systematic debate, investigation and evaluation surrounding all aspects of teaching and learning in the subject.

We would have liked it to be possible for this initial publication in research methods pedagogy simply to consolidate the field by drawing on a rich literature of pedagogical theory and research. But, apart from a few isolated publications, there is as yet no body of work or even a generally accepted approach, around which a pedagogical culture can develop. Our ambition for this book has therefore had to be modest. It is intended to be a small but essential preliminary step towards developing such a pedagogical culture, by enabling teachers in different countries and within a variety of disciplines to establish the extent to which there are common concerns and challenges, and to demonstrate some ways in which they are being met. Since this book appears to be the first in English (and perhaps any language) to address research methods teaching as an important pedagogical interest, we feel it is premature to argue for or against a particular approach to methods teaching. Our aim is to start, as it were, a lot farther back: to raise awareness of the issues and to provide both a stimulus and some source materials for more substantial and systematic future work in the field. The chapters were selected on the basis that they deal with important topics, not because the writers espoused a given ideology or followed a given line of argument.

Our aim throughout has been to address pedagogical issues from the perspective of concepts and principles, rather than to adopt an approach of 'this is what I do in my classroom and this is how you can do it'. A fundamental assumption for the development of a pedagogical culture is that there are skills, knowledge and processes required for teaching a subject that are related to, but distinguishable from, expertise in the subject itself. This has long been recognized in a number of traditional disciplines, where a pedagogical culture, manifested in formal organizations and informal networks, conferences and publications, dedicated to teaching, has developed in parallel with the discipline itself. In fields as diverse as history and mathematics, there is a strong academic tradition of discipline-related pedagogy. Applied linguistics originated when language teachers began to scrutinize their own practice in the light of advances in theoretical linguistics (Corder, 1973) and has since become a vigorous academic discipline in its own right (McDonough, 2002).

By contrast, research methods education has scarcely begun to take shape as a field of academic endeavour. In certain respects the current status of research methods teaching is akin to the situation obtaining a decade or two ago in the teaching of English as a second or foreign language (ES/FL) or of what has been variously styled as academic skills, academic literacy or study skills. When these activities first appeared on the academic scene, they were regarded as simply support or service activities. They occupied a marginal place within university education and were typically taught by junior or sessional staff. There was little interest in, or incentive for, a pedagogical culture to develop around them. Under pressure from a rapidly expanding intake of students from non-traditional and mixed ability backgrounds, however, university managers began to recognize that these subjects have an essential role to play in maintaining standards and retention rates. They were gradually incorporated into the mainstream of academic programmes (Garner et al., 1995), and the teaching of both academic skills and ES/FL is now widely accepted as a significant academic pursuit. As a consequence, a lively pedagogical culture has developed around them, manifested in dedicated professional associations. Theoretical and methodological debates are conducted through national and international conferences, and specialist journals provide an outlet and a stimulus for a growing body of research (Lillis, 2001). Each field now offers a career structure for academics who wish to specialize within it.

A similar upgrading process is, or soon will be, under way with research methods, as it comes to occupy a more central place within academic programmes. The earlier piecemeal, trial and error, acquisition of research skills by a small handful of research students is being superseded by structured coursework. Government and university bodies are calling for the extensive, systematic teaching of research methods to all postgraduate students, as well as to trainee practitioners in a number of fields (QAA, 2004). The academic status of the subject is still not secure in many institutions, as is evidenced by differing views about who should be given the responsibility of teaching it. Where it is regarded as little more than introducing students to some basic information and skills, the task may be given to a junior member of staff or perhaps a current doctoral student. Where methodology is regarded as an essential but rather abstract pursuit, the teaching may be left to more experienced faculty members with a 'methodological cast of mind'. Of course, members of either group can be excellent teachers of research and both are represented among the authors in this book. Early career researchers often display a fresh enthusiasm for research and an inventiveness in their teaching, while senior academics can bring a depth of wisdom and breadth of perspective that make their research methods classes lively learning experiences for their students. But the outcomes are just as likely to be less than optimal. Junior staff may lack perspective and self-confidence; senior staff may be inflexible in their conception of research. In either case, the subject will not be taught as well as it might be. In any discipline, neither showing potential and enthusiasm nor, conversely, having a long record of research will itself make a good teacher. Both characteristics might be said to be a valuable but not a sufficient condition for the effective research methods teacher. Until research methods itself is accepted as central to students' education in a discipline, and a passion for research and ability in teaching it as a *sine qua non* for research methods tutors, students are unlikely to learn how to do research well.

It is only through the development of a pedagogical culture that excellence in teaching research methods can be encouraged and ensured. It is essential for those of us engaged in this field to work together to establish such a culture, to ensure that our collective work develops into an academic and pedagogical undertaking of a high standard. This is, as we said, the intention of this first collection of writings on the topic. The form and orientation of the book have been determined by the inchoate nature of the field. Our approach in selecting the various contributions has been deliberately eclectic, to give as wide a view as possible within the limitations of a single volume of the present state of the art. From its inception some four years ago, we have tried to ensure that this book would be more like a collegial discussion than a lecture; a conversation that reflects original and new insights into the pedagogy of research through the editors' choice of the contributions. By including a wide range of shorter chapters, we have tried to achieve a relatively broad conspectus of current practice as the basis for further conceptualization of what research methods education can become. We also aimed for as wide as practicable a representation of views. The editors are from three different continents, and contributions are included from Australia, Brazil, Canada, Mexico, Nigeria, South Africa, United Kingdom and the United States. The disciplines represented include anthropology, education, nursing, psychology, social work and sociolinguistics. The authors include both senior, experienced researchers and early career academics teaching at both undergraduate and postgraduate levels.

We attempted to maintain coherence among this variety of perspectives and approaches by asking authors to emphasize those aspects of their work that are likely to be of interest to research methods teachers within any social science and in any university and to relate general principles and specific examples, conceptual discussion and classroom applications. There are, of course, points of variation, even discrepancy, between the positions adopted. This is desirable in an initial publication in the field, if only to reflect the enormous range of experience and practice among current teachers. After reviewing the received abstracts and requesting draft chapters from selected authors, the preliminary review process began with our comments as editors on the ideas presented via personal communication with the authors. When we were satisfied with the draft product the publisher put the ideas through a rigorous blind peer review process. All the chapters were sent to three reviewers (two in the UK and one in the US) who are experts in the field of research methodology and pedagogy for a thorough appraisal. Comments and suggestions received from the reviewers were considered and implemented. Once the revisions were submitted to the publisher another round of blind peer reviews was undertaken. We hope that readers will form their own opinions and use whatever academic forum they can find to engage in debate with the writers.

No collection of this size can be truly comprehensive, of course. We have had to take editorial decisions that mean that some aspects of the field are not as well covered as might be desired. Since there is already a sizeable literature on the teaching of statistics in particular, and to an extent quantitative research methods in general, we decided to place the focus largely (although not exclusively) on the more disparate and less widely discussed matters which concern qualitative research or which transcend the quantitative–qualitative division. Even so, there are obvious gaps. A number of methodological and pedagogical topics are given insufficient coverage, either because of editorial decisions or because no relevant contributions could be obtained. They include the relative merits of generic and discipline-specific research methods courses – a topic that surely merits a book of its own – the similarities and differences between undergraduate and postgraduate courses, and the optimal time that should be allocated to them.

Organizing such a wide-ranging collection of writings has inevitably been a challenge. After much discussion and experiment, we decided to follow a pattern that roughly reflects a process of gradually establishing a pedagogical culture. Starting with more general historical and philosophical matters, the sections focus on increasingly specific pedagogical issues. A historical perspective reminds us that, in building a pedagogical culture, we are not starting from scratch or designing courses *ex nihilo*. Research methods have been taught for long enough to enable today's teachers to learn something from earlier debates and experiments, and perhaps to avoid repeating some earlier mistakes. This history has not been examined to any great extent to date, but the two chapters in the Historical Perspectives section represent a valuable start on what should become a fruitful field of investigation. Peden and Carroll document changes in the psychology curriculum at the national level in the United States that have occurred in response to evolving views of the scientific and cultural status of the discipline in that country. A more personal reflection on 30 years of teaching educational research, also in the United States, is given by Preissle and Roulston. These two historical surveys are complementary, not only because they examine different disciplines from different perspectives but also because they bring into focus the predominantly quantitative orientation of one with the predominantly qualitative concerns of the other. The concluding remark by Preissle and Roulston, 'we continue to watch, listen and learn', could serve as a catchphrase for what we hope will become a growing area of interest in the history of research pedagogy – and indeed, for all of the sections in the book.

The Approaches to the Curriculum section opens with Kawulich's discussion of the role of theory in high-quality research. Drawing on her own experience, and the substantial literature, she poses a series of key pedagogical questions, such as: what is the relationship of theory to practice; are theories discipline-specific; and how do theories affect choice of methods? Some of her answers are likely to receive general agreement from other teachers; others may stimulate fruitful debate. Maree examines fundamental questions relating to epistemology in research. He deconstructs some common assumptions prevalent among students of research methods (and, at times, among their teachers), for instance, that experimental methods are *ipso facto* positivist. Against the background of an exposition of alternative epistemologies, such as positivism and social constructionism, he introduces critical realism as a means of transcending their shortcomings and as a basis for both quantitative and qualitative social science research. He also provides valuable advice on teaching research from a critical realist perspective.

The philosophical (epistemological and ontological) choices underlying curriculum design in research methods courses are also the focus of the contribution by Wagner and Okeke. They argue that curriculum choices should not be determined by an unnecessary dichotomy between qualitative and quantitative approaches. Their own research, in South Africa and Nigeria, shows how choices between methodologies are too often ill informed and conclude that students should be equipped to make their own methodological decisions in the light of the epistemological and pragmatic issues surrounding any given study.

Since every context in which research methods courses are run has its own distinctive features, there would be limited value in providing a sort of catalogue of specific degree programmes or courses in various institutions around the world. For those who would find such information helpful, the Internet is a ready resource. Nonetheless, instances of programmes that are structured around important pedagogical principles can serve as instructive examples. The chapter by Pascal and Brown well exemplifies the way in which issues of epistemology and ontology, discussed in depth in the preceding chapters, can be incorporated into the design of a degree sequence, rather than treated as discrete elements. (A similar function is performed for assessment in the chapter by Ward et al.: see below.) Pascal and Brown describe how a programme can incrementally develop students' capacity to build research competence on the basis of a good understanding of epistemological and ontological principles. As well as outlining the philosophy behind their approach, they include examples of class exercises, which can serve as a useful resource of the kind called for in much of the correspondence we received in response to our call for contributions. A further characteristic of their chapter is that it is presented through the individual voices of two early career academics. As we mentioned above, the teaching of methods is frequently allocated to younger staff members who may feel that they lack the knowledge and experience to fulfil the task adequately. We hope that this chapter will be a source of encouragement to such people and as an example for experienced teachers of the sort of creativity that fresh minds can bring to curriculum design as well as to classroom teaching.

The remaining two chapters in this section concern the importance of including in the curriculum a good grounding in the social interaction involved in research. Garner and Sercombe present a simple model of relationship types that has proved a useful heuristic helping students reflect on how they relate to the participants in their research. Given that the quality of data and the most appropriate means of analysing them are influenced – sometimes crucially so – by the relationships established between researcher and researched, the authors contend that a social relations perspective is an essential component of methods courses in the social sciences. One aspect of social relations that is included in many courses is research ethics. In her survey of how the topic is taught, McAuliffe identifies four approaches (or five, if one includes the view that ethics simply cannot be taught). Three of these treat the topic as a discrete element within the course, to be given more or less detailed treatment. The fourth, which she advocates, is to see the ethical dimension 'as a foundational part of the research process' and one that therefore 'needs to be incorporated as a key element in research training and education'. She provides a stage-by-stage discussion of the implication of ethical decisions in the design and conduct of a project, which will be of great value to anyone wishing to learn how to develop this essential awareness among students.

The third section, Approaches to Developing Research Competence, comprises a number of chapters dealing with the more general knowledge, skills and competencies that students need to develop if they are to do good research. Based on the view that research is a series of decision-making processes, Earley presents a framework for developing students as 'reflective researchers'. Three learning outcomes are identified: first, that students will be able to describe themselves as researchers in the context of the larger research community; second, that they will understand how reflection links all stages of research; third, that they will keep a journal. In achieving these goals, they learn both the 'science' and the 'art' of research. In his chapter, Roth writes from the perspective of teaching research as praxis, which aims to obviate the problem encountered by many graduates who find that what they learned about in their methods classes does not prepare them for actually doing research in the real world. Having expounded the theoretical bases of this approach, Roth examines the many complex demands of teaching graduate researchers through a form of 'apprenticeship', using a particular project as a case study. He shows how, rather than attempting to introduce the students to a pre-existing research culture, this approach sees teacher and learner of research as constituents in an evolving culture, which each shapes as much as he or she is shaped by it.

Strayhorn's chapter is an all too rare example of research into methods education (Wagner and Okeke also draw on their own fieldwork in their more theoretically-oriented chapter). Using a self-report questionnaire, he examined the type and frequency of teaching strategies used in methods courses and their perceived effectiveness for students' learning. He found that the two most frequently used strategies (lectures and reading textbooks) were rated least effective, while other less commonly used strategies (such as article critique) were rated highly. He discusses the implications of the findings for the development of effective pedagogy and suggests ways in which more innovative teaching can be developed. Although the sample size was too small to allow for definitive conclusions about such influences as ethnicity and gender, the findings are sufficiently suggestive to point to some directions for important future research.

Another aspect of research methods education that has received too little systematic attention in the literature is the use of computers. Yet, as Nunes points out, computers are transforming our conceptions of how research is conducted, as well as opening up new fields of enquiry that were until quite recently unthinkable.

He writes, 'to conduct research in [many fields] without the use of computers is almost impossible'. This applies equally to quantitative and qualitative studies, which can be effectively integrated with the intelligent use of appropriate software. His chapter provides a brief outline of some of the resources available, either as special packages or through the Internet, together with some practical ways of incorporating the use of technology in all stages of a methods course. In the rapidly changing world of information technology, it is inevitable that such chapters will need to be constantly updated and revised.

The nature and role of assessing students' learning in research methods courses vary widely. In more well-established disciplines, there are 'default' methods of assessment (such as the academic essay and a portfolio of work), but there is no such method in this field. It is therefore an area of challenge and opportunity, but, as Ward, Dickson-Swift, James, Kippen, and Snow comment, assessment is too often treated as a final, add-on item in a curriculum, rather than being an integrated part that helps to enhance learning and motivation. The writers present an example of the use of a wide range of options in a four-year undergraduate programme. Although, in the shorter postgraduate courses in which much research methods teaching occurs, the full scope and extent of their strategies may not be practicable, their detailed discussion of the theoretical issues and the practicalities of their application should be a source of information and inspiration to teachers at all levels.

The fourth section includes chapters dealing with approaches to teaching particular methodologies. It would, of course, be impossible to treat all of the methodologies that are included in courses. Furthermore, particularly in qualitative research, methodology is evolving rapidly. The contributions given here represent a small sample of the range of possibilities and challenges raised by the need to ensure that students develop not only a knowledge of very different methodologies, but more importantly a grasp of the principles underlying them. The selection of exemplary discussions in this section will, we hope, make the goal of developing reflective researchers (as defined in Earley's Chapter 9) more achievable.

Taylor writes about the particular demands of teaching participatory research methodology. Participatory research is based on the premise that 'people know and are capable of identifying and sharing issues [and] analysing and learning from their analysis'. It transcends the traditional distinction between researcher and researched, and helps to avoid the problem of research that answers theoretical questions while leaving unaddressed the real-world problems that gave rise to them. Taylor highlights the motivational effects that engaging with participants can have on students. He also stresses the difficulties: this type of research depends on a degree of self-confidence and maturity of the researcher as well as a grasp of the relationship between concept and practice. There are clear connections here with the social relations approach advocated by Garner and Sercombe.

Practitioners in many fields are increasingly required to acquire research skills as part of their professional education and training. Nguyen and Lam address the particular demands of teaching these students, who may fail to see the relevance of learning how to do research. They discuss a range of ineffective teaching strategies and present alternatives that have proved to be more effective. Like several other authors, they emphasize the importance of adopting a collaborative approach to teaching that takes full cognizance of the students' misconceptions and fears about the subject.

Case study is a common methodology in many of the human sciences, but it is one that is not easy to teach well. Students all too often regard case studies as nothing more than a fallback to be used if the sample population is too small for other more 'substantial' methods. Zucker's chapter demonstrates that case study is a well-developed methodology with a substantial theoretical base and distinctive data gathering and analytical techniques. She describes how rigorous case studies can be designed and implemented, illustrating each point with reference to the investigation of patients with coronary heart disease. Liu and Carspecken give a similarly thorough examination of critical ethnography. They focus on how to maintain a symmetry between curriculum and pedagogy, which is important in all teaching but particularly so in relation to this particular methodology, in which 'the curriculum is the pedagogy'. The principles that guide classroom interactions must reflect and reinforce those of the methodology itself. The authors discuss symmetries of, amongst others, design, relationships and power, and also identify two inevitable asymmetries which must be openly addressed with the students if the methodology is to be successfully learned.

The final section comprises two chapters that address an aspect of growing relevance to research methods education, but one that has as yet been little investigated, namely, the pedagogy of non-traditional students. Grundy and McGinn are, respectively, a student with a hearing disability and her supervisor. Their collaboration in teaching and learning exemplifies how, through sensitive collaboration, the difficulties that students with disabilities encounter in developing research skills not only can be avoided or overcome, but can lead to new breakthroughs in methodology that have potentially wider application. In the final chapter, Flores Farfán, Garner and Kawulich outline some of the challenges of teaching the increasing numbers of students whose epistemologies differ significantly from those that dominate the research paradigm of most methods courses. 'International' students from African, Asian, Middle Eastern, and South American societies (for example), as well as indigenous and immigrant minorities within Western societies, bring to their studies a range of alternative, sometimes fundamentally different, ways of viewing education and knowledge. This raises crucial pedagogical questions. Is the goal of our research methods courses to inculcate these students into the Western paradigm (see Preissle and Roulston, Chapter 1)? Is all research culturally relative? Given the present state of our knowledge (or ignorance), the answers to these questions have to be largely anecdotal. The authors discuss a number of illustrative examples of their own experience in an attempt to identify the issues, address some of the cultural pitfalls and enrich the pedagogy through creative incorporation of alternative epistemological and pragmatic concerns. This section barely scratches the surface of the issues raised by the increasing presence of non-traditional students in research methods courses; this is an area of investigation that offers enormous potential in our quest for a pedagogical culture within research methods.

We have repeatedly expressed our ambition that this collection will serve as a jumping-off point, and an encouragement to the many colleagues who are involved in research methods teaching to develop networks, share ideas, clarify issues and engage in debate. We hope that this will begin to happen at all levels: institutional; local; national; and international. There has inevitably been a great deal of hard work demanded of all the contributors to bring this volume to fruition and we have been greatly impressed by the willingness of all to produce drafts and to rewrite them in response to our editorial suggestions, within tight deadlines. In our dealings with all contributors we have met with enthusiasm and encouragement. A high level of collegiality and collaboration are necessary for a pedagogical culture within research methods to develop, and our experience in editing this book convinces us that the prospects for the future in this regard are very bright.

PART I
Historical Perspectives

Chapter 1

Trends in Teaching Qualitative Research: A 30-year Perspective

Judith Preissle and Kathryn Roulston

Drawing from the literature on teaching qualitative research methods, our own research on the topic and our experiences in developing a qualitative research programme that celebrated its 30th anniversary in January 2006, we examine key trends and central issues in preparing qualitative researchers. Based in the US, Judith Preissle offered the University of Georgia's first designated course in qualitative research in 1976 to five doctoral students in the College of Education. At that time, most aspiring qualitative researchers were being educated as she had been, through a combination of apprenticeship, extensive reading, bits on fieldwork in courses on other topics and trial and error experiences. This preparation had more or less adequately served the small minority of qualitative researchers working in the social and professional sciences to that point in time. By 2006, in contrast, over 50 doctoral students from fields across the university have graduated with our Interdisciplinary Qualitative Studies Certificate, preparing them to practise and teach qualitative research methods and design.

The emerging, interdisciplinary methodology of qualitative research presents us, like other qualitative research instructors around the globe, with both familiar on-going concerns and new challenges. In this chapter we discuss five issues most qualitative research instructors face: (1) representing the interdisciplinary roots of qualitative research; (2) balancing theory and practice; (3) integrating apprenticeships into class-based instruction; (4) balancing credentialism and scholarship while addressing both the intrinsic and the instrumental values for qualitative work; and (5) working with student researchers from many cultural backgrounds and countries using scholarship in qualitative research methodology that has developed primarily in the West.

One problem we wish to avoid in teaching qualitative research is depending on simplistic recipes for research design. One kind of recipe grounds decisions in deterministic epistemological, philosophical and theoretical perspectives. Students are taught that philosophy and theory dictate design and methods. For novice qualitative researchers, this approach poses the dangers of adhering to strict methodological prescriptions with little regard for varying contexts or sensitivity to emergent research problems. A second recipe for research design begins with prescriptions for collecting and analysing data, but ignores epistemological and theoretical assumptions underlying the researcher's choices. A third recipe is based on the premise that the research question drives the development of methods and design with no consideration for either context or the theories and philosophies that frame all questions about the world.

We believe that instructors of qualitative research courses should avoid teaching research design as a linear recipe-like process, and we aim to provide novice qualitative researchers with sufficient understanding of theory to allow them to make appropriate choices. These include considering theories and methods that may be flexibly used to study research problems in social settings. Students can then be encouraged to apply their knowledge of theories and methods to real-world social problems in the context of theoretical discussions and contemporary debates in a range of exercises. The intention is to socialize students into a 'culture of research' (Eisenhart and DeHaan, 2005, 7) and also to foster opportunities for them to demonstrate and develop creative and innovative scholarship. In this approach, theories, methods and questions interact in a mutually defining fashion, and trainee researchers learn to reflect on how choices in each area affect reconsideration of the other areas.

Representing the Interdisciplinary Roots of Qualitative Research

The literatures from which we draw in teaching qualitative research are derived from multiple disciplines, including anthropology, arts and humanities, communications, philosophy, psychology, sociology, and education and other applied fields. This profusion of methodological sources provides rich material for conceptualizing and designing research projects, as well as diverse examples of empirical research from varied communities of scholarly practice. Our experience shows that it can also be an obstacle to students' understanding, for a number of reasons.

First, what is seen as 'normal' science or inquiry varies from one discipline to another (Hammersley, 2004). Students enter our courses with different assumptions about what qualitative research is and should be; they are often familiar with one perspective and tend to valourize it above others. This kind of single-mindedness can be reinforced by the literature of each discipline. Our challenge as teachers is to demonstrate to students the value of learning how different disciplines and fields vary in scholarly culture, style and practice. Support for interdisciplinary scholarship, we believe, begins with inculcating respect for diversity among our newest scholars and researchers.

Second, the profusion of scholarly sources from multiple fields presents a linguistic issue: there is no systematic or consistent use of terminology in qualitative research across disciplines. The task for instructors, then, is to assist beginning researchers to construct preliminary scaffolding for understanding theory, from which students may then refine their understanding of how theories inform their research questions on discipline-specific substantive topics. The benefits for qualitative researchers of working through these challenges and drawing on the interdisciplinary applications of qualitative inquiry, however, are many. For example, the journey of one author (Kathryn) into qualitative research has required crossing disciplinary boundaries from music education into the field of education. Her studies in the sociology of education and collaborations with researchers in other disciplines have assisted her in conducting research informed by alternative perspectives that are less commonly used in her disciplinary home of music education, which historically has relied on multivariate arguments and experimental research designs. One recent research collaboration with scholars and teacher–researchers in reading education (Aaron et al., 2006) inspired a teacher–research collaboration among practising music teachers and university educators (Roulston et al., 2005). Our students have had similar experiences. For example, linguists have framed studies using different sociological theories; language and literacy educators have learned alternative representational strategies from the arts and humanities; mathematics educators have posed deconstructive questions of their data; and science educators have explored applications of narrative inquiry.

Not all qualitative research methods courses are delivered to students from a range of disciplines, of course. We have had intense discussions with colleagues who believe that research methods must be taught only within a disciplinary tradition to assure the congruence between the subject matter and its knowledge production. Some argue that this aim is undermined by what they view as content neutral statistics. Furthermore, programmes in sociology, anthropology, counselling, speech, business and other fields do provide qualitative coursework tailored to their specialties. Nonetheless, the experience of one author (Judith), in running a summer programme in fieldwork methods with colleagues in sociology, was that even content-specific qualitative research methods offerings attract a diverse crowd. Graduate students in the programme came from health professions, hotel administration and other management programmes, education, as well as the social and behavioural sciences (Grant et al., 1999). Although academics do teach qualitative research methods and design to specific discipline groups, to restrict the material to the given discipline denies students access to the valuable breadth of scholarship that can inform qualitative endeavours.

Balancing Theory and Practice

As in many doctoral programmes, our own College of Education students come from multiple disciplinary backgrounds and bring to their studies diverse work experiences and prior learning. Although the majority of our students are pursuing doctoral degrees in education, we also work with students from the social sciences and professional fields other than education. As instructors, we face an initial challenge of assisting students to become familiar with the academic discourses found in writing on qualitative research methodology. Although some students eagerly embrace and immerse themselves in theoretical writings others, some of whom have extensive practitioner experience, find the onslaught of unfamiliar terms and abstract concepts replete with numerous 'ologies' and 'isms' to be overwhelming. Students are faced with learning new terminology and academic discourses. They are called on to read, write and make abstractions from their experience in new and different ways. Initial encounters with social science theory are daunting for some students and prompt their complaints, but we believe it is important to resist calls to resort to simpler descriptions of 'methods' of fieldwork practice or recipes for doing research. As Eisenhart and DeHaan (2005) argue, in an effective doctoral programme 'students must experience firsthand the culture of research' (p. 7). They propose that doctoral students must:

> learn how to pose researchable questions whether requiring quantitative or qualitative methods or data; develop strategies for sampling, data collection, and analysis; learn ways of reasoning and arguing from evidence, means of assessing quality, styles of writing for technical reports and publishable articles, and ways of scrutinizing and constructively critiquing others' work (Eisenhart and deHaan, 2005).

For qualitative researchers to pose 'researchable questions', they need to be competently versed in how theoretical decision-making informs research design and how different epistemological and theoretical assumptions are congruent with different kinds of research questions and research designs (see Kawulich, Chapter 3). To this end, qualitative research courses need to survey a range of theoretical approaches to research and be taught by instructors who represent a range of theoretical and methodological expertise. Through exposure to a wide spectrum of readings and engagement with qualitative researchers who conduct research from different perspectives, students can begin to identify with the theories that will be best suited to their research purposes. Whether students intend to conduct qualitative research for the purpose of understanding, emancipation or deconstruction (Lather, 2004), through directing our students to exemplars of research conducted from different epistemological assumptions, they can be assisted to formulate research questions consistent with the purposes, theory and methods selected or developed.

Our approach to teaching, then, is iterative – aiming for an elaborated understanding of theory, concepts and terms over time. This process frequently resembles back-and-forth journeys between confusion and clarity, as students encounter and struggle with theoretical issues in the midst of the problems that emerge during fieldwork. As Dewey (1939) emphasizes, action and knowledge, theory and practice, are inseparable human activities. Practical engagement in field-related exercises and authentic research activities is integral to discussion of theoretical issues. Reading about the theory and methodology of qualitative research, as our students have reported, produces certain understandings that are illuminated through doing (Roulston et al., 2003). Working through this iteration also can relieve a common problem of novice researchers. Some of our most skilled interviewers and fieldworkers, who rely on interpersonal prowess to gather qualitative data, have tended to delay 'thinking' about what they have until 'later'. As the data accumulate, the propensity may increase to postpone serious analysis. Urging students to recognize that they are 'thinking the data' all along and to learn to think more systematically and self-consciously (see Earley, Chapter 9) helps prevent the confusion brought on by not knowing what to do with the data they have collected.

Yet there are no simple or clear routes to the production of scientific knowledge for qualitative researchers – whether expert or novice. As people increase their knowledge, they also understand the limits of that knowledge. Research often provokes more (and more complex) questions than those that it seeks to answer. This is especially true of research projects on the constantly changing experiences and contexts of human life that are especially vulnerable to this pattern and researchers must learn patience, flexibility and tolerance for ambiguity.

Integrating Apprenticeships into Class-based Instruction

We have argued that adequate theoretical preparation is essential to the education of qualitative researchers if they are to design and conduct worthwhile research and that this theoretical preparation must be balanced with practical experiences in doing research. Students must be able to work through the difficult issues raised in methodological writing. For example, how do researchers conceptualize the participants in their studies? What are the implications of this conceptualization for representation of 'others'? How can masses of qualitative data be reduced to an article length report? What do researchers do when the people they study disagree with the researchers' interpretations?

Many of us who are teaching research methods learned to do research in apprenticeships with senior scholars. We are now faced with providing large numbers of students with research opportunities to work through just these kinds of questions. Both authors began our research careers as apprentices, working closely and individually with a faculty mentor. Lacking the organization and structure provided by class instruction and course work, we often learned through trial and error, reflecting on our mistakes and then writing about what we did next. Our present challenge is to provide our students with a different kind of apprenticeship experience that provides reflective critique and supervision within the different learning environment of structured coursework (see Roth, Chapter 10).

This is possible if beginning researchers engage in authentic research projects to develop skills in all facets of qualitative inquiry, including data collection, analysis and representation, and peer evaluation (Grant et al., 1999). In our own courses, we supervise students in both group and individual projects that allow them to grapple with a variety of issues, including ethical dilemmas (see McAuliffe, Chapter 8) and the influence on research methods of gatekeepers and ethical review committees. Apprenticeships in coursework include the following:

1. *Supervised classroom projects*. In these projects, students conduct an individual project of their own choosing for which they receive the instructor's approval. Given the regulations governing university research in the US, these projects must conform to certain guidelines outlined by each university's Institutional Review Board (IRB) (ethics committee). At our university, these kinds of classroom projects may not involve videotaping, sensitive topics such as sexuality, or children and other participants deemed to be vulnerable.
2. *Individual projects*. Some students prepare research projects and obtain IRB approval prior to coursework. Unlike data developed in class projects, data generated from these individual projects may be used by students in conference presentations and publications.
3. *Authentic team projects*. In some of our courses, students have engaged in authentic projects for which the instructor has gained IRB approval prior to the course (see Garner and Sercombe, Chapter 7). Like individual projects, these assignments provide opportunities for students to engage, for example, in conducting individual interviews and focus groups. As a basis for a course on interviewing, one author (Kathryn) designed a number of qualitative interview studies in collaboration with key persons from different on-campus units, each of which resulted in a report to a client group on a topic of concern to the unit involved. Client groups have included a conference planning department, a university department, and a group of librarians and media specialists. At the end of the course, students presented oral and written reports of preliminary findings to the client group. Team projects have also provided students opportunities to collect and sometimes analyse data for ongoing research conducted by various faculty members at our institution. This provides us with the chance to introduce students to the varying levels of responsibility for research and the expectations for acknowledgment, authorship and such (see Roth, Chapter 10).

As scholars in a research university, we encourage our students to present the findings of their research for local, national and international audiences through conferences and publications. We realize, however, that our students have a great variety of career aspirations and trajectories, and while some intend to pursue research career paths similar to our own, many do not. This represents a different challenge to research methods teachers, to which we now turn.

Balancing Credentialism and Scholarship and Addressing both the Intrinsic and the Instrumental Values for Qualitative Work

As emphasized earlier, we value multiple qualitative traditions as ways to produce knowledge about social life and view research methods as integral to generating knowledge. In teaching qualitative research, however, this emphasis on scholarship sometimes conflicts with the goals of students who undertake advanced research degrees to obtain credentials that assist them in workplaces outside the academy, with no intention of pursuing scholarly careers. For them, learning research methods is simply a requirement in achieving the degree as a means for promotion or higher salaries. In 1979, the sociologist Collins argued that credentialism had become the mechanism controlling professional mobility across higher status occupations in societies around the world: students' 'reasons for going to school are extraneous to whatever goes on in the classroom' (p. 192). Graduate education in the US is experiencing this kind of credentialist pressure. For example, in a 2004 national survey of earned education doctorates in the US, of the 67.7 per cent of 6,635 graduates who had 'definite employment plans' on graduation, only 7.7 per cent mentioned 'research and development' as the primary activity (Smallwood, 2005). Although we expect some students in our qualitative certificate programme will take academic positions, others do not (Preissle, 1999).

Research degrees thus serve two somewhat disparate ends: to prepare scholars to conduct their inquiries and to facilitate career advancement. Given the emphasis on scholarship in academe (see, for example, National Research Council, 2005), as instructors we are placed in the uncomfortable position of managing the gatekeeping demands of the academy to ensure high-quality qualitative research, while avoiding the pitfalls of what Janesick terms 'methodolatory': 'a preoccupation with selecting and defending methods to the exclusion of the actual substance of the story being told' (1998, 48). For example, the documentation of attainment of various 'indicators' is one common method to ensure quality work. Doctoral preparation that relies on many programme requirements may work to restrict the creative aspects of scholarship and reduce doctoral work to the following of recipe-like formulas. Even though such recipes may encapsulate best practice, scholarship must continue to develop and requires a creativity that may not be encouraged by the documentary practices associated with credentialism. We believe that all students, regardless of their motivations for pursuing a degree, are best served by being introduced to the most powerful and creative ways of exploring questions about human experience and that this approach ensures that they are well prepared to design and conduct quality research (Richardson, 2006).

The Hegemony of Western Research Practice

Finally, we address the teaching of qualitative research at the beginning of the twenty-first century, a time of rapid growth in migration and new patterns of virtual work conducted across physical boundaries. We conclude with an issue that concerns us, that of the hegemony of Western research practice. The scholar of the future may well be mobile and multi- or bilingual, relating to multiple geographical spaces as 'home'. Yet we ourselves primarily draw on Western qualitative traditions. Although we teach researchers who come from many countries around the world and who bring with them various indigenous traditions of inquiry, we have had no formal preparation for teaching research to students from non-Western cultures. Our classrooms include scholars who conduct their research and analysis in languages other than English, languages we neither speak nor read. Our students manage their fieldwork in settings physically distant from the institution in which the studies were conceived. New ethical dilemmas await these researchers. Our challenge as instructors is to prepare qualitative researchers who conduct research ethically and can adapt and create the kinds of research practices that are culturally sensitive to their nations of origin. As instructors we strive to develop a reflexive teaching practice in which we comprehend our positionalities and practice openness in working with others. At least three issues are significant:

1. *Gaining entry for research in local communities.* The review procedures used by IRBs in Western institutions reflect expectations that may differ from those for ethical conduct in other countries. Students need to familiarize themselves with these conventions before beginning fieldwork. In the field, there may be a problem in obtaining consent from participants, some of whom may be well versed in the norms of academic inquiry and readily agree to participate and sign the consent forms required, but others may not. Beginning researchers may thus encounter quite different expectations and responses to their requests for consent, and they are advised to 'make haste slowly'.

2. *What happens to data?* Although the repatriation of data is more likely to be an issue in some fields, such as anthropology, than in others, such as education, the question must be considered. Many cultural groups have begun to demand the return of data generated by anthropologists, with thorny legal and social issues to be sorted out in local communities (for example, data may be used in court hearings to settle community disputes over property rights). For researchers engaged in participatory approaches to research, questions about the naming and recognizability of participants in reports and publications arise, along with questions about authorship. With advances in technologies used in research, new ethical questions develop about the display and use of audio and video data in representations of research and how data also might be used for researchers in future teaching and research. While ethical review boards struggle over the legal interpretation of regulations, researchers must work through the very real ethical dilemmas posed by following and translating rules and regulations formulated in one country, but enacted in another.

3. *Translated data.* Many of our students conduct interviews and collect data in languages other than English. Because their dissertations are presented in English, questions arise about the point at which translation takes place – in transcription, during analysis, in representation. What is lost in translation? What transformations take place? How do researchers represent languages other than English in publications, when journal space is limited?

These are three of the many issues in teaching students from across the world. We have found that, with each new regulation applied in our university and with every advance in technology, we, with our students, struggle for answers to fresh questions. Fortunately a growing body of scholarship addresses issues relevant to indigenous scholars. For example, Smith (2005, 92) provides specific strategies for 'building indigenous research capability' that instructors in the West can consult, and a growing literature informs qualitative inquirers conducting research in cross-cultural contexts (Bishop, 2005; Mutua and Swadener, 2004; Smith, 1999).

Conclusions

In this chapter, we have outlined issues that continue to challenge us in teaching qualitative research methods. We have provided no quick fix solutions to any of the following: 1) representing the interdisciplinary roots of qualitative research; 2) balancing theory and practice; 3) integrating research experiences into class-based instruction; 4) balancing credentialism and scholarship; and 5) the hegemony of Western research practice. Our struggles with each of these issues are shared by our students, sometimes in ways that we have yet to understand, and they can have much to teach us about these and other challenges. As qualitative researchers we continue to watch, listen and learn.

Chapter 2

Historical Trends in Teaching Research Methods by Psychologists in the United States

Blaine F. Peden and David W. Carroll

Introduction

Teaching about research methods always has been an integral part of the psychology curriculum in the United States. From 1901 to 1905, Edward Titchener authored a series of 'Experimental Psychology' manuals for students and instructors. The detailed manuals introduced graduate students to laboratory equipment and procedures and defined the subject matter of the new science of psychology. By the middle of the twentieth century, most psychology undergraduates learned about research methods in experimental psychology courses and from textbooks expressing some variation of the course title. At present most psychology undergraduates learn about quantitative methods and analysis (that is, statistics), philosophy of science and research ethics in research methods courses and from similarly titled textbooks. In this chapter, we explore this transformation in teaching research methods by psychologists in the United States. Our chapter is a first step in reviewing the history of teaching research methods and one that we hope will stimulate further inquiry.

This chapter explores when, why and how research methods emerged as a new course in the undergraduate curriculum in psychology in the United States. For the most part the new research methods courses displaced and replaced experimental psychology courses. We regard these questions about the emergence of research methods as interesting and important to psychologists and other social scientists. We contend that the questions and concerns of psychologists that led to models for teaching research methods in the United States establish points of reference for comparing and contrasting methods of teaching research in other countries. Future studies, for example, can compare and contrast traditions to determine whether and how other nations have conformed to or departed from the approach in the United States.

It is interesting to understand the origins of research methods as a separate course because experimental psychology, statistics and research methods courses are intertwined in the psychology curriculum in a complex way. For example, experimental psychology courses have been part of the curriculum for more than

100 years, and statistics has been a separate course since the 1930s for psychology undergraduates (Henry, 1938). In contrast, research methods courses emerged in the 1960s, spread in the 1970s, and became one of the more prevalent and most required courses in the undergraduate psychology curriculum in the United States (Jackson et al., 2001).

It is important to understand the origins of research methods as a separate course for two reasons. One reason is that psychology becomes a more diverse discipline every decade. Despite the overwhelming diversity, the unifying theme is that psychologists understand behaviour using the methods of science (Stanovich, 2007). In the contemporary psychology curriculum the task of instructing undergraduates about the unity in diversity largely occurs in research methods courses. A second reason is that the processes of change we explore in this chapter may apply to other social sciences in the college curriculum. It is quite plausible that other social sciences have followed the psychology model, as it was the first and most systematically developed approach to teaching research methods. In fact, many current social science instructors probably learned about research methods in classes designed primarily for psychology students.

We address three questions in this chapter:

- When did research methods emerge as a separate course in psychology?
- Why did research methods emerge as a separate course in psychology?
- How did research methods emerge as a separate course in psychology?

We answer the first question by reviewing studies of college catalogues to establish a timeline that tracks the incidence of research methods courses. We explore the second question by linking changes in the treatment of statistics/experimental psychology/research methods to discussions and recommendations from the major appraisals of the undergraduate curriculum in psychology. We address the third question by means of longitudinal studies of catalogues and by inspection of textbooks. We conclude by discussing recent trends, suggesting new research and considering to what extent our analysis applies to other social sciences.

When did Research Methods Emerge as a Separate Course in Psychology?

Content analyses of college catalogues provide one way to study trends in curricular offerings for undergraduates in psychology. In fact, psychologists have published major reviews of catalogues six times between 1938 and 1997. In the earliest study of the catalogues of 157 liberal arts colleges, Henry (1938) reported that methodology was a highly-specialized course intended for graduate students, but sometimes enrolled undergraduates. Henry also reported that 27 per cent of the institutions offered at least one laboratory course in advanced experimental psychology for undergraduates. Sanford and Fleishman (1950), who studied a larger and more diverse sample of 330 institutions of higher learning, revealed that 45 per cent of the institutions taught a statistics course and 57 per cent taught an experimental psychology course. Daniel et al. (1965) found that statistics and experimental psychology courses were more common than research methods in their sample of 207 college and university catalogues. Their data reveal that research methods classes were taking root in doctoral universities but not in liberal arts and teachers' colleges.

The data in the 1965, 1973, 1978 and 1997 college catalogue studies clearly show that the 1950s to 1970s were a formative period for undergraduate psychology, and only later in the period did research methods emerge as a separate course. Kulik (1973) included a detailed analysis and discussion regarding statistics and methodology courses on the basis of the catalogues from 643 institutions (see Table 12 in the original report). Specifically, Kulik noted that 52 per cent of the catalogues identified their required course in methodology as experimental psychology and only 13 per cent listed research design as a separate course. Lux and Daniel (1978), who replicated the catalogue study of Daniel et al. (1965) with 178 catalogues, noted that 50 per cent of the institutions taught experimental psychology courses and 34 per cent now taught a separate research methods courses. Perlman and McCann (1999), who updated the Lux and Daniels study by reading 400 catalogues, indicated that the percentage of institutions listing research methods in their college catalogues increased from 0 per cent in 1961 to 42 per cent in 1997. During the same period, the percentage of college courses listing experimental psychology courses remained level at 40–45 per cent.

We have collated the data from these studies regarding the percentage of all undergraduate psychology programmes at three levels of institutions (that is, doctoral, masters, bachelors' and a two-year course) listing the statistics, research methods and experimental psychology courses in college catalogues for the period 1961–2005. Our data supplement those of Perlman and McCann (1999) with recent results for 463 schools from the APA Office of Research for The Profiles of Undergraduate Programs in Psychology for 2003–2005 (http://www.apa.org/ed/pcue/offerings.html). Note that Figure 2.1 plots the data as a function of the year of the catalogues rather than the publication date. Thus, the 1961 figure represents the data published by Daniel et al. (1965).

Figure 2.1 reveals the experimental psychology, statistics and research methods courses as distinct entities. Experimental psychology courses have been part of the curriculum for more than a hundred years and statistics has been a separate course since the 1930s (and perhaps earlier). Furthermore, offerings of statistics have grown slightly over the years, with the largest gains in the last few years. Historically, statistics courses have been more prevalent than either experimental psychology or research methods courses. The story is different for research methods. Research methods appeared as a separate course in the late 1960s and early 1970s and gained in popularity in the last 35 years while the experimental psychology course is less common now than 40 years ago.

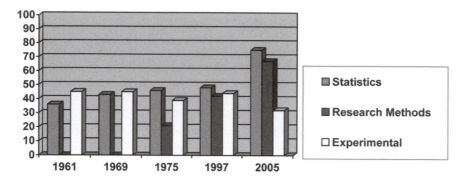

**Figure 2.1   Research courses in psychology curricula from 1961–2005
in the United States**

Figure 2.2 shows the percentage of doctoral, bachelors' and a two-year course, institutions in the United States listing undergraduate research methods in their catalogues. The trend for the three institutions is the same as the overall trend in Figure 2.1; however, the percentages are elevated for bachelors' and even higher for doctoral institutions. By 2005, research methods is well entrenched at doctoral institutions (79 per cent) and bachelors' institutions (77 per cent), and making inroads at colleges that offer a two-year course (20 per cent). Bachelors' degree institutions narrowed the gap by 2005; however, colleges that offer a two-year course still lag far behind the doctoral and bachelors' degree institutions. It appears that doctoral institutions always have led the way with respect to offerings of research methods courses. Henry (1938) described a similar pattern in which larger (that

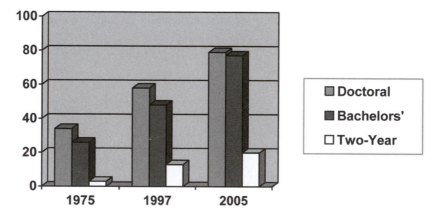

**Figure 2.2   Frequency of research methods courses in different types
of institutions from 1975–2005**

is, doctoral institutions) colleges led the way with respect to offering advanced laboratories in experimental psychology for undergraduates. We speculate that concerns about the methodological competencies of graduate students led doctoral programmes to provide opportunities for their own undergraduates to develop their research methods skills. Presumably, the additional methods courses would help undergraduates enter and succeed in graduate programmes.

Why did Research Methods Emerge as a Separate Course in Psychology?

We explore the answer to this question by linking changes in the treatment of statistics/experimental psychology/research methods to discussions and recommendations from the major assessments of the undergraduate curriculum in psychology:

- the Cornell Conference in 1951 (Buxton et al., 1952),
- the Michigan Conference in 1960 (McKeachie and Milholland, 1961),
- the Kulik Report (1973),
- the St. Mary's Conference (McGovern, 1993),
- the guidelines for psychology majors (APA, 2007).

All the reports appraised the prevailing curricula and all except the Kulik Report (1973) provided recommendations about the content and structure of undergraduate curricula.

Lloyd and Brewer (1992) and Brewer (1997) provided a synopsis of the four conferences and the recommendations of the conference committees. The Cornell Conference in 1951 resulted in the Buxton et al. Report (1952). The committee recommended a curriculum (p. 17) in which the intermediate or core courses included statistics and topical courses. Although the committee plan included the requirement that method be taught with content, the committee also wrote:

> The omission of a course on experimental psychology and the inclusion of one on statistical reasoning require explanation. A separate course on experimental psychology has survived as a token of an earlier day when certain areas in the field of psychology were experimental, others not. In recent years it has been a methodology course, but the persisting problem has been that of finding a content. Methodology empty of content is difficult, dry stuff for the undergraduate, and not productive of much transfer. Basic methodology and scientific attitudes seem to be essentially the same throughout all psychology. If that is true, the learning of methodology as part of each core course is pedagogically an improvement over the traditional separate laboratory course. With regard to statistics, however, a different arrangement seems more efficient. To accomplish anything of permanent value in statistics, a special course seems necessary (Buxton et al., 1952, 27).

Clearly, the main concern here was to champion curricular change in the experimental psychology course. The same concern also set the stage for a new genre of courses and textbooks.

The Michigan Conference in 1960 produced the McKeachie and Milholland Report (1961). The committee identified and discussed various weaknesses in the undergraduate curricula. In fact, the committee specifically addressed the dissatisfaction of many psychologists with the traditional course in experimental psychology. As commonly taught with a laboratory exercise each week, the course seemed infrequently to achieve the objectives of developing positive attitudes toward scientific methods in psychology or of giving students an overall view of scientific investigation (p. 14).

Chapter 6 of the McKeachie and Milholland Report (1961) focused on the experimental–statistical area in part because the committee members 'were unanimous that methodology should be included in the curriculum for majors' (p. 73). The committee further assumed that the introductory course would introduce both quantitative (statistics) and laboratory (experimental) methods to undergraduates and the real question was how to structure further training. The committee proposed three models:

1. Present experimental methods and quantitative methods as part of the laboratory work in other courses (Model 1).
2. Institute separate but parallel or sequential courses, one in experimental methodology, and the other in quantitative methods (Model 2).
3. Establish a separate course in quantitative methods, with experimental methodology covered in the other laboratory courses (Model 3).

The committee also considered and delineated the pros and cons of the three options: infuse both; separate courses; or require statistics and infuse research methods. It is clear that there was much less consensus about teaching research methods than about teaching statistics. The committee also proposed an inverted pyramid curriculum in which methodological and statistical training occurred early in undergraduate education in psychology.

An advisory panel, meeting from July 1969 to June 1972, issued the Kulik Report (1973), which, as Brewer (1997) concluded, was a largely descriptive rather than prescriptive assessment of the undergraduate psychology curriculum. One chapter in the Kulik Report presented a detailed analysis of statistics and methodology courses (that is, statistics, experimental psychology, research design and senior research projects) that allowed psychology departments to evaluate the relative status of their own curricula. For example, the Report affirmed the importance of instruction in statistics and methods for psychology majors and noted that most schools offer separate courses rather than infusing statistics and methods into core courses.

In 1988 the Association of American Colleges convened various disciplinary study groups. The psychology study group produced an article by McGovern et al. (1991). One of the many common goals (pp. 601–602) was that undergraduates have research methods and statistical skills. Specifically, the committee recommended three courses: statistics, research methods, and testing and measurement, and that:

> these skills should be fostered in separate courses, developed in laboratory work, and reinforced by the use of critical discussion of research findings and methods in every course. Whatever the mode of instruction, students should become increasingly independent in posing questions about the study of behaviour and experience and in selecting effective methods to answer those questions (McGovern et al., 1991, 601).

The APA National Conference on Enhancing the Quality of Undergraduate Education in Psychology was held at St. Mary's College of Maryland during 18–23 June 1991. The resulting handbook (McGovern, 1993) entailed the 'most comprehensive analysis and recommendations about undergraduate psychology since bipeds appeared on the evolutionary totem pole' (Brewer, 1997, 438). Furthermore, the Report advocated that:

> the crucial methodology courses should cover experimental, correlational, and case study techniques of research, and they should involve firsthand data collection, analysis, and interpretation. Methodology courses should cover statistics, research design, and psychometric methods, and they should be prerequisites for some of the content courses (Brewer, 1997, 439).

It is noteworthy that the recommendations regarding teaching research methodology did not mention anything about qualitative methods. Furthermore, Jackson et al. (2001) distinguished between experimental and non-experimental (that is, observational, survey, correlational and quasi-experimental) methods, but did not include qualitative methods as a category in their analysis of the demographics of research methods textbooks in psychology.

The Cornell, Michigan, Kulik and St. Mary's Reports all evaluated the prevailing undergraduate curriculum in psychology and typically offered recommendations. The developing picture suggests that research methods emerged as a separate course in the psychology curriculum after the McKeachie and Milholland Report (1961) and gathered momentum following the Kulik Report (1973).

In 2001 the American Psychological Association's Board of Educational Affairs appointed a task force on undergraduate psychology major competencies that produced guidelines subsequently approved by the APA Council of Representatives in August 2006. The APA Report (2007) identified ten undergraduate psychology learning goals and a series of suggested learning outcomes for each goal. Goal 2 pertained to research methods in psychology: 'students will understand and apply basic research methods in psychology, including research design, data analysis, and interpretation'. None of the suggested learning outcomes for this goal includes terms such as 'experiment', 'experimentation' or 'experimental psychology'. Quite clearly, a full transformation from the original view of research in psychology as an exclusively experimental/laboratory one, which is methodologically more inclusive, was now complete. Nonetheless, the goals and related learning outcomes do not mention qualitative research *per se*.

How did Research Methods Emerge as a Separate Course in Psychology?

One possibility is that the individuals attending these successive conferences played a role in the evolution of the research methods course, at least at their home institutions and perhaps more widely. Of course, the picture is murky because we do not know the extent to which the reports were disseminated, read and discussed by academic psychologists throughout the United States. In addition, other factors were contributing to a *zeitgeist* of curricular change. For example, Holder et al. (1958) reported the results of a survey about the views of departmental chairs regarding an ideal undergraduate curriculum for prospective graduate students. Some departments may have been prompted to make curricular changes to better prepare their students for graduate school. In addition, Hepler (1959) addressed the prevailing discontent with the traditional experimental psychology course by depicting students mindlessly performing pre-planned experiments rather than engaging in meaningful research that could stimulate and develop the creative talents of students. Hepler also concluded that the appropriate course was 'basically a methodology course' (p. 638) that engages students in research projects of their own design. This challenge was met by authors who modified the format of existing experimental psychology textbooks or created ones for the new genre, a topic we address later in our discussion of research methods textbooks.

Longitudinal catalogue studies

We can explore how research methods emerged as a separate course by performing a longitudinal analysis of selected course catalogues. We limited the scope of our longitudinal analysis to the curricular offerings by institutions actively represented at the Michigan Conference in 1960. The conference directors, Wilbert McKeachie and John Milholland (University of Michigan); William Hunt (Northwestern University); and Robert Leeper (The University of Oregon) were full-time participants from doctoral institutions. In addition, Lawrence Cole (Oberlin College) and Wilbert Ray (Bethany College) were full-time participants from liberal arts institutions. We contacted archivists at these institutions and requested copies of the psychology course listings from 1955 to 1970. Once we had these materials we looked for changes in the curriculum. We expected that there would be considerable change in the course offerings related to research methods at these schools. In particular, we anticipated a move from experimental psychology courses to research methods courses.

The University of Michigan had elementary experimental and statistics courses in place in 1955. They introduced an honours course in research methods in 1960. In 1961, they removed the elementary statistics course and apparently replaced it with an upper division statistics course. In 1962, the elementary experimental course was removed and replaced, apparently, by upper division courses with laboratories (comparative, physiological, language, perception and motivation). This approach resembles Model 3 recommended by the McKeachie and Milholland Report (1961) (require statistics and infuse methods).

The University of Oregon had an upper division course in research methods in psychology in 1955. They added a statistics course in 1957. One year later, the research methods course was eliminated and in 1964 several new lower division courses in content areas such as perception, motivation and social psychology were added, each with a laboratory. In 1968, an introduction to experimental psychology was added as an honours course. This approach resembles Model 3 recommended by the 1961 Report (require statistics and infuse methods).

In 1955, Oberlin College already had courses in introductory experimental psychology and advanced experimental psychology. In 1961, they introduced a new course in design and analysis in behaviour research. By 1968, the research course was required for their experimental course. In 1970, a new course in research designs and psychometric analysis was introduced and replaced the design and analysis course. This approach resembles Model 2 recommended by the 1961 Report (separate courses).

Between 1956 and 1957 Bethany College revised its psychology curriculum by dropping statistical methods and substituting a requirement for Math 101/102. Other methodology requirements included experimental psychology and tests, and measurements. Another change appeared in the 1963–1964 catalogue in which experimental psychology became a lecture (one hour) and laboratory (two hour) course and the content area courses (cognition and perception, and learning) also changed from a lecture only to lecture/laboratory format. In the same period, the department added a Junior Honors Seminar. This approach resembles Model 2 recommended by the 1961 Report (separate courses) and there is a strong emphasis on laboratory experiences.

It appears that the Michigan, Oberlin and Bethany developments correspond more closely to our expectations than that of Oregon. Michigan moved from the standard experimental course to a research methods course (albeit an honours one) in a series of steps between 1955 and 1960. Oberlin offered a new course in research methods in 1961, even though the instructor did not recall a connection to the conference and called it a coincidence (personal communication with Norman Henderson). Bethany revised their curriculum and emphasized laboratory experience. In contrast, Oregon had a research methods course in place in 1955 and removed it in 1958, so that is not quite the same pattern. More generally, it is obvious that all four schools experimented with this part of their curriculum quite a bit during this period, even though the exact changes differed from school to school, as might be expected given the variety of models offered by the 1961 Report.

The Michigan Report was available to academic psychologists at institutions which were not represented at the Michigan Conference. A case in point is Fresno State College (now California State University, Fresno), home institution of Holder et al. (1958), whose Report recommended curricular changes to better prepare their students for graduate school. When we examined the course listings from 1955 to 1970, we noted a change to emphasize preparation for graduate school between the 1957 and 1958 catalogues. The 1964 catalogue introduced new requirements for Behaviour Research I and II explicitly defined as a 'research methodology course' with the prerequisite of elementary statistics. In 1969, a single research design and methods course presenting research design, statistics and philosophy of science and also featuring student participation in research and report writing replaced the two methods courses. This approach resembles Model 2 recommended by the 1961 Report (separate courses), a curriculum familiar to the first author, who was an undergraduate there.

Research methods textbooks

The first of the new genre of research methods textbooks may be Frank McGuigan's (1960) text: *Experimental Psychology: A Methodological Approach*. In an obituary of McGuigan, Merrill (2000) wrote that McGuigan's volume:

> was one of the first psychology textbooks in which specific details of the scientific methodology were stated clearly and concisely. Prior to the publication of this book, psychology had been defined in textbooks as content oriented, whereas McGuigan intentionally changed to a methodological definition (Merrill, 2000, 677).

Both the PsycINFO abstract and the preface for the 1960 textbook echo this sentiment. In his preface, McGuigan states:

> the present trend is to define experimental psychology not in terms of specific content areas, but rather as a study of scientific methodology generally, and of the methods of experimentation in particular. There is considerable evidence that this trend is gaining ground rapidly. This book has been written to meet this trend (McGuigan, 1960, iii).

McGuigan added that:

> the point of departure for this book is the relatively new conception of experimental psychology in terms of methodology, a conception which represents the bringing together of three somewhat distinct aspects of science: experimental methodology, statistics, and philosophy of science (ibid.).

In addition, we examined the prefaces and tables of contents for other textbooks first published from the late 1940s to the late 1960s. Postman and Egan (1949) presented a traditional experimental text that emphasized content (for example, psychophysics, conditioning, memory and transfer of training) over methods (see the evolution of experimental psychology, December 1999). In the preface, Postman and Egan note that:

> Experimental methods and laboratory procedures cannot, of course, be divorced from psychological facts and principles. Our goal was, therefore, to give a survey of the main empirical findings and functional relationships in selected areas of experimental psychology with special emphasis on the control, manipulation, and measurement of variables (Postman and Egan, 1949, xiii).

In contrast, by the late 1960s, most textbooks were entirely devoted to research methods as opposed to specific content (for example, Plutchik, 1968). Virtually all the new genre expressed the thematic trinity, a trend still present in contemporary research methods textbooks for undergraduates.

Summary and Conclusions

We conclude by discussing recent trends, suggesting new research and considering to what extent our analysis applies to other social sciences. We have noted two trends in teaching research methods in recent years, not discussed earlier in the main body of this chapter. First, both textbooks for research methods and classroom instruction now emphasize research ethics in addition to the thematic trinity of statistics, research methods and philosophy of science. Nowadays, these topics represent the four pillars of contemporary research methods in psychology. Chapter 8 of the present volume (by Donna McAuliffe) supports the importance of research ethics to the contemporary teaching of research methods. Second, another recent trend is for psychology departments to implement year long courses that replace the former sequence of separate statistics and research methods courses. In some sense, this approach is a variation of the second model articulated by the 1961 Michigan Report. We believe the integrated approach has benefited from the development of a new genre of textbooks and become more visible simply because some departments have long employed this integrated approach. Schweigert (1994) authored the first explicitly integrated approach textbook; however, others such as Gary Heiman (1998) and Sherri Jackson (2003) have also published textbooks in this genre.

We believe that there are opportunities for further research regarding the history of teaching research methods. For example, the Jackson et al. (2001) paper is an excellent starting point for a longitudinal analysis of multi-edition research methods textbooks by authors such as McGuigan (1960) and others. There is merit in exploring what undergraduates could and should know about less traditional methods, including methods for historical research and qualitative research. Our impression is that psychology students learn relatively little about other research techniques such as these, although instruction regarding qualitative research is more common in other social sciences (see Chapter 1 by Judith Preissle and Kathryn Roulston; and also Claire Wagner and Chinedu Okeke, Chapter 5).

A question that needs to be addressed is why psychology and other social sciences in the United States explicitly teach undergraduates about the philosophy and methods of science when the so-called hard sciences do not do so. In biology, chemistry and physics, research methods are commonly infused throughout the curriculum through a series of laboratory experiences attached to various courses. In contrast, sociology and political science ordinarily teach research methods in one or more free-standing courses. Psychological instruction in methodology is a hybrid of the natural and social sciences; psychologists prefer the stand-alone courses often taught in the social sciences but initially modelled the course after the natural sciences (that is, experimental psychology). The shift from experimental psychology to research methods courses thus represents a move toward psychology's social science siblings and away from its natural science ones.

Our concern is to what extent our depiction of the emergence of research methods in psychology constitutes a general model for curricular change in other social sciences. This is important, as it touches on the contentious issue of the extent to which various social science disciplines take, or perhaps should take, different approaches to the teaching of research methods. Does the contention that there is a form of research methods generic to all social sciences result from historical circumstances, insofar as other disciplines simply adopted the psychology model? It would be instructive to address this and related questions, although there appears to have been no research in the area so far.

In summary, we have extended the efforts of earlier scholars (Brewer, 1997; Perlman and McCann, 1999) in our examination of how teaching research methods has evolved within the psychology curriculum in the United States. We regard our chapter as distinct from earlier contributions in two ways. First, we have focused on the history of teaching research methods whereas earlier studies have looked at the entire psychology curriculum. Second, we have attempted to answer the question of how the research methods course has become a common requirement in the curriculum. Longitudinal studies indicate that key academic institutions appeared to play a significant role in the evolution of the research methods course. We suggest that similar longitudinal analyses may be useful in better understanding the history of other features of the psychology curriculum.

Acknowledgements

We thank archivists Alan Boyd (Oberlin College); R. Jeanne Cobb (Bethany College); Jean Coffee (California State University, Fresno); Christopher Cox (University of Wisconsin-Eau Claire); Glenda Insua (University of Michigan); and Bruce Tabb (University of Oregon) for providing copies their college catalogues. We also thank Nancy Minahan for thoughtful comments that helped us prepare the final version of this chapter.

PART II
Approaches to the Curriculum

Chapter 3

The Role of Theory in Research

Barbara Kawulich

Introduction

One of the challenges facing the teacher of research methods is that students sometimes find it difficult to understand the role that theory plays in developing and conducting research. This was a problem for me in my own experience as a graduate student in the 1980s and early 1990s. The research courses I was required to take in my master's and doctoral programmes of study were courses on statistics. In those courses, research theory was rarely discussed and, when it was, it was presented in terms of positivism. I believe this may have been the approach in many universities and, as a consequence, today's methods teachers may lack a broader perspective on the relationship between theory and research; or, like me, they may have had to do a large amount of self-directed searching. I believe that a sound understanding of the relation of theory to research practice is fundamental to research methods education. In this chapter, I will share some of the issues about theory that I have found to be important in teaching research methods.

What is Theory?

Kurtines and Silverman (1999) define theory as an explanatory statement used to help explain and understand relations among variables, how they operate and the processes involved. The importance of theory lies in its ability to assist the researcher to identify and organize the connections among various phenomena that may seem unrelated. Researchers need a particular theoretical perspective from the outset to help them answer 'why' questions and to explain various cases or units of analysis in certain situations; theories determine the relationship between concepts that are carefully defined, ways to measure those concepts and what influences them (McTavish and Loether, 2002). Without theory, students tend to come up with questions that are not thought through for a particular setting and are, therefore, not meaningful for the members of that context. Their methods may not be appropriate for the situation and their results may be hard to justify, if not unfounded. Theory should drive the research process from beginning to end, providing a framework for action and for understanding.

In discussions in the literature, the term *theory* is used in three ways. First, it is used to reflect specifically explicated theories that make up paradigms, such as identity theory or social construction theory used in symbolic interactionism. Second, it is portrayed more implicitly in a body of literature that provides a framework for understanding of a subject, such as the literature available on the topic of reading comprehension. Third, *theory* is used implicitly to describe the researcher's assumptions and beliefs about the topic under study, as in sharing one's theoretical perspective on a topic. While using specifically explicated theories is preferable, those who teach RM will have to consider the time available to devote to teaching about theory and the level of students they teach – that is, whether they are teaching undergraduate or graduate students. However one defines theory in his or her research, that definition should be described in detail and justified in the writing to explain to the reader how it has directed and/or influenced the design and implementation of the study and how it affected the analysis and interpretation of the data.

Notions related to *theory* in social scientific research are *paradigm, concept, construct* and *proposition*. Not surprisingly, students sometimes find it difficult to distinguish between them all and to understand their relationship to one another. What is the distinction between a paradigm and a theory and why is it important to our understanding of theory? Babbie (2001) distinguishes between paradigms and theories, defining the former as general frameworks or viewpoints and the latter as sets of interrelated statements that are used to explain some aspect of social life. These theories flesh out the paradigms, offering an explanation for what we observe, while the paradigms offer a way of looking (see Maree, Chapter 4; and Wagner and Okeke, Chapter 5). Silver (1983) views theory somewhat differently: she views it as a way to perceive reality or a means for expressing one's perception of the world. It enables the reader to enter into the researcher's world to understand reality as he or she does. While Babbie defines paradigms and theories as separate but related concepts, Silver's definition of theory incorporates the two conceptual definitions.

Anfara and Mertz (2006) provide an excellent example of the relationship between paradigms, theories, concepts, constructs and propositions, using Maslow's (1954) hierarchy of needs. As a tool for understanding human motivation, Maslow describes various needs that must be met, some of which are more fundamental and necessary than others. In this example, the needs themselves are viewed as the concepts, the levels of needs are illustrated as constructs and these needs are arranged hierarchically (propositions). Maslow showed how lower order needs must be fulfilled before higher order needs; therefore, he concluded, one is motivated to fulfil those more basic needs (theory). Thus, a combination of the definitions of the terms (paradigms, theory, propositions, constructs and concepts) by Babbie, Silver, and Anfara and Mertz, may elucidate for students how concepts are related to constructs, which are arranged according to propositions, which make up theories, which flesh out paradigms (see Figure 3.1).

Figure 3.1   The relationship of concepts to constructs to propositions to theories to paradigms

What is the Relationship of Theory to Practice?

In his discussion of theory driven research, Willer (1992) states that the way theory is structured determines how the research proceeds. He argues the value of viewing theory driven research as empirical research (which students often think of as meaning 'experimental' or 'quantitative'), whether quantitative or qualitative. As noted previously, this theoretical frame may be either tacit/implicit or overt/explicit. Tacit or implicit theory might be described as what you think is going on in the study, while overt or explicit theory would be the specific theoretical framework that assists in the identification of important concepts, operational definitions, development of research questions and interpretation of the data. Theory drives our actions in daily life and in research, whether or not we are aware of that theoretical frame.

One's philosophical and theoretical perspectives, both tacit and overt, drive one's approach to research (LeCompte and Preissle, 1993). It is important for students to learn that this applies to any published research literature; they must also be aware of the theoretical frame they bring to their own research.

Every discipline has its own implicit theoretical framework(s) based on the vocabulary, concepts and explicit theories used in that discipline; these theories determine the types of things that are of interest and the types of questions one asks (Merriam, 1998). In teaching action research to classroom teachers, where the emphasis for me is to teach them techniques that enable them to improve their practice, I do not enter into a specific discussion of explicit theories. I require them, however, to share the implicit theory and related assumptions about the topic under study and to seek out literature on their topic to inform and underpin their study. In this way, their tacit theoretical frameworks become apparent to them and aid them to put aside their personal orientations to view the data neutrally. The works of others, found in the literature review on the topic under study, further provide them with a theoretical framework for developing and understanding their research. The literature provides a basis for understanding, a basis for identifying gaps in the literature and a basis for making a comparison between one's research findings and the existing literature.

McTavish and Loether (2002) also point out the value of the literature review as a means for understanding how prior theory has affected others' work, what concepts are important to the topic under study, how others define various concepts, and what questions other researchers deem to be important. Theories are used to guide research design and to let us know when the research is complete; McTavish and Loether contend that theory is critical for identifying concepts and the situations in which these concepts may undergo change. Many instructors require students to set aside a separate chapter for the literature review as a means to 'structure the inquiry, identify gaps in the literature, outline principal theoretical lines of thought, and generate potential research possibilities' (Clandinin and Connelly, 2000, 41). However, Clandinin and Connelly suggest that the literature may be interwoven throughout the final research product in a less formal way than having a separate literature review chapter.

One cannot properly implement a study without a guiding theory. As LeCompte and Preissle state:

> research designs are improved radically – in applicability and generalizability, in credibility and validity, and in precision and reliability – by explicit attention to the influence of theory throughout the design and implementation process (LeCompte and Preissle, 1993, 137).

Quantitative studies that do not include general theory, particularly those oriented toward causal analysis, may leave the researcher unable to explain why some variables affect other variables (Mahoney, 2004). Sherraden (2000) suggests that theory provides an integral basis for knowledge building in applied social research and in basic research alike. An exception to this is the use of grounded theory approaches, which are used to generate theory by grounding the findings in the data, rather than from a particular theoretical perspective. Grounded theory also may be used to test theory or to further develop it.

The pervading role of theory is summarized in Figure 3.2. This figure illustrates that theory is important to all aspects of research. Theory directs the types of questions asked and determines which potential participants can best inform one's study. For example, in her study of HIV-positive adults' meaning making, viewed through transformational learning theory, Merriam (2006) illustrates how sample selection was guided by her research question, which was derived from her theoretical framework.

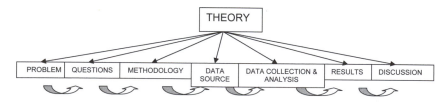

Figure 3.2   The role of theory in research

In my role as a teacher of research methods, I frequently use my own ethnographic research as an example of how various theories yield different types of questions for study. For example, from the perspective of feminist theory, my investigation of Muscogee (Creek) culture (Kawulich, 1998, 2004), which is a matrilineal subculture of the patriarchal mainstream culture, focuses on these women's choices and their perspectives of their role in the culture and how their roles differ from those of the men in that culture, while a cultural theory approach might focus on how they perceive their socialization in Muscogee (Creek) culture to have affected their life decisions. Using identity theory, by contrast, leads to questions about what it means to be a Creek woman. If I took a critical theory approach to my work, I might ask, 'How do the women of this culture perceive that their role as leaders differs from that of the male leaders?' The theoretical viewpoint guides my thinking in developing questions, selecting participants, collecting data in various ways, in analysing that data and in presenting it. If theory determines the types of problems to be studied, it also provides the framework for looking at a problem. The theory and, hence, the problem determine what questions need to be answered by the study. The questions lead the researcher to use a particular methodology, guided by a theory that is appropriate to answer those questions. Theory and methodology also direct the researcher's role in selecting and interacting with participants and in determining what data should be collected to answer the research questions. Theory also determines one's approach to analysing the data collected and how one interprets, presents and applies the findings of the research (LeCompte and Preissle, 1993). Data viewed through a particular theoretical frame would generate different interpretations, similar to the way various theories generate different questions.

Is the Use of Theory Discipline-specific?

Williams (2000) suggests that theory used to guide research often is 'derived from a particular specialism' (p. 158). Various disciplines tend to use particular theories more often than others and there seem to be differences in how various disciplines view the use of theory. In some disciplines, it is evident (from a historical perspective) why certain theoretical perspectives predominate. For example, in anthropology, several key figures of the twentieth century were in some way associated with institutional anthropology in New York City with the American Museum of Natural History. Frank Boas, who was an assistant curator at the museum in the late 1800s, for example, trained or worked with many of the twentieth-century's anthropologists, including Margaret Mead, who was an adjunct professor at Columbia University with Boas, Ruth Benedict and Alfred Kroeber, among others. Boas's influence shifted the focus of prior anthropological work from the traditional typological/racialist physical anthropological approach to one that focused on the individual in the culture and on how the culture was structured internally. His approach emphasized historical study (looking at processes exhibited in cultural traits) and psychological study (looking at how individuals from different cultures think and view the world). Boas's influence on the field of anthropology coloured how anthropologists of today view their discipline and how they conduct their research (Lesser, 2004).

Another example of the relationship of theory to discipline exists in sociology. Ritzer (2000) notes that, in preparing his fifth edition of *Modern Sociological Theory*, he once again added systems theory to the book because of the increased visibility of and attention to the work of Luhmann in international sociological research. Ritzer describes the theories included in his book as having stood the test of time, as having wide application and as addressing important social issues. He suggests that these theories developed from the importance of such social factors as political revolutions that addressed social order, the rise of capitalism and socialism, the increasing importance of feminism, urbanization, changes resulting from religious influences and the growth of science and technology. These factors have influenced how various sociologists over the last two hundred years view the world around them and, thus, have influenced the generation of and reliance upon various theories found in the discipline.

So, of what importance is theory to the research in various disciplines? In education, classroom practice relies on tacit and formal theory alike, as it is carried out within the teachers' framework of assumptions and beliefs (Deng, 2004). Prevalent theories used in education include constructivism, change theory, leadership theory, cognitive theory and others, such as theories by Bandura, Vygotsky or Maslow. The discipline of sociology relies on such theories as structural functionalism, conflict theory, symbolic interactionism and exchange theory among others (Ritzer, 2000). The discipline of psychology also emphasizes the use of theory in research design, implementation and interpretation. Of the many branches of psychology, only a couple will be mentioned here. For example, typical theories found in educational psychology include Bandura's social cognitive learning theory; Vygotsky's (1989) cultural historical theory of psychological development; and Piaget's cognitive development theory. Counselling and psychotherapy studies frequently use such theories as psychoanalytic, Adlerian, existential, person-centred; Gestalt, reality, behaviour, cognitive behaviour or family systems theories in therapy (Corey, 1996).

Anthropologists readily rely on theoretical frameworks for guiding research design, implementation and interpretation. Bernard (1994) describes two basic types of theory used in anthropological studies. Ideographic theory is elemental theory that applies to a single case, while nomothetic theory applies to many cases. Typical theories associated with anthropological studies are cultural materialism, sociobiology, structuralism, structural Marxism and, psychological and cognitive idealism, for example, Harris (2001).

Other disciplines, such as archaeology and social work, do not rely as heavily on the use of theory. In the case of archaeology, Bamforth (1999) suggests that, since the 1960s, theory has become a primary pursuit of some archaeologists; yet, he notes, the practical, applied nature of archaeology, that is, the precise collection of artefacts and features and their relationship, is very concrete and may be considered by some to be atheoretical. He notes that archaeology is rooted in observation and evidence, but the interpretation is grounded in both explicit and implicit theoretical background knowledge and generalizations. Archaeology typically is not carried out to test hypotheses; therefore, experimental designs are not appropriate. Further, this discipline does not lend itself to replication; hence, Bamforth suggests that theory should be used in archaeological studies to help the researcher identify evidence, design data collection procedures, assess the strength of findings and enhance understanding. These studies typically use mid-range theories to connect archaeological data to human behaviour or use culture theory to explain that data. Mid-range theories are those which contain fairly concrete concepts that can be operationally defined and empirically tested, as opposed to grand theories, which are more abstract and lend themselves less to empirical testing. These (and other) theories and their uses in this discipline have received increased emphasis in discussion in the past decade (Bamforth, 1999).

Social workers also rely on the use of theory. However, Thyer (2001) believes that much of social work research is not theory-based and that little attention is paid to theory or at least it is rarely articulated. Thyer suggests that not all research needs to be theory-based. For example, he lists the following types of research as being atheoretical: needs assessments; descriptive studies; epidemiological research; some forms of qualitative inquiry; policy analysis; demographic studies; cross-cultural studies; meta-analyses; studies on methodological innovations; historical studies; empirically oriented risk assessments; predictive studies; evaluations of clinical interventions; agency programmes or community practice. Yet designing these types of research with a theoretical underpinning could provide a deeper, richer interpretation of results.

Williams (2000) suggests that there is a trend toward preparation of social researchers, rather than sociologists or educationalists, for example: 'What is odd then about considering social research as a discipline, is that its *raison d'etre* is a set of tools for investigation' (p. 163). Social research, he points out, does not have a body of theory that explains what the world is like. While it has its foundation in epistemology as the framework for using methods for investigating a problem, Williams notes, it lacks ontological foundations that other disciplines have. He emphasizes the importance of the role of theory in social research, when he states that producing social researchers with no grounding in a particular discipline is similar to producing technicians who conduct research without regard for theoretical implications and these technicians may conduct research that produces untestable results.

In a recent informal survey of 22 graduate level research methods texts from the fields of education, anthropology, sociology, psychology and general social sciences, I found that four did not address theory, 11 addressed the role of theory in a few pages of one chapter, four of them devoted a chapter to the subject of theory and three of them addressed theory as an integral part of research and covered the role of theory in the research process throughout the book (though one of these texts, Anfara and Mertz, 2006, is an edited volume specifically examining the role of theory in research). Evidently, not everyone agrees that theory is important in the teaching of research methods or methodology.

How do Theories Affect One's Choice of Methods?

Sherraden (2000) proposes that theory and method are inextricably related aspects of social science inquiry. He describes theory as 'the specification of how we think things work, so that this thinking is subject to empirical test' (p. 5). The theoretical perspective determines the questions the researcher asks and thus influences the methods of collecting and analysing data that will answer those questions. Bergman and Coxon (2005) contend that various approaches to research yield different answers to the same or similar questions, no matter how carefully one attempts to carry out the research. They suggest that 'metatheoretical approaches make different assumptions about human thought and action and, thus, are likely to accumulate, code, analyse, and interpret data differently'.

Various subject area disciplines tend to favour particular methods for collecting data. For example, ethnographers tend to use interviews, participant observation and documents for data collection to learn about cultural constructs, while researchers focused on studies of group behaviour may use focus group interviews or observation techniques to answer their questions, as noted by LeCompte and Preissle (1993). In their presentation of narrative inquiry, Clandenin and Connelly (2000) supply a variety of methods for collecting data, including storytelling, autobiographies, journalling, field notes, letter writing, conversations, interviews, family stories, documents, photos and life histories, all of which can be viewed as field texts for analysis. Denzin and Lincoln (2000) indicate that various disciplines rely on certain methods or research practices. For instance, education has a history of using ethnographic methods; anthropology relies on participant observation and ethnographic methods, as do sociology, communication and cultural studies; cinema and literary studies rely on textual, hermeneutic, feminist, psychoanalytic, semiotic and narrative analysis; while history, biography and archaeology have a history of using archival, material culture, historical and document analysis, and medicine, communications; and education have relied on discourse and conversational analysis.

Hence, the researcher's standpoint, personal philosophies and theoretical perspectives affect his or her choice of methods; to ensure that the research questions are answered through the data collected and analysed, the data collection techniques must match the theoretical constructs (LeCompte and Preissle, 1993). For example, in my ethnographic study of how Muscogee (Creek) culture affects the women's life choices, participant observation and ethnographic interviews serve me well to answer the research questions. Culture theory derives from sociocultural anthropology and focuses on society and culture, particularly the study of customs, beliefs and traditions of social life. Since I am interested in cultural aspects of the women's lives, culture theory directs me to use ethnographic methods of data collection to answer the research questions and guides my investigation of how being socialized in the culture influences the community members' lives. It is important for my students to realize, however, that, while I rely on these theories for much of my own research and while I present examples to them from this research, there are other theories used to underpin research studies beyond these, which they may find to be more useful in their research.

It is not only in qualitative research that theory plays such a determinative role. Teachers of quantitative research also should place emphasis on the importance of theory in the entire research process, not just in the interpretation stage. In quantitative studies, theory may be used to direct the development of the hypotheses for the study and the means for testing those hypotheses. Theory determines the variables to be studied and the interpretation of the relationship among those variables. Yet this is not always made clear. Sometimes a particular theoretical framework may provide the impetus for a mixed methods design. For example, in educational psychology, cooperative learning (the theoretical perspective) may generate hypotheses to be tested and, at the same time, may generate questions that are answered qualitatively. The teacher may develop a hypothesis to test to determine whether the learning has taken place and also may observe students or interview students about their perceptions of the learning process.

How do we Incorporate Teaching Theory into a Semester-long Course?

Since different disciplines focus on particular theories and different paradigms subsume particular theories, several questions arise. First, to what extent do we need to teach particular theories within the disciplinary context? Second, do we need to teach about the role of theory? Third, if so, how can instructors of research methods provide adequate coverage of applicable theories within a one semester course? The previous discussion, I hope, has shown that various disciplines in the social sciences view theory as an integral part of teaching research methods, though to varying degrees. The discussion above also illustrates that the role of theory, whether implicit or explicit, is an integral part of the research process. It is impossible to provide a thorough discussion of explicit theories in a one semester course, but a cursory coverage of applicable theories is possible. Some instructors may argue that a survey of theories is a waste of time; however, some of us believe that an overview of theories is a good way to raise student awareness of the role of theory in research.

My own experience with theory as a student has made me aware that an insufficient grounding in theory poorly prepares students to conduct research. I regard it as important to expose my doctoral students to a broad range of theories from a variety of disciplines. I set aside three to four weekly class sessions at the beginning of the 16 week semester for their discussion of various theories that are used to underpin qualitative research, while the rest of the sessions focus on development of problem statements, research questions, data collection methods, analysis and write-up. Initially, I lectured on various theories and how they influence research design, data collection, analysis and interpretation. This approach did little to arouse their interest in the differences between these theories, so I handed over the instruction of the theories to them. I asked them to select a theory from an extensive list I gave them to present to the class and to provide a summary handout on the theory: its originator(s); the questions it generates; typical methods for collecting data; and how the theory typically is used. This considerably heightened their attention to theoretical constructs, their discussion of them and their retention. At the end of the course, each student has a stack of summaries of various theories that he or she can rely on later when deciding upon a theoretical approach that appeals to him or her, or that provides questions to guide the dissertation process. Further, I have found that my doctoral students find innovative ways to present these theories. One student, for example, in presenting postmodern theory, handed each classmate a card with a different comment about the life of Walt Disney as presented by people who knew and worked with him. By looking at the individual statements, one gathered a single viewpoint of the man and his work but by looking at the statements collectively, one obtained a more complete, sometimes very different, picture of his life, actions and interactions with others.

Several years ago, when I was teaching a two semester qualitative research course, I was able to allot more time to the discussion of theory. The one semester course I now teach does not allow for as much discussion on this topic, but students can be directed to tables in texts that cover the topic. A good example is provided by LeCompte and Preissle (1993, 128–33) in which they compare various aspects of functionalism, conflict theory, symbolic interactionism and ethnomethodology, critical theory, ethnoscience or cognitive anthropology, exchange theory, psychodynamic theory and behaviourism. While it is impossible to cover all available theories, I can share with students an example of how theory frames a study. The example uses a critical feminist theoretical framework and the problem addresses Muscogee (Creek) women's perspectives of leadership; the overall research question might be, 'How do they perceive their roles as leaders as compared to male leaders?' The methodology would draw from ethnography and the data sources would be Muscogee women who serve in leadership positions. The data collection methods would include interviews, observations and document analysis, and data would be analysed using narrative analysis. The results in this example focus on issues related to the traditional role of men as leaders, the importance of helping others in the culture and serving as a role model for other women – themes identified in the data. The discussion would centre on how the results support other works, such as various feminist leadership models and feminist critical theory. I also use actual data from this study to illustrate how to code and analyse the data. At each step, students are shown how critical feminist theory guides what the researcher does and how he or she interprets the findings. Students then are required to carry out a short qualitative study during the semester and illustrate a theoretical frame throughout their study.

Summary

Theory, both tacit and explicit, is an integral part of the research process from beginning to end. It is important in the development of questions: in creating a research plan; in determining what types of data should be collected and from whom; in determining how one should collect the needed data; and how it should be analysed and interpreted. Theory seems to be emphasized more in qualitative research than in other types of research; however, because of the role that theory plays in the research process, from beginning to end, it is important for those of us who teach research methods to emphasize how important the theoretical underpinnings of the study are to each step in the process. In this way, we are better able to teach students that atheoretical research may be viewed as inferior to research that is framed and guided by explicated theory. This chapter is not meant to be the definitive justification for theoretically-based research, but is intended as a beginning point for future discussion of the role that theory plays in quality research. Some questions that arise for me include, 'How can we as teachers of both qualitative and quantitative research methods incorporate discussions of theory into our already packed curricula?' and 'What techniques do others use to teach the value of theory in the research process?' I hope these and similar questions will prompt the readers to engage with the place of theory in teaching research methods.

Chapter 4

Critical Realism and Teaching Empirical Methods

David J.F. Maree

Introduction

Reasons for choosing qualitative, quantitative or both methods for inclusion in a methods course are complex and multifarious, and these reasons do not always involve a clear explication of the theoretical assumptions that the lecturer has used when designing the course (Wagner and Okeke, Chapter 5). Frequently even those teaching experimental methods within a quantitative paradigm resign themselves to being labelled positivist. One can avoid certain basic epistemic mistakes such as believing that positivism and measurement equates to being scientific (and being interpretative or constructionist is *not* scientific!) by examining some basic assumptions about what science is and what reality is.

The aim of this chapter is to provide the research methods teacher with a particular theoretical basis for teaching empirical and quantitative methods. The theoretical perspective explicated in this chapter is called Critical Realism (CR) and was chosen as a fruitful way to regard empirical work that needs to negotiate itself between the problems that positivism presents, on the one hand, and those of constructionism, on the other.

Roy Bhaskar gave form to Critical Realism beginning in the mid-1970s in two important works, namely *A Realist Theory of Science* (1975) and *The Possibility of Naturalism* (1998). CR's stance against postmodernism and positivism did not endear itself to many theorists and only later more works and debates surrounding CR arose. Bhaskar (1975), in the context of natural science, polemicized against positivism and Kantian transcendental idealism by opting for transcendental realism to emphasize the focus on a mind independent reality. The same themes occurred in the context of the social sciences (Bhaskar, 1998). CR negotiates the line between empiricism, on the one hand, and idealism, on the other. As examples of empiricism and idealism, the perspectives of positivism and constructionism will be discussed.

Positivism

Positivism refers to the development of logical positivism or logical empiricism in the 1930s. (These terms are more accurate descriptions of positivist thought than the term 'positivism' although I shall use the latter for the sake of brevity.) A number of philosophers and scientists gathered in Vienna to discuss matters of importance and were called the Vienna Circle. They were persons such as Carnap, Neurath and others. They drew heavily on the work of Wittgenstein, and Karl Popper also debated with them (Hanfling, 1981).

Positivism is a strict empiricist enterprise which declared that only those statements that reflect a reduction to an observation statement can lay claim to meaningful knowledge. In other words, if someone tells me 'it's raining', I would regard that statement as meaningful and as a knowledge claim as soon as I observe that it is indeed raining or indicate what I would do to verify the claim (Ayer, 1946). Thus, scientific knowledge can be based only on observable statements. There were various moves to approximate claims about certain so-called unobservables as knowledge claims. For instance, if the needle on an amp meter moves a certain distance, one can speak of a certain amount of electric current flowing, even though it is unobservable (Hempel, 1965). Positivists had a great issue with unobservables and in this sense they were anti-realist. Forces such as cause or concepts, such as truth, cannot be observed and thus cannot be meaningfully spoken about within a scientific context.

The 'realism' part of CR refers to the reality that one investigates. It does not, however, refer only to that reality we can see and touch; if it did, it would be called 'empiricism'. The empiricist believes that the only aspect of the world worth investigating is the observable part. This would be true of the positivist as well, who would reduce everything worth investigating to what can be observed or at least to a statement that can be tested as being observable. Everything lying outside this realm would be nonsense or not meaningful. Behaviourists would also count as empiricists since they deny the meaningfulness of investigating mental things: only that which can be observed, namely behaviour, should be investigated. Behaviour can be viewed as externalized thoughts. Some behaviourists and positivists do not deny the reality of the mental, but only that it cannot be sensibly investigated.

The realist goes further than the empiricist, in believing that there are unobservable things – stuff beyond observables such as structures, powers and mechanisms – that are worth discovering and investigating.

Hume was an empiricist and from his empiricist philosophy followed an intense scepticism about what we can know from our surroundings by means of observation. However, one consequence of his empiricist view, namely, that knowledge should have its roots in the senses, is the problem with causality or the fact that all that we can perceive when looking at events are those events that follow regularly on from each other. We cannot observe something such as 'cause' or a 'necessary connection' between events. A simple example might suffice: look at two billiard balls, the one is moving towards the other, bumps into it and then the second one starts moving. One sees two events, the movement of billiard ball A and then that of B. We tend to say that because A bumped into B, the latter started moving and therefore A caused B to move. However, Hume says all that I saw was two events happening in conjunction. Someone doing the same experiment over and over sees only a constant conjunction of events but never the 'thing' called a cause. All that we have, then, is a constant conjunction of events and because we are psychologically inclined to form an association between constant events taking place, we believe that there is something like a cause.

A law is thus based on the observation of a constant conjunction of events (and some psychological habit-forming inclinations). The problem is twofold: 1) a constant conjunction of events usually can be observed only in closed systems, that is, where mechanisms are controlled that only the particular set of events can be observed; 2) events are identified with what they establish, namely, laws. This has the absurd conclusion that only when events play out is a law established. However, should a law not be universal, that is, apply in closed and open systems alike? The problem with the brand of empiricism underlying positivism is the ontological conflation of laws and events. It sees real things only in one dimension, namely, the one where we experience observable events.

To get past this positivist view of science to the root of the defining characteristics of science we need to ask the transcendental question, namely, how is science possible, or more specifically, what are the conditions that must prevail for science to be possible? We note that science is possible and taking place, so some conditions in the world must be such that it allows science to take place (Bhaskar, 1998). The answer is, in short, that reality must be *structured* and *intransitive*. It is structured in the sense that events do not exhaust the real and it is intransitive because it exists independently of human minds.

Some Assumptions of CR: Open and Closed Systems

CR distinguishes between three levels or domains of reality, namely the domains of the empirical, actual and the real. The domain of the *empirical* restricts science and what is real to what we can experience. The domain of the *actual* restricts science to actual events taking place. In the domain of the *real* the mechanisms, powers and structures of reality are revealed and discovered. These mechanisms and powers can be unobservable (but real) and the process of science is aimed at discovering and revealing deeper levels of reality. The positivist collapses the three domains into that of the empirical. This means that reality for the positivist is restricted to experiencing actual events. Thus, event regularities are all that the positivist has to show for what is real. We can call this an epistemic collapse of the three domains because when an actual collapse takes place, or rather, when the three domains coincide, then we have a brief closed system normally brought about by an experiment (Collier, 1994).

A closed system arises when we are able to isolate a causal mechanism – this is what normally happens when one does a scientific experiment. Note that the positivist or empirical realist does not allow the postulation of unobservable mechanisms responsible for actual observed events and only has the luxury of typifying events, as they occur, as laws (Collier, 1994). Nature is an open system with a number of mechanisms responsible for a number of potential and actual events. A mechanism can be real but never or rarely realized or when it is realized it can go by unobserved. An event can have a number of mechanisms as cause and it is this multifariousness and the difficulty to observe spontaneously occurring events with singular causes that makes nature an open system and necessitates experiment. It is only with experiment, by creating a closed system, that we can control a system to try and isolate a single mechanism underlying certain events (Bhaskar, 1975; 1998).

'Laws' or tendencies are identified when mechanisms and powers are isolated (the term 'law' has the sense of something always taking place, no matter what; thus, we rather speak of a tendency, because in open systems a law, when exercised, can be thwarted or not have observable effects). We identify a tendency when we create a closed system. As anybody knows that has been involved in experimentation in the science laboratory at school, experiments can go very wrong: things blow up; inaccurate measurements are made; the resistance of a surface confounds results; and they all have to do with the human experimenter and the open system he or she is trying to control.

The science we read about in textbooks that, for example, explain the laws of motion, can be demonstrated only in closed systems. Our billiard ball example can be extended to an experiment to determine whether momentum is conserved when one ball strikes the other. However, this can be illustrated only in an environment in which we can control the movement of one ball exactly and are able to make accurate measurements of the velocity of the balls. If the system ceases to be closed, outside influences, such as the weather, rough terrain or lack of visibility, can make it nearly impossible to do some experiments. Imagine trying to do the billiard ball momentum experiment on rough terrain, such as a gravel road, while it starts to rain and in the dark!

Further, we can illustrate the particular law of linear momentum only by controlling a number of variables while meddling with one. Reality, however, is never closed and, in the open systems that we live in, some so-called laws never get actualized or even observed but this does not mean they are less real. A social system is an example *par excellence* of an open system.

The point of experimental activity is that, if we do not distinguish between events and mechanisms underlying those events, then we identify law and event as ontologically the same thing. How do we explain that laws work even in open systems although they are not always realized or observed? In order for scientific (experimental) activity to be intelligible, one needs to assume that reality is structured and that mechanisms are responsible for events in open and closed systems alike.

What is the problem then with positivism? Of course, the critical realist uses experiments and observation as much as the positivist does, but whereas the positivist account of laws is restricted to empirical invariances (a constant conjunction of events) in closed systems, the critical realist account situates laws and mechanisms underlying events in open systems.

The Transitive and Intransitive Dimensions

CR views reality as independent from the human mind and interpretation of reality as fallible and provisional. Bhaskar (1975) made a distinction between the 'transitive' and 'intransitive' dimensions as objects of knowledge claims. This distinction is quite important because it highlights the epistemological mistakes one can make when conflating the two.

The *transitive dimension* is where we interpret reality – it is the domain of our theories and explanations and as such can be the object of our critical gaze as well. Knowledge is fallible and theories can be tested and revised. Interpretations can be argued about, revised and criticized. The mistake of constructionism is to equate reality and interpretation. This is an example of the epistemic fallacy (Bhaskar, 1975), that is, that *what* we can know is conflated with the way reality *is*.

CR is 'critical' because, despite its affirmation of a mind independent reality, it realizes that the human interpretation and understanding of that reality is far from exact: it is fallible, corrigible and tentative. Our interpretation, understanding, descriptions and theories cannot be equated to what is interpreted, understood or described. CR takes an explicit fallibilistic standpoint towards claims of knowledge and its theories: we can always be wrong and our theories need to be revised in the light of new evidence. The 'critical' also alludes to the constructionist and interpretivist who say that reality and what goes along with it somehow are intertwined with our language. Constructionists would say that changing one's interpretation means that one's perception of what is real changes. Language and constructions of reality are the final authority of truth. The critical realist counters by upholding the fallible and tentative nature of explanation and understanding.

The *intransitive dimension* is the domain of the real which is independent of the human mind. This reality is relatively stable, because there are structures that endure despite the flux and changes. It is also stratified and not one-dimensional, as the positivists let us think by restricting reality to the level of the actual, namely, to that which we can experience and observe when such events are actualized or take place.

The Quantitative Imperative

Measurement has played a significant role in the history of science. The billiard ball momentum example above illustrated the close connection between measurement and a closed system. The popular belief about positivism is that it ruthlessly endorses the quantitative imperative (although Michell (2003) found evidence that the quantitative imperative did not play such a strong role in the positivists' view of social science and psychology). The reductionist positivistic assumption that most scientific methods ought to be modelled on that of physics probably played a role in convincing social scientists that quantification is the hallmark of scientific work. Thus, a particular impression of what 'real' scientific work involves and the particular historical situation of social science and psychology led to social scientists' adopting measurement as a key element of their methodological approach – the so-called 'quantitative imperative' that it is necessary to measure things in order to be scientific (Michell, 2003). Psychology is a discipline that naïvely adopted a version of the quantitative imperative which led to an almost pathological blindness to what fundamental measurement in the science really entails (see Michell, 1997; 1999 for an insightful discussion and overview).

If measurement is to be on the same footing in the social sciences as in the natural sciences, it must be applied to things that can actually be measured. Michell (1997) regards it as part of the psychologist's task to find out whether the construct can actually be measured and to find an appropriate way to measure it. It makes sense to measure length because humans have devised measures that stay the same, irrespective of context. Stevens' early definition of measurement as the 'assignment of numbers to things according to a rule' was misconceived from the start (Michell, 1997), since assigning a number to a thing or event does not guarantee measurement in a fundamental sense, for several reasons.

First, as Wright and Linacre's (1989) article title says: '*Observations are always ordinal; measurements, however, must be interval.*' Merely assigning numbers to observations could at most provide ranking. Ranking does not equal interval measurement and fundamental measurement is always interval or at least ratio. Fundamental measurement requires having a linear scale, that is, the spacing between units means the same across the range of a scale. Social scientists construct Likert-type scales (which implies ranking of observations) and add the items to obtain a total score. The total score is then all too quickly utilized as an interval scale.

Second, a measuring instrument should not be dependent on the characteristics of the sample. It is similar to having a flexible measuring stick for length that, depending on the samples' average, minimum and maximum length, is adjusted so that ten equal intervals always fit in despite its actual length. This is precisely what happens with psychological and social measurement.

Rasch measurement is probably the closest model to that of fundamental measurement (Bond and Fox, 2001). It converts scores to a linear interval scale and separates the estimation of item properties from that of the sample. Measurement based on the classical test theory cannot separate sample and test characteristics – the difficulty of items and the reliability of a test always depend on which sample one uses. One thus gets a test whose properties depend on the characteristics of a sample and we have seen that the ideal of measurement is to have invariant measures.

Thus, measurement, first of all, should not be seen as the hallmark of science, as the discussion of CR and positivism has shown. By rephrasing the transcendental question above to whether the conditions of the possibility of science can be linked to measurement, it can be seen that it is not primary. Measurement is linked to the tools of science to reach its goal, namely, depth explanation or the uncovering of causal mechanisms. The image of science positivism constructed, which as we can see is wrong according to CR, was carried over to relativism and the postmodern trend of constructionism.

Constructionism

Constructionism arose as a reaction against positivism and foundationalism in science at the beginning of the previous century. The search for a scientific method that provides true knowledge and the search for an assured foundation for the edifice of scientific knowledge were overthrown by the work of, among others, Thomas Kuhn, Rorty and Feyerabend. There is no method that can lead to truth or certain knowledge (and the basis of empiricism and its positivistic variant) namely, observation, guarantees true and certain knowledge was turned inside out by these postpositivist theorists when they showed that observation is always theory laden. This simply means that observation takes place through the lens of theories, background knowledge, assumptions and perspectives. It was subsequently realized that scientific work was done in social contexts and that if no universal criteria for truth, method and knowledge existed these were socially determined and constructed. The shift from universal to local criteria emphasized the relative nature of science.

This sort of methodological and epistemological relativism found willing participants in some constructionist proponents in the human and social sciences and it was realized that people, more collectively than individually, create the truths they are willing to work and live with. For science this meant that knowledge is socially constructed and substantively subjective rather than objective! A simple example will suffice: the constructionist says that something such as 'personality' does not exist and is a mere fiction or creation of the human mind (Burr, 1995). It can be replaced by other categories and other 'realities'. Even the category of gender can be questioned and reconstructed. By contrast, the realist asserts the independence of reality from the human mind: there is something separate from the human mind that does not depend for its existence on the human mind.

Critical Realism in Social Science

Bhaskar (1998) said social science can be a science in the same sense as natural science but not in the same way. This means that social reality is structured and intransitive, that is, there are mechanisms underlying events and there are intransitive objects to be studied. Although things such societies and groups exist, there are some ontological limits placed on their nature (Bhaskar, 1998): 1) the existence of social structures depends on the activities they regulate; 2) social structures are concept dependent, that is, their existence depends in some way on the concepts people have of them; and 3) social structures are only relatively enduring, thus their tendencies (laws) are not universal in terms of space and time as the case is in natural science. However, social structures still form intransitive objects of study despite their concept dependence. The mistake of constructionism (and hermeneutics) is the collapse of language and being.

Because social reality is fundamentally open, with a multitude of mechanisms and tendencies at work, it is Bhaskar's (1998) opinion that it is almost impossible to do social science experimentation in the same way as in the natural sciences. If experimentation is impossible, then the social scientist has to find other means of studying social reality. Bhaskar proposes that the social sciences should investigate the open system as the natural science does its open system, finding a replacement or 'partial analogue' for experiment (Collier, 1994). According to Bhaskar:

> once a hypothesis about a generative structure has been produced in social science it can be tested quite empirically, although not necessarily quantitatively, and albeit exclusively in terms of its explanatory power (1998, 62).

In the natural sciences experiment is a form of work to isolate a mechanism and establish a tendency. A tendency allows prediction which ought to hold when the mechanism gets isolated. However, in the social sciences one starts off with so-called proto-theories or explanatory attempts (Collier, 1994). To transform the attempt into a theory it needs to be tested, and it can be tested only as an *explanation* of what has occurred. In natural science a causal mechanism can be isolated in a closed experimental situation in response to a causal hypothesis, but in social science an explanatory theory that explains better than other theories needs to be devised to account for the data. In essence, social science explanation is retroductive. It still accounts for causal mechanisms, that is, structures underlying events and phenomena, but not in an experimental way. An example is evolutionary psychology (or evolutionary biology or palaeontology) where the data is there to be observed and from it a coherent theory that explains the situation best has to be devised. Thus, some sub-disciplines in both the social and natural sciences cannot follow an experimental approach by creating a closed system and isolating a mechanism. Experimental approaches are more suited to some substrata (see below) in psychology, such as cognitive and neuropsychology, than others, such as social psychology or depth psychology.

The Stratification of Reality

I think that CR allows for creating closed systems, albeit limited, in social and psychological reality. This is based on Bhaskar's (1975) view of reality as stratified. CR distinguishes different strata or levels in nature, each with its own structure, mechanisms and powers. The relationship between these strata is important. The concept of stratified reality runs counter to reductionism, which says that phenomena at one level can be wholly reduced to mechanisms at a lower level. Bhaskar (1975) argues that biology cannot be reduced to chemistry because there are emergent mechanisms on the biological level that cannot be accounted for by mechanisms at the lower level. Nonetheless, the higher level presupposes the lower one.

Although, like nature, the social and the psychological operate within an open system, it is more difficult to produce closed systems in the former domains. Nevertheless, it is not impossible to approximate closed systems, depending on the stratum. The stratified nature of the social and psychological allows for different methodological approaches. As an example, in the domain of the psychological, one could differentiate between the levels of the biological, psychological and the phenomenal. Below the biological come other levels, such as those of chemistry and physics. Each level emerges from, but is not reducible to, the lower levels. Each level is governed by its own trends or laws from which one cannot predict the laws at a higher level. On the biological level we have the functioning of the brain and limbic systems responsible for human behaviour and functioning. The psychological describes human functioning in psychological nomenclature (for example, depth psychological terminology or folk psychological concepts). The phenomenal describes first person experience, such as consciousness, beliefs and desires. On the phenomenal level qualitative or interpretative methods are more appropriate and closure cannot easily be obtained. Closure becomes easier the lower one goes and measurement becomes correspondingly more appropriate. For instance, it is easier to measure reaction time than a personality construct on the psychological level.

In order to uncover mechanisms operating in the social and the psychological, various methods can be used, depending on the research question and the stratum. Measurement is but one tool and it is dependent upon the hard work of producing an approximate closed system.

Teaching Empirical Methods in Social Science

Critical Realism underlies the strong interplay between theory and empirical work. Explanations are tested empirically (in the way empirical is defined in CR) and the results inform further interpretation. The research student must learn to avoid assuming that measurement equates with empirical observation and is therefore scientific. Method should be appropriate to the stratum examined. When measurement and, of course, statistical analysis are used, they form only part of the explanatory/testing process. Theory (and thus explanation, understanding and argumentation) guides measurement – not the other way around (Bond and Fox, 2001).

The value of CR for teaching empirical methods in the social and psychological sciences is considerable. It does not provide a method and it is certainly not a method – it informs our discovery process. The methods teacher ought to be aware of the ontological and epistemological assumptions of research and avoid collapsing epistemology with ontology. CR provides a way of avoiding this epistemic fallacy and the problems of both positivism and constructionism. It thus provides a more appropriate description of the scientific process and hence a sound basis for teaching research methods than either positivism or constructionism. The most salient points of value to the methods teacher can be summarized as follows:

- A distinction must be made between mind and reality: the real cannot be constituted by the mind but of course it colours our interpretations. However, social realities are intertwined with our interpretations: they are concept dependent.
- Our interpretations and explanations are fallible and revisable.
- Contra positivism, closed systems rarely occur naturally because we live in an open system.
- Hence restricting our explanations to event regularities or actual experiences fundamentally impoverishes our explanations.
- The researcher needs to understand that given the autonomy of the ontological and its differentiation, science aims at deep explanations: there are a *multitude* of *mechanisms* and powers – some exercised, others latent – that give rise to events and phenomena.
- Reality is thus stratified and no single mechanism exists that can account for an event or phenomenon: different strata addressed by other disciplines and sub-disciplines can contribute to understanding phenomena.

The social scientist works with realities that are not always accessible by means of direct empirical testing and observation. The perceptual and causal effects of mechanisms are apparent around us: people are agents, they meddle and they change history. In the same way the domain of the social provides the necessary life world for scientists to operate in – the one presupposes, but cannot be reduced to, the other. Because the social/psychological is open in a more fundamental way than nature is, closure is difficult and observation of regularities and tendencies is even more difficult. However, realizing that we are working with a depth-ontology, that is, with a reality that is differentiated into the real, actual and empirical, we can avoid the pitfalls of empiricism by restricting the real to what can be experienced in events actually taking place. We also realize that our interpretations and meaning-making activities (that is, our theories) are fallible and provisional, and that it is hard work to explain and test them against reality. In this way even the empirical social scientist can move forward uncovering mechanisms pertinent to the social/ psychological without fear of overstepping the boundaries by making too bold a claim about the truth of the findings. Social science research is always open to discussion and criticism and never final, but it is about something that can be explained independently of the fallible constructions of the human mind.

Chapter 5

Quantitative or Qualitative: Ontological and Epistemological Choices in Research Methods Curricula

Claire Wagner and Chinedu Okeke

Introduction

This chapter examines one of the choices that academics often feel constrained to make when constructing research courses: whether to teach a quantitative or qualitative methodology (or both). We explore the usefulness of selecting curriculum content by making a distinction purely on a methodological level. We begin with a brief discussion of the principles and practices on which quantitative and qualitative research operate that brings to the fore the philosophical assumptions that underlie the differentiation between these methodologies and the reasons that inform their uses. We examine the criteria given in the literature for including either or both of these methodologies in the curriculum of a research course. We conclude that choosing between methodologies (or even combining methodologies) does not necessarily imply an attendant philosophical framework and argue that constructors and/or teachers of research courses need to be more aware of unexamined ontological and epistemological assumptions and about what we subsequently teach students.

Historical and Philosophical Assumptions

The debate on research methodology has a history that dates back to the eighteenth and nineteenth centuries' philosophy of science. The debate centres on what the source and nature of knowledge about the social world are supposed to be. The major philosophical currents of these periods include positivism, historicism, neo-Kantianism and pragmatism. From these philosophical currents, important ideas leading to the development of research paradigms emerged. For instance, the central aim of research within the confines of positivism is to discover universal laws through the positive data of experience, pure logic and pure mathematics (Haralambos and Holborn, 1995). Social scientists adopted this mode of conception of knowledge from the natural sciences (Giddens, 1997). Researchers within this orientation rely on controlled and systematic collection of data and during the conduct of research, 'persons or events are broken down into discrete … (and) directly observable units with behaviour that is separate from and unaffected by the observer' (Brink, 1991, 14).

However, anti-positivist researchers, influenced by the historicist, neo-Kantian and pragmatist philosophies, dismiss the positivists' assumptions as speculative and reductionistic. Taken jointly, the anti-positivists believe that human life is highly diversified and that the positivists' expression of it does not reflect its diversity. They therefore place emphasis on a deeper investigation of underlying meanings in order to uncover the distinctive cultural dynamics from which such forms of life had evolved. Anti-positivists are interested in analysing the conditions under which knowledge is produced while recognizing that observers within the social and physical world can do so only through paying attention to the distinctive character of humans. Generally the subject matter of the anti-positivist researcher is the understanding of the distinctive nature of human social interactions (Glesne and Peshkin, 1992).

What began as a collection of individual opinions through the positivists', historicists', neo-Kantians' and pragmatists' ideas of the eighteenth and nineteenth centuries gradually conflated into opposing epistemologies, or ways of knowing, the outcome of which is two distinct contemporary research orientations, each resting upon certain philosophical assumptions about the way knowledge of the social world is acquired. Researchers speak in terms of: positivism versus relativism; determinism versus interpretivism; hypothetico-deductivist versus inductivist; objectivism versus subjectivism; and of course quantitative versus qualitative approaches.

Thus for many theorists, this development is a case between two competing approaches and their methodologies (that is, positivism equals quantitative research and anti-positivism equals qualitative research). But for many others, it is a matter of different research methods with varying degrees of benefits and limitations suited for conducting particular kinds of social and behavioural enquiries. It could be asked to what extent this dichotomization, especially in terms of methodology, has helped the conduct of social research? And how does this division provide students with the epistemological consciousness that the real world of research seems to demand today? Before we engage with these questions, we provide a brief overview of quantitative and qualitative methodologies.

Overview of Quantitative and Qualitative Methodologies

Quantitative research is designed specifically for the identification and description of variables with a view to establishing the relationship between them. Quantitative researchers, therefore, study larger population samples as a prerequisite for valid, reliable and easily generalizable findings (Roberts, 2002). They use descriptive, correlational, quasi-experimental and experimental methods. Data analysis is usually executed through descriptive and inferential statistics and is often computer aided. Inferences are then drawn from a sample to the population based on the processed data.

Qualitative research implies recognition of processes that are not readily susceptible to measurement in terms of quantity, amount or frequency (Carney et al., 1997). Its emphasis is on capturing or obtaining an in-depth understanding of the interactional processes as manifested during a particular study (Wainwright, 1997). The qualitative researcher works at greater depth with a relatively small number of participants in order to enhance the quality of the responses (Brink, 1991) and mostly prefers interpretative methods, such as focus group discussions, naturalistic observation, and, unstructured and semi-structured interviews. Analysis in qualitative research starts with the management of data through the assembling of field notes, coding and searching for categories or patterns. Analytic methods include ethnographic, sequential and discourse analyses, the constant comparative method; analytic induction and grounded theorizing (Glaser and Strauss, 1967; Wildy, 1999), data-specific, content or context analyses (Callahan et al., 2003).

These, in very broad terms, are what we mean by quantitative and qualitative methodologies in the sections that follow.

Three Viewpoints on the Content of Research Courses

There is self-evidently a link between an academic's conception of research and what and how we teach our students about research (Brew, 2003). The origin and nature of our beliefs can be attributed to discursive practices (implicit linguistic practices that control our speech and behaviour): 'In an educational context ... legitimated discourses of power insidiously tell educators what books may be read by students, what instructional methods may be utilized, and what belief systems and views of success may be taught' (Kincheloe and McLaren, 2000, 284). It is essential to reflect on these values and perspectives when designing research curricula (Chin and Russo, 1997).

In relation to the choice of research methods curriculum, three main views are found in the literature concerning epistemology and methodology. They are that the curriculum should comprise:

- predominantly or solely quantitative methods,
- predominantly or solely qualitative methods,
- a systematic combination of the two.

Although some writers argue that there is no longer any justification for a dichotomy between quantitative and qualitative methodologies (Patton, 1996), many courses address either one or the other. It is likely that one or the other of these is preferred in any given course and that students are explicitly or, more commonly implicitly, taught that this is the 'correct' way. Tashakkori and Teddlie (2003) found that research courses in the US are 'either qualitative or quantitative' (p. 61). They furthermore reported, 'graduate students are often encouraged to choose a "track" early on in their education'. This is commonly termed mono-method research. Even when quantitative and qualitative approaches are taught in one course, they are often presented as alternatives with little connection to each other. Textbooks tend to perpetuate this separation by having different sections for quantitative and qualitative research or concentrating on only one of the approaches, although there are some texts (for example, Neuman, 2000) that avoid or transcend the division.

A third viewpoint on curriculum content is a paradigm of diversity in which qualitative research and quantitative research augment each other, a concept that is debated in the literature. This is referred to as the third methodological movement by Gorard et al. (2004), but is more commonly known as mixed methods research; it is described by Tashakkori and Teddlie (2003, 62) as 'the type of research in which a qualitative and quantitative data collection procedure ... or research method ... is used to answer the research questions'. Qualitative and quantitative methods are seen as compatible in a paradigm some refer to as pragmatism. It can be argued, however, that this is a new type of hegemony, which can be termed 'pluralism' and which is advocated to satisfy different socio-political needs. Habermas (1971) maintained that all theories and methods have legitimacy, but at the same time he was conscious of the fact that integrating different procedures is 'of central significance for the logic of the social sciences, which have only fully developed in the 20th century' (p. 185). The problem with using only one approach is that '[t]aken on their own, each such approach is an inadequate, one-sided explanation of those phenomena that it seeks to explain from a particular methodological perspective and set of theoretical assumptions' (Bohman, 1999, 59). An alternative way of viewing methodological (and theoretical) pluralism is in economic terms; social scientists can accept research contracts irrespective of which theory or methodology is required.

There may be several variations on these three basic views of curriculum content that need not be explored here. What is important is that many teachers of research methods courses assume (consciously or unconsciously) a methodological approach, which determines what social science students are taught.

Justifying a Choice of Methodology

How do we teachers choose which methodology to adopt? What drives our choice? Do we choose a specific methodology (or a combination of methodologies) because we believe that it is the best way to investigate the phenomenon we are researching? Or is the way in which we do research dependent on our ontology (the way in which we look at the world) or our epistemology (our way of knowing)? There are also external reasons, apart from the quest for knowledge and solutions to problems, arising from our academic and personal lives, that help to determine the choice. For example, Mouton and Muller (1997) state that non-governmental organizations and other grant-making bodies in countries like South Africa tend to favour adopting qualitative approaches, in keeping with the demands of international funding agencies. In other developing countries, such as Nigeria, grant-awarding institutes specify the research approach, usually favouring methods compatible with statistical analyses (Ohuche and Anyanwu, 1990).

In a study of theses completed between 1991 and 1999 across seven departments of education at five universities in Nigeria, Okeke (2003) describes a research enterprise that shows awareness of neither the epistemological dynamics underpinning the choices that we make when doing research, nor the methodological duality that informs the conduct of educational research. The study revealed a predominantly positivistic–quantitative research tradition and a subsequent review of postgraduate research programmes at the universities confirmed, predictably, a relationship between the methodology used in the theses and the curricula of research methods courses. Seventy-five doctoral students were asked for their opinions on:

- the quantitative research approach,
- the qualitative research approach,
- the overwhelming use of statistical tools in the conduct of all research at schools,
- the best way to teach research,
- their general impression of the postgraduate research course.

One response from this study is significant for our present discussion. The participants were unanimous in their comments in relation to the mono-method approach to research. They felt they did not have any academic freedom in the choice of research method. According to one respondent:

> the use of questionnaires and the application of statistical tools … has since become a tradition. Even if the approach fails to satisfy my research needs … it does appear that any other form of research other than quantitative will be unthinkable.

The participant's views were in general agreement with the view expressed by another participant:

> students need to be exposed to other research approaches, to enable them to choose a more appropriate method depending on the nature of the investigation being conducted.

It could be argued that certain methods are more suitable to specific disciplines and therefore that it may not be the supervisor's assumptions so much as the nature of the discipline (and/or the topic). Any cursory examination of recent research will, however, show that both qualitative and quantitative methods are used in the field of education, for example. The findings raise fundamental questions about the epistemological choices made by Nigerian postgraduate students when conducting research for their theses. The question must be asked, whose research is being conducted, the student-researcher's or that of the supervising team? Can universities afford to educate students (especially at the doctoral level) to conduct mono-method research when they will graduate into a world that needs reflective practitioners of research? See Brannen (2005) and Tashakkori and Teddlie (2003).

In summary, personal and institutional interests often appear to replace epistemological and methodological relevance in the quest for understanding the social world. Furthermore, pressures from outside the research communities can define the goals of research in terms other than the pursuit of knowledge and hence determine which research tradition is adopted. In the light of these pressures, how can teachers of research methods make balanced and informed curriculum choices?

Does the Method Fit?

Some authors of research texts argue that researchers should maintain the link between ontology, epistemology, methodology and method (Babbie and Mouton, 2001; Mertens, 1998). At the one extreme of this viewpoint is the argument that only certain methodologies and methods can be applied within a specific ontological stance. From this perspective, the assumptions framing the ontology and epistemology of some approaches preclude the use of certain ways of researching the social world. For example, some feminists have called for researchers working from a feminist paradigm to abandon all quantitative methods (but for an alternative view, see Eagle et al., 2000). Laudan (1996) argues that research traditions establish methodological rules and norms for the collection of data and for testing theories. Thus a researcher will choose a method as the best (or only) one on epistemological grounds, but also perhaps because he or she has formed a habit and developed expertise in that approach and is disinclined to learn or practise different thoughts and behaviours (Brannen, 2005). Chamberlain (2000) goes so far as to call these researchers 'fundamentalists – the literal interpreters of the one true way, the followers of the canons and commandments of the method' (p. 288). The key question for this approach is clearly, does the method fit the paradigm?

Another version of epistemological determinism sees the research question as the deciding factor (Chamberlain, 2000). In other words, the researcher uses any methodology that he or she sees fit to answer the research question or achieve a specific aim – sometimes referred to as paradigm relativism (Tashakkori and Teddlie, 1998). Seel (2000), for example, advocates methodological plurality if psychological research is to remain useful to practising psychologists as well as to society in general. Empirical knowledge should thus (although not necessarily always) be useful in practice. The term 'practical', however, does not only mean 'useful' or does not have to be connected to practice in general, but can refer to a particular purpose (Bohman, 1999). Ashworth (1995) recommends that the teaching of qualitative methods should begin with the practical aspects of qualitative research and move to philosophical aspects at a later stage.

This approach can be criticized for glossing over the fundamental differences that remain between quantitative and qualitative research despite efforts to resolve them through triangulation and mixed methodologies. Postmodernism suggests, however, that methodological debates are futile, and advocates a questioning stance towards standard ways of performing research with the aim of improving its practice.

From which Paradigm should we Teach?

Given the contention that different viewpoints about researching human behaviour manifest themselves in differences between curricula, one may ask if one particular methodology can or should be preferred over another. The corollary of this question is, will training in one methodology or another produce better researchers? Or should training in both methodologies be the norm? Or should students be trained in an entirely new approach, such as postmodernism?

Wagner (2003) surveyed the content of 82 social science research courses across 24 South African universities and conducted in-depth interviews with academics who teach undergraduate research courses to explore their beliefs about how the curriculum should be constructed. She found that 61 of the courses included both quantitative and qualitative content, but with a much stronger emphasis on the former. It is interesting that the interviewees (n=9) who taught a mixed methods course described quantitative and qualitative research as equal in status, but continued to make quantitative research the most fundamental aspect of their curriculum by including more topics commonly linked to this approach.

One of the beliefs about the research methods curriculum that was identified on the basis of the interviews is that courses should be constructed around the critique of traditional approaches. Almost all of the interviewees described their training as 'traditional', following a narrow, usually positivistic and quantitative, concept of research. Many of the research courses that they now teach have, however, been recently redeveloped to include a broader approach. The participants in the study described how their own perspectives on research were changed by one of three processes. The first was that undergoing a paradigm shift made them critical of traditional mono-method approaches. In all cases they had shifted from a purely quantitative curriculum (the one in which they had been trained) to a quantitative and qualitative curriculum. Second, some participants believed that disciplines are transformed when senior academics with rigidly traditional views retire and leave the discipline open to younger people. Younger, reforming participants agreed that if they form a critical mass in a department they are able to change the shape and content of the research course without too much resistance. The third impetus to change came from participants who had themselves had more pluralistic training and hence had a broader perspective on what the curriculum of a research course should entail.

Nonetheless, as Collins (1999, 4) warns, one should not sacrifice everything pertaining to the traditional: 'Traditional research methods are very important to all researchers, as these methods have been used for years and have served to build a foundation of robust knowledge.' Dick (1997) suggests that we need to be amenable to innovative ideas about ways of conducting research, without replacing the old methodological orthodoxy with a new one. Providing students with a grounding in both quantitative and qualitative methodologies will, on the one hand, equip them to answer almost any research question they might encounter but, on the other hand, it will tend to weaken their grasp of any particular epistemology. This raises the danger of creating a new hegemony of methodological pluralism that may be at the mercy of the latest academic fad.

Not all researchers advocate multi-methods research courses. Lincoln (1990, 87), for example, questioned her confidence in 'two tracked' research courses, calling them 'training for schizophrenia'. She advocated a commitment to either a conventional or an emergent paradigm and intensive training in the chosen model. This runs counter to the argument, mentioned above, that the research question, and not the researcher's epistemological standpoint, should drive the methodological choices.

We would argue that the either/or approach to curriculum design is inappropriate, and contend, with Silverman (2001), that '… the choice between different research methods should depend upon what you are trying to find out' (p. 25). Too often the decision between including quantitative or qualitative methods in the curriculum is made on false premises. Courses are constructed around distinctions on a methodological level, which are then often justified on the basis of a specific ontological and epistemological stance. But the ontological and epistemological connection is by no means clear-cut. Within the one epistemological framework (for example, humanistic research) there are researchers who work with numerical data and statistical analysis and those who use interpretative techniques such as discourse analysis (Polkinghorne, 1992). On such grounds, various authors argue that there are many and diverse epistemological and pragmatic influences on choice of research method:

> There is no single method that is privileged in the production of knowledge about human existence. Each method, including those that employ numeric procedures and those that employ qualitative procedures, is a lens that can bring into focus particular aspects of human being … Choice of method for a particular project depends on which is most useful for addressing the research question (Polkinghorne, 1992, 233).

> In themselves techniques are not true or false. They are more or less useful, depending on their fit with the theories and methodologies being used, the

hypothesis being tested and/or the research topic that is selected. So, for instance, behaviouralists will favour quantitative methods and interactionists often prefer to gather their data by observation. But, depending upon the hypothesis being tested, behaviouralists may sometimes use qualitative methods – for instance in the exploratory stage of research. Equally, interactionists may sometimes use simple quantitative methods, particularly when they want to find an overall pattern in their data (Silverman, 2001, 4).

Furthermore, Terre Blanche and Durrheim (2006) point out that researchers may work in more than one paradigm at the same time depending on practical requirements. Social science researchers should carefully consider constructing their identity as being linked to particular methodologies (Gorard et al., 2004). We agree with these authors that using certain methodologies and research methods does not automatically translate to adherence with assumed attendant paradigms. We would prefer that students have the ability to argue the link between ontology, epistemology, methodology and method instead of choosing a methodology and fitting everything else around it. This contention is not advocated to enable future researchers to establish economic eminence or for teachers to follow academic fashions. Rather, we would like students to have the potential to become more than good practitioners of methodologies.

Conclusion

As the title of our chapter indicates, methodology is often related to ontology and epistemology. Moreover, quantitative research is equated to positivism and qualitative research to paradigms that oppose positivism. The literature on the content of research courses and research by the authors of this chapter seem to reflect this distinction between methodologies. We argue that choice of research methodology and a method is partly epistemological and partly pragmatic and that students should be equipped and encouraged to make decisions on these grounds instead of on purely methodological grounds. We would like to instigate contemplation among teachers of research courses about what part (if any) methodological fundamentalism plays in the way that they construct the curriculum and what they teach students.

Chapter 6

Ontology, Epistemology and Methodology for Teaching Research Methods

Jan Pascal and Grace Brown

Introduction

We were interested to write this chapter because we wanted to share our experience of teaching research within a small school of social work, at a regional campus in Victoria, Australia. We teach approximately 120 students across four years of an accredited Bachelor of Social Work degree. We are passionate about research. As current PhD students, undertaking research within the discipline of social work, we continually engage in a critically reflective research process as we move from practice to research, to theory and from researcher to teacher, to student and back again.

We aim to teach research methods within a developmental sequence. This sequence begins with an exploration and understanding of ontology, epistemology and methodology. This understanding provides a basis for teaching both qualitative and quantitative methods. The developmental sequence of 'philosophy then methods' is translated into student-centred learning that involves facilitating critical thinking in Year 2 and implementing research design in Year 3 within an undergraduate Bachelor of Social Work (BSW). This sequence is foundational to the process of more independent research that evolves in BSW Honours and Postgraduate research. The sequence also forms a firm foundation for practice research within the field of social work, but could equally be applied to other professions and disciplines.

We commence student learning with an exploration of ontology, epistemology and methodology and the relevance of this to the field. We suggest it is important for students to understand the embedded assumptions within a diversity of research traditions (see Wagner and Okeke, Chapter 5 of this book for further discussion). This not only facilitates critical thinking, but also has implications for social work practice contexts. We then discuss ways in which these philosophical underpinnings are translated into an experiential pedagogy. These learning techniques include practice relevant case studies, developing research proposals and data analysis laboratories.

Both 'pure' and 'applied' methodology and methods are foundational for postgraduate research projects. We continue our developmental sequence with the discussion of becoming an independent researcher through fostering a deeper critical analysis and synthesis, which leads to an understanding of research philosophy, methods and application. We suggest that in applied fields, such as social work, nursing and public health it is both the doing (methods) and the understanding (methodology) of the research process that provides the possibility for enhancing professional practice.

We have written the chapter as we would teach: as a learning dialogue and in the first person. Often we speak in one voice, but at times we discuss our individual standpoints, indicating this with the use of our initials. Thus, our overarching aim in this chapter is to share with you our reflexive connections between educational theories, our teaching research practice and its application for professional contexts.

Educational Theoretical Framework

It is not possible, nor our intention, to engage in lengthy debate about educational theory within this chapter (for a comprehensive discussion see Zuber-Skerritt, 1992). Nonetheless, it is important to note at the outset that our teaching is broadly informed by the principles of reflective and experiential learning (as in the works of Kolb, Dewey and Lewin), and critical and reflexive research (Fook, 1996). These principles are discussed briefly below.

Lewin's experiential phenomenology was developed as a method of observing behaviour, experience and action within social contexts (Zuber-Skerritt, 1992). Lewin's action research and fieldwork theory highlighted the integration of theory and practice and the implications for social change. This was in contrast to more quantitative research methodologies of the time (Zuber-Skerritt, 1992). Lewin's social and relationship focus is integral to professional social work and echoes social constructionist models (Mullaly, 2002), and is therefore directly compatible with our teaching philosophy and practice.

Additionally, Kolb developed the experiential learning model into a four-stage cycle of learning. According to Zuber-Skerritt (1992), this model demonstrated 'immediate concrete experience is the basis of observation and reflection' (p. 96). Further to this, Dewey developed a dialectical process of learning that transformed observation and reflection into action (Zuber-Skerritt, 1992). Action research incorporates a problem solving process. Again, this connects research to the everyday tasks of social work practice, theory and research.

The work of Fook (1996) assists us to integrate educational theory with teaching research methods as a form of reflective social work practice. Students are encouraged to regard the links between practice, research and theory as relevant to all social work activity in the field. Fook (1996) suggested that a '… reflective approach affirms the importance of experiential and interconnected ways of knowing the world, and favours more emancipatory and participatory research practices' (p. 5).

Our educational theoretical frameworks support the inherent notion of adult learning principles that seek to empower (Freire, 1972) our students to engage with the complex discourses of social research (Secret et al., 2003). Thus, drawing upon the principles of Lewin, Kolb, Dewey and Fook, the aim is to educate our students in the observation, experience and action cycle of research. From a social work education perspective, the social construction of social problems and a commitment to reflective practice is enacted through the design of curriculum and teaching material. In this way, educational theory is utilized to inform the teaching of research methods.

The following section outlines content and provides examples from teaching in lectures and seminars. A presentation critiquing the strengths and limitations in the curriculum is then given.

Second year (JP)

This subject is a beginning encounter with research methods for undergraduate BSW students. In teaching a foundational research subject, I aim to build a base knowledge of research ontology and epistemology, as well as knowledge of qualitative and quantitative methods. Initially, the starting point is identifying and clarifying attitudes and assumptions about undertaking a research subject in an undergraduate BSW. I have often observed that students are anxious or mystified by the subject and its relevance to social work. Through exploring their assumptions of research, students are encouraged to view research as having direct application and benefit for practice (see Table 6.1 for examples of discussion questions).

Table 6.1   Questions for exploring students' assumptions about research

1. What image comes to mind for the word 'research'?
2. What characteristics does a researcher possess? List the qualities you think it takes to be a researcher.
3. How do you feel about research? How do you feel about doing a research subject?
4. Do you think research is important for social workers? Why or why not?
5. Who do you think should do social work research? Read research? Can you imagine yourself doing research?

Furthermore, I emphasize that students, and not only academic experts, can do research. In the following session, students are asked to formulate a research plan based on a case scenario. Students are 'theory free' at this early stage, and this second exercise creates both anxiety and a sense of creative freedom. In fact, students already have an existing, albeit tacit, knowledge about research. Students are asked to call upon their own experience and knowledge of research. Students typically characterize research within the quantitative approach, discussing evidence, statistics, hypothesis and proof. Despite these early but limited assumptions, this exercise acknowledges students' tacit knowledge (Polanyi, 1966).

Further, as many of our students are young women, the research planning exercise is based on social work research with young single mums (see Table 6.2

for outline of the research planning exercise). Although students are not necessarily young single mothers (some are older, male or child-free), nonetheless, students relate to the material both personally and as student social workers. The exercise points to the personal and professional relevance of social work research. These initial sessions incorporate discussion about sociocultural assumptions about research and social work. Thus, by the end of the second session students have begun to explore values, assumptions, tacit knowledge and experiential learning (Zuber-Skerritt, 1992).

Table 6.2   Research planning exercise

Scenario: You are part of a team of social workers in a regional Community health Centre. After discussion with the Maternal and Child Health Nurse, your team becomes aware of a group of young single mothers with new babies. These young women are feeling socially isolated. How would you research their needs?

Task: Using your current knowledge base, how would you go about researching the following social work issue?

Discussions about assumptions lead to an exploration of ontology and epistemology of research methodology. Students are introduced to these philosophical concepts in order to explore their own values about being, knowledge and reality, but also as a foundation for understanding the embedded assumptions in research methods. Here too are implications for practice as questions arise about evidence-based practice, objectivity and the importance of subjective experience in professional contexts with research participants and social work clients. In short, what is highlighted here are the embedded assumptions of scientism.

After these somewhat abstract discussions about values and philosophy, I apply these concepts to research methods. Here I present an overview of the research process, first, from a qualitative and then a quantitative approach (Sarantakos, 2005). Again, this is linked to a practice case study involving researching the needs of patients with HIV. Students find the exercise intellectually challenging, but engage with the social justice and poignancy of the HIV scenario. This heuristic device facilitates awareness that research methods are transformative, ethical and practical, and not merely abstract philosophical skills, and have application for professional practice.

The next few sessions focus on critical literature appraisal. Students are challenged by literature reviews as they seem similar to an essay, while having a very different purpose. The temptation is to merely describe the work of others, or to be hypercritical, without understanding the limitations inherent within all research designs. This is particularly the case when students criticize qualitative articles for not, in effect, being quantitative. This is where understanding ontology and epistemology becomes beneficial to the challenging task of appraisal.

Furthermore, students are required to be competent in literature searching. This includes the use of online material such as electronic journals, databases and websites. Herein lies the challenge for students' developing skills of critical appraisal of research literature. The first challenge is identifying empirical literature (including systematic reviews and meta-analyses) as distinct from theoretical or discussion papers. Second, and more significantly, is the challenge for finding credible sources of online empirical literature. This is not a comment on credibility of how research design is explicated in the journals (although this may be the case), but rather that students have trouble distinguishing between government reports, funded research, bias, ideological assumptions and threats to credibility. Thus, the explosion of information available to students requires sophisticated critical thinking, as well as technical skills.

Moving in a reflexive arc, we return to specific methods in more depth, with the intention of developing a mini proposal. Here I outline traditionally used qualitative (Creswell, 1998) and experimental designs (Rubin and Babbie, 2007); I intentionally leave the 'doing' of methods until later in the subject so that students have an opportunity to develop methodological and critical understandings. Otherwise, the tendency is to leap ahead to how to 'do' research, without sufficient awareness of the foundations. At this stage of the subject, students are required to demonstrate a beginning, but sound, understanding of the methods and process of research. This is demonstrated through a critical literature review assessment task. From their standpoint of research 'consumers', they are then encouraged to become research 'producers'. This is simulated in the next assessment task of producing an abridged research proposal.

Third year (GB)

The third year research subject brings together two groups of students. The first group consists of students continuing their third year of the four-year bachelor course. The second group of students enter the course at third year as graduate entry students. This subject builds upon the theoretical foundations of second year and graduate entry students' practice experience. It is an iterative process, requiring a revisiting of qualitative and quantitative methods, but also makes direct links to practice. That is, students come to see research as social work in the form of practice, including: programme evaluations; needs analysis; funding applications; interview and survey skills; critiquing reports; and statistics.

Throughout the semester in this subject, the life experiences of students are drawn upon in the class, many of whom have been professionals or may have some experience of research. The connection between experience and knowledge about the research process needs to be made obvious. For example, most human service organizations collect statistics that are utilized for programme planning or undertake investigations regarding client needs from time to time. Agencies also collect information that relates directly to funding criteria that reflects and informs policy contexts. Students are often engaged in these processes at work but have not recognized such processes as 'research'. Students undertake an exercise that highlights direct application of research methods to policy contexts (see Table 6.3).

Table 6.3   Class exercise demonstrating policy contexts

You are a worker in a large government department responsible for implementing government policy relating to addressing the problem of suicide amongst youth in the State of Victoria. You have been given the task of planning state wide programmes to address this problem. The first step you need to consider is who should be involved in this planning process and why they should be involved. Discuss this first step with the other people in your group.

The theoretical experiences of students who are continuing from their second year, and who may have studied the research process in other subjects such as sociology or psychology, are fostered. When undertaking small group activities, a mix of students from the 'continuing' and 'graduate entry' subgroups is encouraged, so that links between theoretical and practice knowledge can be made more easily. Small group activities are designed to facilitate knowledge sharing and dialogue that link student knowledge to theory and practice. The culture of the classroom is that everyone has something that can be shared and developed for learning. This way of teaching bears relevance for mixed ability adult learners in the same class. Therefore, the expertise of both groups of students who come together in the third year of the programme is utilized.

As the semester progresses, the class content mirrors the research process; that is, classes are workshopped to assist students to formulate a research proposal (the final assessment task). Workshops include: formulating the research question; ethics; literature; methods and analysis; and dissemination of results. Thus, the subject reflects both practice and research processes.

Many students, even those who have knowledge of the research process, come to this subject fearing the subject will challenge them beyond their capacity. With this in mind, the first session concentrates on exploring the views students have about research and what it means to be a researcher. Rigorous debate about the purpose of research is encouraged, as is discussion of the role research can play in bringing about social change. The 'experts only' myth is debated and reinforces the need for social workers (including students) to undertake research once they have learnt the skills. Through these debates and discussions, students importantly begin to see the relevance of undertaking research in their future employment. Students also learn that research occurs within a social and political context (see Table 6.4).

This leads well into the next session about research ethics. In the ethics class student understandings about personal, professional and societal values are revisited. Discussion and debate about the purpose of research, and why and

Table 6.4 **Class exercise demonstrating social/political/ethical context of research**

If we think of unemployment as a social problem where would you go to find out about the following social facts relating to unemployment? –   Who is affected?   Where do they live?   Who do they live with?   How old are they?   How would those experiencing the problem be described in socio-demographic terms?   What constitutes the condition of unemployment becoming a negative, harmful or pathological condition?   Who judges unemployment as a problem and why do they judge it this way?   What social values are being threatened by the existence of the condition of unemployment?   Who supports/opposes resolution to the problem of unemployment?   What is the current political context relating to the condition of unemployment?   What is the current government policy relevant to the problem of unemployment?

for whom the research is being conducted, lead to an examination of sources of bias or value-laden research. Ethical issues that occur at all stages of the research process, from inception through to dissemination are discussed and debated, and include topics such as ethics approval, informed consent, privacy, anonymity and confidentiality, physical and mental distress, research sponsorship, misconduct/ fraud and ownership of research results.

The session on utilizing the literature includes accessing a wide range of information from libraries, the World Wide Web and government departments. The session addresses the purpose of the literature review for formulating the research question and identifying existing research and gaps in knowledge. Students are taught the way in which literature supports research design and planning; and skills for writing the literature review. 'Continuing' students are encouraged to assist 'graduate entry' students by passing on knowledge relating to accessing information at the library, and many students choose to utilize the library orientation programme.

The following sessions move through topics that lead to the development of the research proposal. Topics include: formulating the research question; deciding on a methodology and methods including data analysis; designing a programme plan; undertaking an evaluation; and seeking funding/designing a budget. The programme planning and evaluation component of this subject is integral to student learning as applied to working within human service organizations and highlights these methods as another form of social work intervention (for a programme planning exercise, see Table 6.5).

Classes in this subject utilize a workshop format. For example, students are asked to consider a topic of interest for their research proposal to bring to class so that it can be developed in class with the lecturer and fellow students.

Table 6.5   Programme planning exercise

You are a worker in a small community health centre that has recognised problem gambling to be an issue amongst the client group presenting for emergency relief. Your task is to begin the planning process for establishing a programme that will provide suitable intervention for this client group. The first step you need to consider is who should be involved in this planning process, discuss this first step with the other people in your group. When thinking of who should be involved you may like to consider people from your auspicing organization, from the community, and from a variety of institutions, such as government, advocacy groups etc.

The process continues week by week as students work through all the steps of formulating their research proposals in small groups.

Throughout this subject teaching continually emphasizes the theme of research as a mechanism for social change. A key strategy for enacting this is dissemination of results. Class topics include writing, publishing, forums and participants' feedback. Dissemination can lead to social change, awareness, betterment of lives, informing social work practice and building the profession through sharing knowledge.

SPSS: A Critical Reflection

To recapitulate, throughout this chapter the authors have tried to demonstrate the connection between ontology, epistemology, methods and professional application. The following illustration provides an example of what happens when these methodological foundations are not attended to sufficiently.

First, some preliminary background is required. During the third year, students undertake a 14-week agency placement. This shortens the teaching semester for third year subjects to only six weeks. The research subject is blocked for five hours over six weeks. Curriculum changes in other subjects have also impacted on the third year research subject. As a result, the third year research curriculum is crowded. It now includes in-depth exploration of methods, as well as programme design and evaluation, descriptive and inferential statistics and using SPSS software.

In teaching in such a crowded curriculum, there is insufficient time available for deep learning about quantitative methods. Thereby, students enter the SPSS laboratory sessions with lack of underlying epistemology of quantitative design and statistical analysis, and few demonstrate intuitive aptitude or previous experience. While students can learn to push buttons and print outputs of descriptive and inferential statistics, it is observed that they often lack interpretative data analysis skills. This compounds fear and dislike of statistics and encourages surface learning (Knight, 2002): that is, doing without knowing.

This is the only part of the subject that does not bear direct practice relevance, particularly for rural practitioners. Many agencies in the field do not use SPSS due to the expense and resource limitations. When using quantitative data analysis software, it would be prudent to use practice relevant software. Further, the present focus in curriculum on SPSS as an assessment task precludes attention to qualitative data analysis packages. As part of our critical reflection, the authors question if such a focus derives from hegemonic assumptions regarding positivism in the social work curriculum.

Further Research Contexts

Practicum (GB)

In the fourth year, students undertake a project-style field practicum. For many students this is a first opportunity to put research theory into practise. Students enjoy this opportunity to apply knowledge to real life social work practise. This engages students in the critically reflective spiral of knowledge, research and practice. These processes are iterative and coexistent.

Students undertaking practicum continue the process begun in the classroom. The field practicum further develops research skills debated, discussed and practiced by students in the small classroom groups. 'Real life' research occurs in practicum through: preparation of research proposals that may have a funding submission component; undertaking needs analyses for human service organizations; practicing interview and survey skills as part of agency research; and writing up the outcomes of research conducted. The impact of this reinforces the relevance of research for social work practice and students experience the research process as an important conduit for bringing about social change.

Honours

The third year subjects indicate students with potential for higher degree learning. The second and third year subjects have provided the foundations from which Honours students can develop independent research skills. The key research skills we aim to foster include: identifying and developing a question; critical literature reviewing; and methodological understanding. Students also encounter the ethics approval process. Further, students engage in research fieldwork and data analysis, many for the first time. These are complex learning tasks requiring high order analysis and synthesis of information that extends learning from previous research subjects.

Within the BSW degree, the Honours year is embedded within the fourth year curriculum, requiring students to complete course work, field practicum and Honours concurrently. As supervisors this includes both educative and supportive aspects to assist students to complete the demands of a rigorous process, with the additional difficulties associated with undertaking rural social research. Many of these difficulties are structural and include distance, isolation, access to resources and peer support. For academics, rural contexts can necessitate broad knowledge across fields of practice, multidisciplinary literature and qualitative and qualitative methods. In short, there is a need to be creative and resourceful in undertaking the supervisory role.

Research consultation and supervision

As early career academics in a small school of social work at a regional campus, the authors are contributing to creating a culture of research. This includes the role of supervisor to students undertaking higher degrees. This role also includes acting as consultants for: higher degree students (not formally being supervised); past students now working in the field on agency research projects; and individuals from human service organizations.

As postgraduate students, academic knowledge and skills are emphasized in order to form a basis of mutual understanding with undergraduate students. The ups and downs of the research process; the personal journey we are all engaged in; the joy of discovery; and the moments of self-doubt are all shared. In this way, the cyclical process of researcher, to teacher, to student is continued.

Conclusion

This chapter has outlined the teaching process. It is posited that, a developmental sequence of ontology, epistemology and methodology assists students to form a firm foundation for practice research within the field of social work. Beyond methodological understanding, the teaching aims to instil the passion for research. Through engagement in this cyclical process of reflective researcher–teacher–student, knowledge and learning about research as tools for social change is enacted and shared.

Chapter 7

Research as Social Relations: Implications for Teaching Research Methods

Mark Garner and Peter Sercombe

Introduction

Doing research in the social sciences implies participating in a range of relationships. The nature of these relationships and their role in the successful conduct of the research vary considerably. The least personal are the formal relations with funding or auspicing institutions. Relations within the wider discipline community often include some more personal communication, but are for the most part conducted through some form of written communication, in which the social element is more or less absent. In all of these relationships, the researcher is the central, common element and has rights and obligations with regard to the other parties (Erickson, 1986).

Relations with the subjects of the research, however, typically involve interpersonal interactions and are social in the most direct sense. The way in which these social relations are developed and maintained critically influences both the conduct of the research proceeds and the quality of the data that are obtained. This is self-evident for certain methods, for example, participatory research (see Taylor, Chapter 14) and case studies (see Zucker, Chapter 16), but any study that involves some personal contact, however slight, with the participants will be influenced to some extent by the nature of that contact.

It is essential for the researcher to be sensitive to these relations and to develop the skills necessary to ensure that they are conducted in a manner that is not only ethical and humane, but also as conducive to the research outcomes as possible. Reflection on one's own experience as social science researcher will show the extent to which the conduct and outcomes are determined by the mutually defining social relations with the participants.

Yet social relations are rarely explicitly mentioned in research methods courses. An informal survey of around two dozen Master's programmes that we conducted prior to introducing a new degree at a British University revealed, despite different methodological emphases, a broad consensus on what constitute the essential research skills in the social sciences. These can be simply summarized as the capacities to:

- read, synthesize and evaluate the research literature,
- formulate a research question and, where relevant, associated hypotheses,
- decide what data are relevant to answering the research question,
- identify a study population from whom data can be gathered,
- select one or more appropriate methods for gathering data,
- apply the method(s),
- systematize the findings,
- analyse and draw relevant conclusions from the findings.

Certain aspects of social relations, such as ethics, are included in most methods courses. Participatory methodological approaches, such as ethnography and action research, as well as data gathering techniques, such as focus groups and case studies, may also involve some discussion of how to interact with those who are the object of the research. Further, many of the contributions in this book attest a widespread view of research as praxis, the interplay of theory and application, reflection and action. Praxis is an inherently social process: Roberts (2000), drawing on Freire, characterizes it as critically conscious dialogue with others.

Nonetheless, social relations seem to be rarely, if ever, focused on as a topic deserving of study in its own right. One reason for this may be the lack of an easily grasped framework within which social relations in research can be described and discussed. An experienced researcher can readily give general advice to students about how to interact with informants, but it is much more difficult to describe them in a way that draws attention to key features of relationships and how they influence the collection of data. A simple model for describing the relationship types that a researcher may expect to encounter helps students to grasp the concept of praxis within a social relations framework, especially as teachers can draw on their own research experiences for illustrative examples.

In this chapter, we discuss an attempt at introducing social relations into the curriculum of our research methods course for postgraduate students of applied linguistics and sociolinguistics. There are many models of social relations in the literature (Erber and Gilmour, 1994), but many are too complex for use in teaching students who have no background in social psychology. One accessible model is Fiske (1992), which we have used (with slight modifications) as a means of focusing on, among other things: the ethics of sociolinguistic research; the practical conduct of fieldwork; and the interpretation and evaluation of data. In the remainder of this chapter, we give a brief summary of Fiske's model, describe how we presented the social relations component of the course, and reflect on our own and the students' reactions to it.

Fiske's Model of Social Relations in Research

Fiske (1992, p. 689) postulates that the:

> people in all cultures use just four relational models to generate most kinds of social interaction, evaluation, and affect. People construct complex and varied social forms using combinations of these models implemented according to diverse cultural rules.

His four models of relationship types are predicated on those aspects of interactions that people attend to and on those personal attributes that are meaningful to the interactions. The types are defined according to two intersecting scales:

- equality ↔ inequality
- independence ↔ interdependence

Fiske treats these as 'either/or' categorical dimensions, but it is more helpful for our purposes, and arguable on theoretical grounds, to treat them as parameters (that is, points along a continuum). In brief, the four models are as follows. (For a more extensive treatment, see Garner et al., 2006, where we examine its application to research ethics.)

An *equality matching* (EM) relationship is characterized by equality and independence. EM relationships are based on in kind reciprocity, as each participant continuously monitors the relationship to ensure that the benefits derived from it balance his or her contribution to it. Focus groups used for collecting research data depend for their success on the effective maintenance of EM relationships between researcher and informants. Too great a degree of interdependence can undermine the necessary detachment of the researcher from the information being presented and too great an inequality (in either direction) may threaten participants' desire to share information.

A *market pricing* (MP) relationship is characterized by inequality and independence. It is based on proportionality and participants focus on 'rates of exchange', of which the archetype is of course money. Research using paid participants – for example, experiments involving university students – involves this type of relationship. In others the payment may be in kind, for instance, when a researcher in an immigrant community gives English lessons in return for community members' participation in the research.

EM and MP relations are both transactional, predicated on the independence of the participants, who are free to choose whether to contribute or not, either through 'give and take' (EM) or through 'buying and selling' (MP). The transactional parameter is not uncommonly regarded as the *only* measure of social relations, on the assumption that people remain in a relationship only as long as they are receiving sufficient reward from it. This is, however, too restrictive a view to account for a large proportion of human relationships, including many of those entered into during the research process (Mills and Clark, 1994).

An *authority ranking* (AR) relationship is characterized by inequality and interdependence. Here, social relations are not simply a matter of unequal power, but of mutual dependence, which also involves obligations. The AR model most closely resembles the relationships involved in positivistic social research. The researcher determines the theoretical framework and knows what data are sought and why. The informants are required to provide data on demand – for example, by filling in a questionnaire – and have no access to the theory or control over the intended outcomes.

A *communal sharing* (CS) relationship is characterized by equality and interdependence. What each participant contributes to the relationship is complemented by the contributions of others. This sort of relationship is found in consultative approaches to research. On the basis that they have information and understandings that may be of value to the research, subjects have access to the theory and intended outcomes. They may, and often do, have some input into how the research is planned and conducted. The obligations of reciprocity are thus essential to maintaining the research relationship. The attempt to build a CS relationship is a presupposition of ethnographic approaches to research and, in particular, ethnomethodology (see Agar, 1980; Malinowski, 1935).

If we treat the defining characteristics as parameters and not categories, Fiske's four models can be seen as ideal types in terms of which various kinds of research relationship may be classified. A given relationship is described according to how much it resembles, or is dissimilar from, one of the types. Asking students to place a given relationship along two parametric axes, as shown below, can be a valuable stimulus to class discussion.

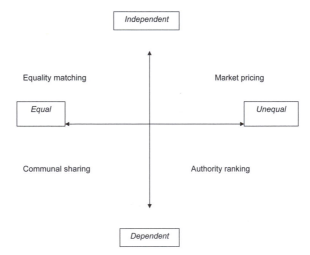

Figure 7.1   Four models of social relations

The social relationship between researcher and participant can also evolve, and is frequently negotiated as work progresses. Furthermore, it is possible, perhaps even probable, that the relationship is likely to be perceived differently by the parties involved, and disparate views of what is taking place in the research process may lead to misapprehensions that can impede the research (Garner et al., 2006, discuss real examples of such problems). Research is much more likely, therefore, to be successful if the researcher is both aware of his or her own perceptions and expectations of the relationship and sensitive to those of the subjects.

It is important to note that we are not advocating here a course in 'how to make friends and influence people'. The issue is not personal development (in the popular sense of that term), but a critical and academically well-informed perspective on one of the more elusive and complex processes of the many that are involved in doing social science research. The objective of including it as a topic within the research methods curriculum is that students will develop an understanding of research methods as praxis: that they will learn not simply how research is done, but how to do it themselves.

Can a practically relevant understanding of social relations, however, be explicitly taught or can it be acquired only through the trial and error of experience? Will students perceive it as of theoretical relevance to methodology as well as of practical use? This was the question we attempted to answer in the project reported in the next section.

Teaching Research Methods with a Social Relations Emphasis

The opportunity to put forth the idea of a social relations component arose when we received funding from our university's teaching and learning committee to develop a practice-oriented research methods course. It was to be conducted over successive semesters, in each of which a different group of students worked as 'research assistants' to the teaching staff, who were conducting a study of perceptions of identity among international students in Newcastle in the United Kingdom.

Like some others reported elsewhere in this collection, the course was designed around students' active participation in the various stages of the study. Students helped to design the research tools, identify potential informants and gather data. Data were collated and compared, and the findings developed collaboratively. At every stage, there was discussion of conceptual, methodological and ethical issues. In addition, throughout the semester there was a consistent emphasis on social relations.

We aimed, in the first two classes, to develop students' awareness of the inherently social nature of research, by presenting and discussing a version of the framework outlined above. The next four classes were devoted to different methods for data gathering. As well as the theoretical framework and implementational issues involved in each method, we also considered the kinds of relationships with the subjects that each one could be predicted to engender. Two of these methods – survey questionnaires and structured interviews – need no further explanation. Two other, much less widely familiar methods were also introduced, namely Q-sort and scrap books. The former requires the informant to sort and re-sort a series of statements on a rank-ordered scale; it is usually applied in quantitative studies, but has also been applied in qualitative research (Brown, 1993; 1996). Scrap books are a common activity in primary schools, but would seem to have potential as a research tool, particularly in identity and self-perception studies. The participants, working in a group, are provided with a large amount of pictorial material, such as magazines, brochures and even junk mail, and asked to cut out pictures and text from them and paste them into a book, adding whatever drawings and words of their own they want. When finished, the book is to represent themselves to the others in the group. Group members discuss and interpret one another's books in an open session. These research instruments require different amounts and kinds of social interaction between researcher and informant, which provides an opportunity to reflect on the role of social relations in the research.

After the data gathering tools had been introduced, the students were divided into four groups, and each group was allocated two of the methods. The students then applied these methods to gathering data. Since the study was investigating identity among international students, and the majority of the class were themselves in that category, they first piloted the methods on other members of the class.

This enabled them not only to familiarize themselves with the techniques involved, but also to experience the relationships between researchers and researched. We aimed for them to gain an insight into emic and etic perceptions of both researcher and researched. Emic and etic are concepts derived from phonology (phonetics and phonemics) that Pike (1967) extended to the study of culture. The former comprise observed phenomena; the latter are the cultural meanings assigned to them. The researcher's task is firstly to make an etic description of behaviour and then, through interaction with the informants, to arrive at a construction that reflects as closely as possible their own emic perceptions.

Our students then identified two small (n=3–5) study samples consisting of international students outside their own degree programme. They used their methods to complete the data gathering process into informants' perceptions of their identity and ways in which it may have changed since coming to study in the United Kingdom.

The results were collated and their implications discussed (see Sercombe and Garner, 2005, for a report of the findings). Each method was assessed for its effectiveness and ease of application. The students also kept a weekly journal in which they reflected on their learning experiences.

As well as assessing the research tools, the students discussed their relations with the subjects, the ways in which the various data gathering methods influenced and/or defined these relations and ethical issues that had arisen. The social relations model provided the framework for description and evaluation. The results included both qualitative and quantitative data, each of which tended to lead to different kinds of research relationship. At the end of the semester they evaluated the extent of their success, in tackling the research question; and the kinds of relationships that had formed between themselves and the subjects of the research; and, finally, whether the social relations focus had been instructive.

Students' Views of the Social Relations Approach

Regardless of the methods used, all students involved, during the research period, gained some degree of hands on experience of conducting social science research and establishing social relationships in the process of collecting data. We asked students to reflect on the course in the final class discussion, and further in unstructured interviews conducted during the semester following their research methods course. What follows is a summary of their views.

A number of positive aspects of the learning experience in the course were identified. There was unanimous approval of the praxis-oriented approach, which the students felt had given them an opportunity to 'get their hands dirty' by actually doing research. They felt it gave them a clearer understanding of the demands of designing a project that is theoretically valid as well as practicable. Further, they had encountered the sorts of organizational difficulties (for example, people not turning up for interviews; unclear tape recordings; tape recorders running out of battery power; tapes ending without their realizing it; questionnaires not being completed) that are an integral part of social science research but are rarely mentioned in textbooks. Paradoxically, however, some students tended to interpret this as a failing of the course itself. Having been given the role of 'research assistants', they perhaps felt that the lecturers, as 'principal researchers', should have been able to prevent such logistical and practical problems from arising at all. This is an unavoidable risk in any 'learning by doing' approach to pedagogy. Some students will be so discomfited by the mistakes they make or the things that fail to turn out as predicted that they will be unable to learn from them. For our part, we learned from the reaction of these few students that we must be careful in future to raise students' awareness at the beginning of the course that problems are inevitable and that the ability to cope with them as they arise is essential for a competent researcher.

In general, however, the majority appeared to have found the course a sort of 'rite of passage', after which they began to think of themselves as researchers. Being engaged in a real research project under relatively stress free conditions thus helped to demythologize the activity and cast it as one that can be creatively and successfully tackled by relative novices to the process.

As far as the introduction to data gathering methods was concerned, some students felt they were disadvantaged by not becoming sufficiently familiar with all four of the research tools employed in the overall project. There was disappointment expressed at not having been more closely involved in the employment of more than two methods (and experiencing the means, functions and benefits of triangulation). In this respect, it was argued that the praxis was not realistic and less useful than if students had been exposed to the principles of a range of research methods.

As a result, the methodological learning outcomes were not achieved in every case. Some students thought that the exercise of using two methods had been intended to make them specialists in those methods, rather than as an exercise that contributed to academic development. Having mastered them, they felt that this was all they needed and were not inclined to think of all methods as potentially useful as they began to engage in their own research projects.

Given the time constraints of a weekly, two-hour class, it is not easy to see how this problem can be overcome. On the other hand, there is an argument that it may not need to be: Perry (2005) emphasizes the difficulty of doing research while also trying to understand the principles that underlie it. He argues that most graduate students do not need to know how to use the full panoply of methods (as they will probably only ever use one or two), suggesting that students' primary need is an understanding of underlying research principles.

Approaching research as a form of systematized professional human relationship was generally perceived as stimulating and enlightening. In particular, having acted as informants in the trial of the research instruments had given them a useful perspective when they began data gathering with their own sample. A number of students had been interested to discover that a researcher–researched relationship can be a continually negotiated liaison, rather than simply a static, impersonal and transactional association. The two parameters (equality–inequality and dependence–independence) of the model outlined in section 2 proved helpful in focusing on social relations as an aspect of the research process. What is less clear, however, is whether the four specific relationship types are sufficiently easily grasped to enable students to apply them to the description of their own interactions with informants.

There were some negative views. A few students were of the opinion that the social relations approach exaggerated the importance of the relationship between researcher and researched. They felt that, as the informants were adults (mostly postgraduate students), their interests were purely pragmatic and transactional. A couple thought that only ethnographic research needs to take social relations into consideration.

Conclusion

Social relations, in particular those between researcher and subjects, are a fundamental dimension of the research process. We have argued that they should be included in the curricula of research methods courses. They are rarely mentioned, however, in the methodological literature, and a great deal of theoretical discussion and pedagogical experimentation is needed to develop an appropriate approach to teaching them. A fundamental requirement is a framework for the study of social relations that is both theoretically well grounded and easily grasped by students who have little or no background in social psychology. It must also have descriptive validity, insofar as it casts light on significant aspects of the research process. In this chapter, we have briefly outlined one possible model, based on Fiske (1992), that may have an application in research methods courses. Our attempts to use it in classes, however, suggested that its usefulness may be limited to the parameters of description.

Although we have focused on social relations, there are clearly many other elements that need to be taught in research methods. These need to be integrated into a course that is coherent and as comprehensive as possible. In the hope of stimulating interest in and debate about the nature of the research methods curriculum, we have reported on our attempt to integrate a social relations perspective into a course. The course was designed around teaching research methods as praxis and involved the students as 'research assistants' in an ongoing research project. The aim was to involve them in the whole process of social science research, and thereby to engage them with underlying principles and some of the methods that are derived from these principles, and the sorts of practical issues that can arise in implementing them. It also focused on the different social relationships that arise in the course of implementation, in an attempt to raise students' awareness of the relational dimension of the data that they gather in the course of doing research.

The orientation of the course seemed to give the majority of students a sense of confidence in their capacity to undertake research of their own. The focus on social relations aroused their interest in how they interacted with informants and how this may have influenced the data that were collected. By exploring the relationships from the perspective of both researcher and subject, they developed a valuable perspective on the conduct of fieldwork.

Chapter 8

Incorporating the Ethical Dimension in the Teaching of Research Methods

Donna McAuliffe

Introduction

Teaching research methods in the humanities and social sciences necessitates also teaching the fundamentals of applied ethics. Alongside methodological considerations and the debates between qualitative and quantitative research lie the important aspects of social research that have to do with concern for the human condition and our duty as social scientists not to cause harm in the conduct of research in the public domain. While the teaching of research methods traditionally focuses on an understanding of research design; conceptual frameworks; literature review; generation of research questions and hypotheses; methods of data collection; statistical and qualitative analysis; and ways to disseminate findings; attention also needs to be paid to ethical considerations that inform all the parts of the research process. Students who learn about how to conduct research in social sciences also need to gain a clear understanding of a range of ethical issues so that they are well-equipped to engage in industry-based or further academic research postgraduation. By building ethics into the research teaching agenda from the beginning and setting ethics up as the foundation for rigorous and quality research design, students will learn to appreciate the need for careful attention to ethical considerations that will ultimately make them more competent in conducting research in the social sciences environment and more competitive in applying for research grants.

An overt approach to integrating ethics into research teaching, by treating them as two sides of the same coin, serves to elevate to a level of greater importance the critical issues of accountability. Researchers are accountable to many stakeholders, including research participants, those who fund research, and the public who are the consumers of research findings. Researchers also need to be accountable in relation to issues of duty of care; duty to not cause harm; integrity; honesty; and non-coercion. Ethics cannot, therefore, be separated from research and an integrated approach is particularly important in the arena of education where students first learn the basics of what is and what is not acceptable in the field.

This chapter focuses on teaching students how to do social science research in a way that incorporates some important and basic ethical considerations, as well as their implications for the way in which the students go about planning, preparing for and conducting their projects. In particular, it deals with confidentiality; privacy and anonymity; informed consent; voluntary participation and coercion; data storage and security; anticipating and managing issues of potential harm and research with vulnerable groups; issues of subjectivity; and the researcher role. The chapter also addresses the role of research ethics committees and common protocols for obtaining ethical approval to proceed with research that involves human subjects.

The Place of Ethics in Social Research: Why Incorporate the Ethical Dimension?

Researchers must begin to consider ethical issues before they begin a research project. Ethical problems can be avoided only by planning carefully and consulting with appropriate individuals and groups prior to doing the research. The failure to conduct research in an ethical manner undermines the entire scientific process, impedes the advancement of knowledge and erodes the public's respect for scientific and academic communities (Shaughnessy et al., 2003).

A survey and review of the significant body of literature written about social research reveals a diversity of opinion about the place and positioning of research ethics. There appear to be four approaches taken by those writing texts for researchers and students. The first is to treat research ethics as an important area of expertise, deserving of its own special place in literature and thereby warranting a brief mention but not a deliberate integration into texts on research methods (Punch, 1998; Steinberg, 2004; Yates, 2004). The second is to concentrate solely on the topic of research ethics, providing case examples and detailed exploration of philosophical obligations (Greggory, 2003; Stanley et al., 1996). The third, and most common approach, is to dedicate a chapter to exploration of research ethics, and to refer back to this chapter in discussions about different stages (Royse, 2004; Ruane, 2005; Rubin and Babbie, 2007). The fourth approach is to integrate research ethics into each stage and phase of the research process, exploring possible ethical concerns at the levels of question formulation, sampling, data collection and research writing (Marlow, 2005). With reference to the earlier point about accountability, this integrated approach is more likely to keep ethics in the forefront of students' minds, ensuring that they are always questioning what they are proposing to do and how, and whether there is any likelihood of harm or deception.

From a pedagogical perspective, research methods courses tend to follow one of these four approaches. There are those courses that by design acknowledge the importance of ethics but refer students to additional reading or advise them to consult relevant ethical codes or guidelines, or to take a more specialized course in research ethics. Then there are courses that are designed specifically for the teaching of research ethics, although these are primarily at postgraduate level and are often offered by external private consultancy trainers. Perhaps the most common approach is for a research methods course to dedicate a lecture or proportion of time to research ethics and to include questions on ethics in assessment. Finally, there are those courses that use a fully integrative approach where research ethics are set up as the foundation for sound methodological decisions, and discussions are built in to the teaching of different phases and stages of research design (Sar et al., 2002).

The importance placed on research methodology by those who teach it determines to a large extent how research ethics is included in curricular design. A long-standing debate in the psychological literature that has extended into business and the biosciences is whether it is even possible for 'ethics' to be taught at all. This is reflected in repeated calls in the literature for ethics education based on empirical research and examination of cases where ethical protocols have been breached, often in very serious ways. In reference to the biosciences, Eisen and Berry (2002, 38) contend that 'research ethics education in the biosciences has not historically been a priority for research universities despite the fact that funding agencies, government regulators, and the parties involved in the research enterprise agree that it ought to be'. In the field of social work, Gibelman and Gelman (2001) argue convincingly that 'research courses at the MSW and doctoral levels must include content pertaining to ethics in research and to procedures for reviewing research protocols'. In health care, Aita and Richer (2005, 124) state that 'every researcher and professional working in the healthcare field should understand the risks and benefits of their research to the individual and society, and the personal dimension of research ethics'.

For those involved in the teaching of research, there are ample resources that set out clear protocols for the ethical conduct of research with human participants. There is also no shortage of literature and other material that sets out the history of abuse of vulnerable individuals and groups in the name of scientific, psychological and sociological research, and the many cases that have come to light over the years provide a strong rationale for inclusion of research ethics in undergraduate and graduate education. As far as Australia is concerned (and most other countries will have equivalent resources), the National Health and Medical Research Council (NHMRC) have developed a 'National Statement on Ethical Conduct in Human Research (2007)' and 'Guidelines for Ethical Conduct in Aboriginal and Torres Strait Islander Health Research' (NHMRC, 2003). These comprehensive statements set out the functions and responsibilities of Human Research Ethics Committees (HRECs) and provide guidance on research with vulnerable groups (such as children, young people, persons with an intellectual or mental impairment, persons highly dependent on medical care, indigenous peoples).

In addition to this national statement, which is founded on the ethical principles of integrity, respect for persons, beneficence and justice, most professional disciplines have their own respective codes of ethics or standards of conduct that set out responsibilities in relation to research activities. The Australian Association of Social Work (AASW) Code of Ethics (1999) sets out 14 points under Research (S4.5.2) covering issues such as informed consent and voluntary participation, confidentiality and/or anonymity, protection from harm or distress, accurate reporting of findings and storage of research materials. The Australian Psychological Association (APA) Code of Ethics sets out 18 points under 'Research' and a further 9 points under 'Reporting and Publication of Research Results'. The Australian Sociological Association has a Code of Ethics that focuses on research and has a total of 45 points that cover research conduct, teaching, distribution of results and publishing. For teachers of research methods in social sciences, there is therefore substantial content readily available, and the many sections of these various codes provide rich resources for the development of case scenarios and problem-based learning modules to assist students to apply the guidelines to hypothetical situations in the classroom context.

Ensuring Rigour in Social Research: How to Incorporate the Ethical Dimension

If ethical concerns lie at the heart of good research, then we need to consider how the ethical dimension can be effectively incorporated into a research design. Essentially, the question as posed by Yates (2004, 159) is 'which is more important: the protection of research participants' rights or the "value" of the research?' An increasingly widely accepted protocol for designing sound research that ensures that these crucial issues are considered is the importance of subjecting the research to critical appraisal by external ethical reviewers by submitting an application for ethical clearance or ethical approval. These 'external experts' take the form of what have become known as HRECs, or Institutional Review Boards (IRB) (Melville, 2005; Waldrop, 2004). Such bodies have been established within a culture of risk management, where minimization of institutional liability is paramount (Melville, 2005). If a research project is planned to take place in a hospital, for example, where patients are to be interviewed about their perceptions of health care, the research team may be expected to submit documents to the research ethics committee to show how they would protect the confidentiality of responses and what steps they would take to ensure that no harm would come to the participants. If a researcher intended to conduct a large-scale survey with school students about drug and alcohol use, they would be expected to demonstrate how he or she would ensure anonymity and obtain informed consent. In the case of minors involved in research, it could be that parental consent for participation would be required. HRECs and IRBs generally have protocols that need to be followed and may require consent forms to be worded in a particular way. Typically, a researcher or research team prepares and submits a number of documents for review, which might include:

1. A standard application for ethical approval or clearance – this would be a document that would set out the aims, methods and significance of the research project, with attention given to recruitment and sampling of participants; informed consent (and any inclusion of vulnerable groups or people with impaired capacity); confidentiality and/or anonymity assurances; secure storage of data; reporting back and dissemination of findings; and potential risk to participants in terms of harm or distress. Some of these issues will be discussed in more detail in the following section.

2. A participant information sheet – to be given to research participants to ensure that they are fully aware of the aims and intentions of the research, what will be discussed during an interview or focus group, and whether interviews will be audio-taped, that participation is voluntary and that they can withdraw themselves and their data without penalty, that their anonymity will be assured and nothing from the research taken into the public domain will be attributed back to them, and that they can have access to the results of the research.

3. An informed consent form – which sets out in an agreement that can be signed and witnessed, the obligations of the researcher and participant. In combination with the information above, this is also known as a 'research contract' (Yates, 2004, 162). There are many examples of informed consent forms, as well as checklists to ensure that all the important points have been covered (Reamer, 2005, 38; Royse, 2004, 53). Participants are given a copy of this signed form to keep.

4. A 'gatekeeper letter' – which might be required from an agency that is assisting in some way with the research. Such a letter could, for example, be provided by an organization (for example, a particular department of a hospital, or the principal of a school) to say that they are aware of a research project and are prepared to assist the researchers to recruit a sample of participants from the people who use the health services or attend the school.

5. Interview schedules or surveys – to ensure that questions are not likely to cause harm or distress, or if there is the potential for distress, that the researchers have addressed (in other documents) how they intend to manage this. As research questions often change following pilot testing of surveys or initial interviews, it is the responsibility of the researcher to resubmit any changed documents to the relevant ethics committee for further approval.

Students in research methods courses must have a basic knowledge of the reasons for such procedures and be familiar with the forms and processes. In teaching research methods, the above processes and potential ethical approval documents are minimal knowledge requirements for conducting sound research. If students are taught only the mechanics of conducting research, then they are likely to falter when it comes to justifying interviewing children without parental consent or observing homeless people without their knowledge. If students are made aware of ethical considerations in the early stages of research education, they will have a much better foundation for thinking about all of the potential ethical considerations that would warrant consideration. This may significantly influence the way that research questions are constructed: the choice of methodologies; sampling frames; recruitment strategies; and ways of collecting data. Constructing research in an ethical vacuum poses risks not only to participants, but also to researchers who could easily find they have walked into a minefield of unanticipated ethical concerns. Consequently, it is worth noting some of the specific areas that can become problematic in terms of ethical considerations.

Confidentiality, Privacy and Anonymity

There is often confusion between the concepts of confidentiality, privacy and anonymity. One of the key concerns in social science research is whether information gained from participants can ever be truly confidential. All information gathered by interview is essentially collected in an identified form. That is, the researcher has interviewed someone and has knowledge of who he or she is, and what they said. While this information can certainly be de-identified by assigning code names or pseudonyms to the data transcripts, there is still an onus of responsibility on the researcher to ensure that a person's identity is not disclosed through provision of information in a public forum and that responses cannot be linked to identifiable individuals. Research undertaken in small communities or with elite groups (such as politicians, judges, high profile media personalities) can raise difficult issues for confidentiality and anonymity. In some cases, people do not want to be de-identified or anonymous. They have a point to make and they want that point attributed to them by name. It is important that researchers do not take lightly the concerns about confidentiality and anonymity in relation to identity, and that promises and assurances are not made that may not be able to be kept (Ruane, 2005). Students need to be made aware of these issues when considering their sample and possibly the location of the research.

Sometimes extending research to a national or international level can minimize potential for identification. In addition to anonymity of identity is the issue of confidentiality of information disclosed during a research interview. Researchers are not immune to legal subpoena and do have a duty of care (as do all citizens) if there is the potential of harm to someone. If a research participant discloses to a researcher that he or she intends to harm another person or themselves, the researcher may not be able to uphold any assurances of confidentiality of information that may have been given. As Melville (2005, 379) notes:

> Simply turning off the tape recorder during an interview will not suffice, nor will simply destroying the tapes. Social research often skirts around these issues. Participants must be fully aware before the study commences about the information a researcher might need to disclose to authorities and the consequences of having to do so (for example, legal proceedings).

Informed Consent – Voluntary Participation and Issues of Coercion

Informed consent, and how to ensure it, is an issue that is repeatedly raised in research texts because of the commitment that researchers have to not coercing participants into involvement in activities either that they do not understand or about which they have been given insufficient or misleading information. Teachers can provide students with examples of situations in which informed consent is doubtful, and discuss ways to manage this (for example, asking the research participant to explain in his or her words what the research is about and what he or she understands he or she is required to do). There are a number of conditions that it is argued must be met to ensure that consent to participate in research or evaluation is voluntary. Ruane (2005) defines four of these conditions as:

- competence,
- voluntarism,
- provision of full information,
- comprehension of that information.

Researchers often face difficulties with informed consent when engaging with vulnerable groups such as minors, people with impaired capacity, or people from different cultural traditions who may not have adequate comprehension of the language in which the research is conducted. Ethical approval will not be granted by an HREC or IRB if there are any concerns about competency to provide informed consent, possible coercion, or if participants are misinformed about the purposes of the research.

This, of course, raises questions about the value of covert research, that is, research that takes place without the knowledge of people engaged in it in some way. It is important for students to note that this is a contentious debate. Some writers take the hard line that no covert research is justifiable, while others take the view that there could be justification for 'the greater good' and advancement of knowledge (Greggory, 2003). It is also very important, in relation to the concept of voluntariness, that participants are made aware that they can withdraw from the research at any time without penalty (for example, having a service stopped or access to resources minimized) and that their data can also be withdrawn (although this is much more problematic if data is part of a focus group or observational research). Sin (2005, 281) argues that 'the constant renegotiation of consent is underlain by the understanding that the complexity of research demands different forms of consent, some more explicit than others, depending on the stage and nature of the research at different points in time'. It is important, therefore, in teaching research methods that students understand the components of consent and are prepared to negotiate potential difficulties in the obtaining of this consent.

**Anticipating and Managing Issues of Potential Harm or Distress:
A Dual Dilemma**

Research in the social sciences often involves exploration of sensitive issues that have the potential to cause some degree of psychological distress. This potential is heightened, depending on the research topic and questions and methods used for collection of data. A researcher could, for example, administer an anonymous quantitative survey about experiences of sexual assault, but would have no way of knowing the impact of questions on respondents. Or the researcher could conduct qualitative in-depth interviews with sexual assault survivors, which allows much greater ability to gauge and assess levels of potential distress and to have strategies in place to manage them. HRECs expect any potential risk to be examined in some detail, as one of the foundations of ethical research is the principle of not causing harm. All ethical codes that outline research responsibilities enshrine this principle. A typical strategy for managing potential distress is to have supports and referral sources available for research participants if needed. A particular dilemma is posed for the social science researcher who has a background in a discipline, such as social work, psychology or counselling, where the boundaries between objective researcher and 'helper' can become blurred (McAuliffe and Coleman, 1999). While there is an abundance of literature that discusses implications of research involvement for participants, there is little that addresses the complexities for the researcher. As Davison (2004, 381) points out, 'few (researchers) had been advised during research teaching or early supervision sessions that it is possible to encounter unexpected emotional distress during research, or that this would be a suitable topic to explore in supervision meetings'.

Teachers of research ethics in social sciences should draw students' attention to the possibilities of vulnerability and related subjectivity, particularly where researchers might have an 'insider status' (that is, have themselves experienced the phenomenon that they are researching). Insider researchers can bring a wealth of knowledge and experience to the analysis of sensitive topics, significantly increasing the richness of data, but students need to be taught that supervision should be used wisely so that the 'emotionality of the research process' can be openly acknowledged and worked with in a constructive way (Davison, 2004).

Conclusions

The ethical dimension, it is argued, is an integral and foundational part of the research process and, as such, needs to be incorporated as a key element in research training and education. This chapter has explored how research ethics are typically incorporated in both literature and education, and emphasis is placed on teaching research that is ethical in all stages of the process. As risk management and liability frameworks become increasingly important and instances of scientific misconduct and unethical research practices come to light, it is important that students are familiarized in research methods courses with the expectations of institutional ethical review processes. Students should be taught how to prepare a document for ethical approval by a Human Research Ethics Committee or Institutional Review Board; how to structure a Participant Information sheet and an Informed Consent form; and how to obtain gatekeeper letters (*and the form of such letters*) from organizations and stakeholders. These elements can all be built into assessment, with a requirement, for example, that students prepare the documents in relation to a proposed piece of research. Furthermore, students should be exposed during teaching on research methods to the debates about: overt and covert research; confidentiality; privacy and anonymity; and the elements of informed consent. Students should also be encouraged to assess all potential research within a framework of potential risk, both to participants and to themselves as researcher and to work proactively towards developing strategies to minimize risk. Finally, those teaching research methods need to model for students an authentic interest in the pursuit of sound and rigorous research built on solid foundations of integrity, respect for persons, beneficence and justice. The reputation and continued development of social science research relies on this foundation.

PART III
Approaches to Developing Research Competence

Chapter 9

Developing Reflective Researchers

Mark A. Earley

Research methods education typically focuses on acquiring skills. This is essential, as graduate students often need to be able to produce a thesis or dissertation as their final degree requirement. To successfully navigate what for many is their first major research study, however, students must also be introduced to the fact that research is not just a set of skills to learn and apply. There is no generic research template to which researchers can turn for every study they conduct. Research is entirely context bound and no template or skill set will apply to every context. Therefore, it is necessary for research educators to also help students develop the *mind of a researcher*, recognizing that research is as much art as science. In this way, students are better equipped to understand the implications of various decisions they make while conducting a study – implications for the study, for the profession, and for themselves as professionals in their respective fields.

This chapter begins with a few 'beliefs' I have about research and how it might be taught to students in the social sciences. First, *research is a process*, which *Webster's Dictionary* defines as 'a series of actions, changes or functions bringing about a result' (retrieved 17 February 2006 from http://dictionary.reference.com/search?q=process). This series of actions carried out by researchers is not linear – the process is cyclical and iterative (Creswell, 2005; Maxwell, 2005). In other words, research is not a series of isolated actions – each step, each action and each decision relies on, is informed by, and informs other steps and actions in the process. Further, these research actions and steps are themselves processes. For example, researchers cannot complete a literature review without having clarified their purposes and these purposes are typically narrowed and refined based on the literature review. The *process* of conducting a literature review overlaps with the *process* of determining and refining a purpose for study. This is a way of thinking about research that instructors need to infuse throughout their research methods courses.

A second belief I hold is that a researcher does not 'do' research by simply following a series of steps. Rather, a researcher engages with these processes. What I mean here is researchers both 'think about' and 'do' research. When researchers select and narrow their purpose, write research questions, review the literature and design a study, they are making choices and solving problems (Pietersen, 2002). The choices researchers make usually clarify what is important to them as professionals in their field of study (Mooney, 1957). Researchers make these choices regardless of the philosophical or methodological underpinnings of the study. Behavioural psychologists conducting experimental studies have as many choices as community sociologists have when undertaking ethnographic research. Throughout the design process, and as researchers move into data analysis and writing the research report, they continue to make choices that influence the finished product. Does a survey researcher leave an outlier in the data set or remove it? Does a researcher using path analysis need to transform a variable prior to analysis or leave it as is? On which epiphanies in a participant's life history will the researcher focus? An observer can never capture every nuance of a setting – what to leave out? Because instructors can never hope to capture every unique research context their students might encounter, an important goal for research methods courses must be to provide students with the tools and habits necessary to make these contextualized decisions on their own – to think about while doing research.

Considering research as a series of processes in which the researcher makes a number of decisions, the skills we help our students develop must include how to understand and reflect on their context and processes. Every methodological approach (for example, quantitative, qualitative, mixed methods, arts-based, evaluation and action, among others) has its own processes to consider; yet they are all processes that require the researcher to be an active decision-maker. To be able to make better decisions in these varied contexts, 'it is important ... to recognize that an understanding of any situation must be based on an appreciation of the context, and also of the different and possibly competing perspectives which might be involved in interpreting the situation' (Fook, 1996, 4). Understanding and appreciating one's own research context does not just happen: researchers must be reflective practitioners to move beyond following steps and truly engage with the research setting.

The purpose of this chapter is to present to research methods instructors a framework for developing reflective researchers; that is, researchers who engage in and learn from the process of studying a particular topic or phenomenon. Engaging with these processes and learning from them first requires the student to develop the requisite skills in research design and data analysis, which many research methods courses and texts already accomplish to various degrees. However, engaging with and learning from the research process both require the researcher to move beyond these skills and reflect throughout the course of a study.

To introduce this framework, I draw from two other theoretical frameworks: reflective practice and experiential learning. These allow me first to describe the researcher as practitioner and then to describe the research experience as an experiential learning setting, referring to Kolb's 'Experiential Learning Cycle'. I then combine the two ideas to describe the habits of the reflective researcher that research methods instructors can introduce to their students. I close with suggestions for applying this framework to the research methods classroom with examples from my own teaching in the field of educational research. My hope is that by introducing students to the habit of reflective practice, they will learn to appreciate the very personal and contextual nature of research conducted in any field with any methodology.

Researcher as Practitioner

The title 'practitioner' is often applied to those who apply a specific set of skills and knowledge to their work in a particular profession. Nurses are practitioners engaged in the care of patients in a variety of settings – they bring specific skills and knowledge to these settings. Teachers are practitioners engaged in the education of today's youth, who will become tomorrow's informed citizens – again, teachers have a specific set of skills and knowledge they bring to the classroom setting. Researchers are also practitioners engaged in (among other activities) the process of discovery and knowledge production, bringing to their research settings specific skills and knowledge about both the topic of study and the research process. Students in our research methods courses are future research practitioners acquiring the necessary skills and knowledge to be effective researchers – either as 'producers' of research, or as 'consumers' (Creswell, 2005). No matter how students apply their knowledge postgraduation, they benefit from an understanding of the reflective processes researchers undertake.

Although it is not the intent here to fully describe and analyse the diverse literature related to reflective practice, two essential points can be noted. First, what we mean by 'reflection' varies across contexts and is not in any sense limited to any one definition (Kreber, 2004). Second, what seems to set reflective practitioners apart is their ability to move beyond the technical work of their field (Schön, 1983) and begin to consider, 1) why the work is done, and 2) what impact the work has on the community served. Many fields embracing the reflective practice concept see this habit of thinking about one's work as opposed to simply doing one's work as a way to increase practitioners' own sense of their professional identity, which in turn is meant to increase their impact and effectiveness as professionals. For example, Palmer (1988) stresses that 'good teaching cannot be reduced to technique; good teaching comes from the identity and integrity of the teacher' (p. 10). This statement should be applied to research as well: good research is more than technique and comes from the identity and integrity of the researcher.

Donald Schön's work (for example, 1983; 1987) is most often cited as the foundation for describing the habits of reflective practitioners. Of his many contributions, one in particular is relevant here, namely the distinction between reflection-in-action and reflection-on-action. Reflection-in-action takes place as the practitioner recognizes and '[makes] sense of surprises, turning thought back on itself to think in new ways about phenomena and about how we think about those phenomena' (1987, para. 7). Researchers not engaged with their process will miss these 'surprises'. Although it is necessary to introduce students to the various steps in the research process for them to acquire the skills and knowledge they will bring to the field, it is just as important to introduce them to this idea that there can be surprises. The ability first to recognize and then to reflect on these surprises is less commonly taught.

Schön's (1983) notion of reflection-on-action is equally important to researchers. Here, reflective practitioners look back on an 'action', such as a recently completed research study: and question; what happened; why it happened; how it happened; and what can be learned. This reflection most often leads to new insights about the 'action'; reflective researchers, therefore, gain a new understanding of how research can look in their discipline, what role research plays in their discipline and how they, as researchers, are professionals. This reflective practice assures researchers play a role of more than just technician and truly begin to understand the research settings they investigate and how their own investigations affect the field in general.

Research as a Learning Experience

What should be evident from the description of the reflective practitioner is the learning that takes place while conducting research – learning not limited to seeking answers to research questions. Any research setting is a learning environment into which a researcher enters. Researchers enter a study with 'research questions' to be answered, but there are many times during and after a study when researchers can learn more than just how their research questions are to be answered. In-depth data exploration and analysis, and paying attention to respondents or participants (whether through survey responses or interview responses) inform the researcher about the details involved in studying this particular topic. Researchers learn more about how to 'do research' as well (Evans, 2002): each completed study brings new insight into how to carry out a similar study or a study on the same topic, the next time the researcher has the chance. This is especially true in cases where the study is part of a larger research agenda. More practice and more experience studying the same topic increase the abilities of the researcher to conduct future research. This learning process is fuelled by the researcher stopping to reflect on the study, both while it is ongoing and soon after it is complete.

This process of learning from and through experience is best described by Kolb's 'Experiential Learning Cycle'. As with the reflective practice literature, it is well beyond the scope of this chapter to explore the full model described by Kolb and expanded upon (and criticized) by others. Rather, I borrow this framework to describe one way in which reflection can be a critical part of the learning process and therefore critical to the research process. In general terms, the experiential learning cycle includes:

1. concrete experience (for example, conducting a study, or engaging in any of the individual steps of the research process),
2. observation and reflection,
3. forming abstract concepts, and
4. testing in new situations (Smith, 2001).

An important aspect of this experiential learning process is the *personal* or *contextual* nature of learning (Moon, 2004); these same characteristics apply to research.

Applying this framework to researchers, the 'concrete experience' can take two forms:

1. the overall experience of conducting a study, and
2. the engagement with the individual processes involved in conducting a study (for example, developing a research question, selecting participants, data analysis).

Introducing each of these processes as 'learning experiences' encourages research methods students to consider each as more than just a 'step' in the process – students begin to see how the various phases of a study are interconnected and dependent on each other. Students also begin to understand how their own decisions affect not only one particular phase but each of the other phases as well. This emphasizes the need to be purposeful and reflective while engaging in research.

Learning Objectives and Activities for Developing Reflective Researchers

Kraft (2002) argues that 'reflection is a purposeful activity, not mere day-dreaming' (p. 178). It is up to instructors in research methods courses to adopt learning goals, activities and assessments that include purposeful reflection in order for students to begin developing this habit. I present teaching and learning activities associated with three potential learning goals for students, as well as feedback options for instructors as examples of how I integrate these learning goals into my own educational research methods courses. My purpose here is to provide instructors with models that can be adapted to any research methods classroom, independent of the level of the course, methodological content of course (for example, quantitative methods, qualitative methods, arts-based methods, historical methods) and field in which the course is taught (for example, nursing, education, sociology, library science).

Because reflective practitioners reflect on both their *practice* of research and *themselves* as researchers, integrating reflective practice into a research methods course should happen in two contexts: students' reflections about *themselves as researchers* and students' reflections on *specific aspects of the research process* (that is, developing a research question; conducting the literature review; designing the study; collecting and analysing data; and writing the final report). To this end, I present here the following learning goals:

1. Students will be able to describe themselves as researchers who are part of a larger research community,

2. Students will understand how reflection links various phases of the interactive research process, and
3. Students will develop the habit of keeping a research journal.

This is not, of course, an exhaustive list of the possibilities. Rather, these are examples that I hope will inspire research methods instructors as they consider integrating this reflective researcher framework into their current courses.

Learning Goal 1: Students will be able to describe themselves as researchers who are part of a larger research community

The purpose of this learning outcome is twofold. First, I want students to understand they are not the only researchers in their fields. There are others from whom they can learn, and networking with individuals in the field is important. Second, I want students to be aware of how their own research will contribute to the larger field in which they work. To encourage this, I have engaged students in a variety of activities (not all of these in the same class, however).

One activity I use in every course is an exercise at the end of Chapter 2 in Joseph Maxwell's (2005) text, *Qualitative Research Design: An Interactive Approach* (note that I use all of his exercises throughout the text in all of my courses; this is just one example). In this exercise, Maxwell encourages readers to write a memo about their purposes for undertaking the research they are about to conduct – these purposes can include, for example, personal purposes (to graduate, to learn more about a topic, because this affects my work, etc.) or professional purposes (to get a job, to solve a problem in their work setting, etc.). Maxwell introduces readers to a variety of purposes to consider, as well as encouraging readers to reflect on their different identities that might influence their research (for example, 'self as teacher'; 'self as student'; and 'self as parent'). This memo activity is very thought provoking for students: it is one of the first assessments they write for the course. Rather than grading it, I give students feedback (typically this involves asking them questions about what they wrote) and encourage revision throughout the course.

A second activity I have used in some of my courses involves students in searching for what I call 'research community spheres'. Students draw a series of concentric circles on one sheet of paper. The innermost circle is labelled 'ME'. I then have students fill in successive circles from inside out with larger groups of researchers working in their area, groups of which they are a part. For example, the typical second sphere is students' cohorts in their graduate programme. Additional spheres include local, state, regional and national professional associations that incorporate researchers in the students' field of study. I encourage students to find at least two individuals and/or one professional association at each level.

For example, much of my own work is in teaching and learning introductory statistics. At the local level, there are a few individuals at my institution interested in statistics education and a few more at various institutions around the state.

There is a regional group, the Mid-Western Educational Research Association, which includes some researchers in this area and a national group (the American Educational Research Association) that includes many more researchers in the area. There are several other groups (national and international) as well. I walk students through my own 'spheres', indicating names of individuals and how we have connected over the years, as well as how these connections have influenced my own work.

Learning Goal 2: Students will understand how reflection links various phases of the interactive research process

This second learning outcome moves students from reflecting on 'self as researcher' toward reflecting on various phases in the research process: developing research questions; conducting the literature review; designing the study; analysing data; and writing the report. Each of these has various pieces associated with it (for example, designing the study includes selecting participants, selecting quality data collection sources and preparing a timeline, among other issues) and I spend one or two class sessions introducing students to each phase. These also work into students' final research proposals, a required capstone assessment for all of my research methods courses. My purpose with this learning outcome is to encourage students to stop and reflect on what they are doing (Schön's notion of *reflection-in-action*) as well as how what they just did connects to other phases. As one possible assessment, students can also apply Fook's (1996) notion that researchers must appreciate 'competing perspectives' by generating alternatives for their decisions and evaluating their relative merits.

As an example, the literature review is a vital piece of the entire research process, in which research questions can be refined, instruments selected and evaluated, data analysis options reviewed and current study outcomes compared to those presented in the literature. So, as students are engaged in reviewing their own literature, I require them not only to draft a small-scale literature review but also to discuss how the process affected their research questions and design choices. To do this, students may create a list of the various forms their research purposes or questions took (for example, each time they were revised) with a brief description of why they made each of the changes. If a particular journal article or book influenced their thinking, I ask them to cite those references in this discussion.

A second way I encourage students to reflect on the process of research is by asking them questions about their work – typically, 'Why did you do it that way?' I let them know ahead of time these questions are not meant to indicate they did something wrong. Rather, I want them to be able to describe what factors they considered and what choices they made. This eliminates very quickly the urge to say, 'because that's the way it's done'. I do not accept that as a response. This also helps students become more aware of the 'art' as well as the 'science' associated with conducting social science research. Students become more aware that they do indeed have choices – they are never, in any research paradigm, locked into a particular study design simply because 'that's the way it's done'. At the same time, when combined with the personal memo described for Learning Goal 1 above, students become very aware of how they as researchers do have an impact on the study, regardless of their underlying paradigm, based on the choices they make each step of the way.

Learning Goal 3: Students will develop the habit of keeping a research journal

This outcome should be self-explanatory. My purpose is for students to have one spot where they document and store all of their reflections. I introduce the concept of a journal on the first day of class and remind students weekly to write in their own journals about research in general, themselves as researchers and/or their own studies. I check with students after about a month of class to make sure they are doing this – I do not ever grade these journals, but rather record them as completed. For some students this is a familiar activity, as they are used to journaling in their personal lives or for their work. For other students, keeping a journal is not easy and can even be a major challenge. I encourage students to use a variety of media, including writing, Internet blogs, drawing, poetry, music or recording their thoughts with a micro-cassette recorder. I tell them what is most important is that they do it: the particular product or process is not important. Some instructors use portfolios in place of journals, so students can collect all of their coursework and reflections together. The literature on portfolio assessment is vast and too complex to introduce here, but I encourage interested instructors to make use of this type of alternative assessment (and others they know of) where possible and appropriate.

Conclusion

The purpose of this chapter was to present alternative learning outcomes that research methods instructors should be addressing in addition to (not in place of) the skill acquisition outcomes common in research methods courses. The aim is to enable students not only to do research but also to think about research. This will also benefit research methods instructors as they learn not only what their students can do but also the kind of professional researchers they are becoming. This, in my own experience, makes teaching the course much more enjoyable because I am not restricted to teaching a 'how to' course. I can engage students in discussion about the 'whys' of research and encourage them to learn not only the science of research, but the art of research as well. Once students have completed their coursework, they move into their respective fields with a deeper understanding of the research process and their own role in the research community. Reflective researchers not only connect more personally with their research; they also understand how their research connects and applies to the larger field in which they work.

Chapter 10

Apprenticeship: Induction to Research through Praxis of Method

Wolff-Michael Roth

Aporias of Learning Research Methods

It is a well-known fact among educators that the epistemologies teachers espouse mediate the learning environments they create (Tobin and McRobbie, 1997). In my experience, the same can be said for graduate programmes in the social sciences. Thus, on several visits to German and French universities – specifically to research groups focusing on knowing and learning in the natural sciences – I found graduate students engaging in empirical studies without any prior preparation in the ways of how such research might be conducted; much like in the early years of anthropology, these graduate students simply went into the field and conducted their research hoping that what they did would lead to useable and useful outcomes. The situation in most North American universities is just the opposite. Graduate students frequently are required to take several courses in research methods or methodology prior to designing research and collecting data. When they actually attempt to begin their research, these students often do not know where to begin even though they have studied methods texts and done very well in the associated courses (Roth, 2005b). Typically, students in many North American universities say, 'I want to do a quantitative study,' 'My research will be an auto/ethnography,' or 'I will do qualitative research,' without actually knowing *what* they want to research and *why* this research might be of interest to anybody.

There are contradictions in both of these approaches, which, because they are so widespread, cannot be relegated to the category of extreme cases; they constitute mainstream approaches to graduate student training in the research methods of the social sciences and humanities. In the first approach, the students generally have a good idea about what they want to research but do not have opportunities to work with practitioners who already enact the required research practices in competent ways. In the second approach, students are overly concerned with method and methodology, and this concern becomes the driver of the research problem. Furthermore, graduate students do experience difficulties enacting research methods – as captured in the notion of a 'theory–praxis gap'.

In order to try to overcome these problems, I have developed a personal approach described here that I hope will be useful to other researchers. In my teaching and role as supervisor, I have aimed at introducing students to research method as *praxis* (Roth, 2005a). My students do research alongside someone else in my research group and learn to write research by writing with the teacher; the same practitioners have taught graduate classes on research method in a similar way. This approach is solidly grounded in a theoretical framework that conceptualizes knowledge in terms of knowledgeable participation in social practice. In this chapter, I:

1. articulate cultural-historical activity theory as a framework that explains why the approach is successful in the production and reproduction of scientific communities and individual scholars, and
2. provide a description of the approach of inducting graduate students into research methods by doing research.

Theoretical Grounding

Many graduate students find themselves in one of two epistemological paradigms when it comes to learning how to do research, including design, data collection, data interpretation and writing: discovery learning or information processing. In the former paradigm, the graduate students are asked to find out how to appropriately research their chosen phenomenon on their own. Finding or working out the appropriate method is considered to be part of the requirements for getting a graduate degree – the typical advice for budding ethnographers was to find a tribe and then to figure out the what (question) and how (method) of research. In the latter paradigm, methods and methodology courses are provided as vehicles to transfer knowledge to graduate students, who then are asked to apply what they presumably learned. Research studies have shown that in the first approach, students do not progress as far as they can because they generally do not benefit from the practices that a culture already has worked out (Delamont and Atkinson, 2001). In the second approach, the problem lies in the fact that knowing is conceptualized apart from doing, so that there is no relationship between how well students do in university courses and how knowledgeable they are in enacting research. In recent years, a number of theoretical frameworks have gained ground, which, though different in their framing, have several underlying commonalities:

1. A focus on praxis as the relevant site for enacting and researching knowledge,
2. A corresponding focus on the particulars of the contextual, contingent and distributed aspects of knowing, and
3. A focus on the mutually constitutive nature of biography and history (for example, Holland and Lave, 2001).

All of those theories have in common that they are grounded in a structure/agency dialectic – whereby structures enable and constrain the observed actions, but actions are possible only because of available structures of consciousness and world (Sewell, 1992).

From the perspective of praxis-oriented theories, doing research is but another form of human agency, characterized by its particular *modus operandi*. It is a particular mode of scientific production, which mediates cognition, perception and human action through the salient motive, tools, division of labour, community and attendant rules (Engeström, 1987). The research activity system in general and the individual and community of research practice in particular are produced and reproduced in each action oriented toward a goal that contributes to realizing the motive. Because formal learning environments and the world outside school differ with respect to the motive (doing well in a course versus producing publishable research), there normally is a gap between what students can learn in a research methods class and what they need to know when they do research on their own (Roth, 2005b).

In praxis-oriented theories, knowledgeability is understood in terms of activity motives, which means that it is expressed only in praxis itself. More so, numerous sociological studies have shown that what professionals say they have done and what they actually do may be incompatible and with it the competencies displayed in the two situations – praxis and talk *about* praxis. This has considerable consequences for learning: it is understood in terms of changing participation in a changing culturally mediated praxis (Lave, 1993). A number of modes of thinking and doing, often the most vital ones in a particular practice, therefore are appropriated through participation in praxis involving face to face interactions. Numerous ethnographic studies show that this also holds for accomplished scientists, who, when failing to reproduce a particular experiment or procedure based on protocols and published articles, tend to visit another laboratory where the relevant practices are already successfully enacted (Collins, 2001). If experienced scientists often cannot reproduce a practice based on methods descriptions, how can we expect inexperienced graduate students to do so?

The upshot of such considerations is that to learn research method one has to participate in research *praxis* – which is the very site where graduate students in science learn research method and develop identities as scientists (Roth and Bowen, 2001). It is not surprising then that in his well-known workshop on the practice of reflexive sociology, Pierre Bourdieu (1992) states that there is no way to acquire research practices other than to make students experience it in practical operation or to experience how the scientific habitus realizes itself in the face of practical choices and dilemmas. Here, it is not sufficient to observe someone else doing research – for, as in watching sports on television, little is learned that allows observers to be competent practitioners themselves. Rather, newcomers have to enact research praxis so that they can find in their actions the relevance of the instructions they have received or read.

Praxis of Graduate Training

My own graduate students, therefore, begin to do research as soon as they enter their programme and my research group, both at the MA and PhD levels. They generally are supported through some project for which I received funding so that through their research, the students realize the project and their theses. In the course of their two or three years, respectively, they produce a minimum of three and six international conference papers/research articles, respectively – and this independent of any prior skill that they might come with when they first enter my laboratory. They learn to do research by doing research: they learn to do interviews by first watching me and then increasingly taking over. They learn to analyse data by analysing data with me and then increasingly taking on the analysis themselves. They also learn to write research articles by writing them with me, again requiring a lot of corrections and rewriting on my part until at the end of their programme, they are highly competent in writing research articles themselves.

Collecting data sources

To assist my students to develop data source collection practices, I spend some time with them in the field. For example, in the ethnographic study of a fish hatchery, a doctoral student and a research assistant began accompanying me after I had already established contact, achieved entry and received consent, and had begun data collection. The two were to take the project over from me. Initially, they followed me around in the site and sat quietly at the table during the first interviews. Later, they observed on their own, only occasionally touching base with me during the day when they had a question. In interviews, they began to ask questions all the while leaving me with the main responsibility of moving ahead. Increasingly, however, they took on more and more of the questioning until they conducted interviews on their own. A second doctoral student, whose thesis was almost entirely focused on the hatchery, learned to do ethnographic fieldwork in general, and interviewing more specifically, as he participated with others more experienced in these methods.

The hatchery was far away from our university, so that we decided to stay for periods of time. In the evenings, all members of the team met to discuss the events of the day. We wrote research notes before and after these evening meetings, and shared them with the others. In this way, the new researchers became aware of the phenomena that they had not been aware of before or they discovered that something they had observed had a particular relevance to the ongoing data collection.

These meetings also served as a means to reflect on our research practices. Such reflection is a necessary component of the praxis approach, for learning to do research in general and to collect data in particular by doing what someone else does is limiting because it does not articulate the reasons for acting this or that way. On the other hand, the experience of collecting data was necessary for the new researchers to reflect about the relevant aspect of research methods in the first place. That is, jointly collecting data and reflecting on data collection in the evening allowed these new researchers to learn by thoroughly practical means and by elaborating their practical understanding through critical reflection, which led to explanations of and for their actions.

Having established a research group, I often no longer have to accompany new students into the field. Other participants in my group have developed sufficient competencies and become mentors of newcomers. Thus, in an ongoing project, a masters student, who had already spent five years within an environmentalist group, two of which as researcher for her MA study, inducted a new doctoral student to the site where he, too, would conduct his research. He learned to write research notes from the institutionally junior person and conducted his first study under her auspices. Two years later, another MA student wanted to work on a project involving the environmental group; this time, the PhD student inducted the new person to the field site, observation and interview methods. In turn, the new MA student became the mentor in the field site of an even more recent doctoral student. In this way of operating, the institutional status of a person reveals little about who is the teacher/mentor and who is the learner. Thus, one of my current graduate students had begun right after completing her undergraduate degree, a double major in anthropology and biology. After two years of working for me, and before beginning an interdisciplinary masters programme, she had developed such tremendous competencies that she came to mentor and induct doctoral students and postdoctoral fellows.

Analysing data sources

In my laboratory, graduate students learn to analyse data by participating in collective data analysis sessions. The sessions work like this. Someone in the research group brings some data source he or she has collected, which could be a videotape, transcript, audio recording or any other material artefact from the field. We make the artefact available using a computer and video projector. After the owner of the data source has provided some background about the origin and context of the materials, we watch, listen to or read the materials presented. As soon as someone wants to make an interpretive comment, the owner of the data source stops the display. The person presents his or her comments, which may then lead to a discussion. During the discussion, and as a way of substantiating the divergent analyses that are put forth, the data source is replayed as often as needed. These meetings are rich sources of ideas for how to frame the data sources, which theoretical frameworks apply, the nature of relevant theoretical constructs, possible categorizations, etc. Thus, we usually do not get beyond a few seconds or minutes into a videotape before a two-hour meeting has come to its end. Once participants feel that nothing else of substantive nature is to be added, the data source owner continues presenting materials.

To allow the data owner to participate in the discussion without having to worry about taking notes, we videotape each data analysis session. The data source owner then takes this secondary tape and extracts from it relevant categorizations and ideas. He or she usually moves to test the categories in the remainder of the entire set of data sources, which therefore constitutes the beginning of a grounded theory.

New members in the research group participate in the sessions, contributing and subsequently reflecting on others' and their own contributions. If they are the data owners, they also have a set of diverging interpretations that they can test and play against one another in their personal search for sense and meaning. Because the members of my research group are engaged in very different studies, very different interpretative methods come to be enacted during the collective analysis. Thus, video-based interaction, discourse, conversation and narrative analysis are but some of the forms new members in my research group would encounter on a regular basis.

Writing research

In most graduate programmes, the masters or doctoral thesis is viewed as evidence that students are capable of and have demonstrated research competence. Writing research thereby appears after the training period. There is a contradiction, however, in that many graduate students find it next to impossible to publish the results of their research. This shows that they have not yet developed the required competencies that would allow them successfully to enact this last phase of a research project. I believe that the writing phase is an integral part of becoming a researcher. My goal is that after someone has received an MA or PhD degree, they can conduct and write research on their own. In the meantime, I participate to a decreasing degree in their writing for publication. Here is how it works.

After having submitted their data sources to collective analysis – sometimes this will be repeatedly with the materials from a particular study – the graduate students continue the analysis, confirming and disconfirming hypothesized categories and writing draft analyses. At the same time, they engage in intensive reading of articles from the journal that they have tentatively chosen in which to publish their work. This prepares them for the genres of writing research acceptable to the audiences of the chosen journal. Eventually, the students come to a point where they know the claims that they want to present and defend in a particular article. I ask them to write something resembling an abstract focusing entirely on the claims and then I work with them to identify exactly what the stated purpose of the article will be.

Once students submit their drafts to me, I go beyond simply commenting and outlining what works and what does not work. I actually add and change some of the writing so that they see how something might be presented. Our standard practice is to use a tracking feature so that students can follow the changes made and, if necessary, ask about why a particular change has been made. Generally, I do not rework the entire article but focus on one part, rework it to some extent, and then ask the student to work through the remainder following my example. In the next round, I work on the revised section, again reworking parts of it and requesting further reworking to be done. In this way, we work through each section, allowing the student to rework section after section based on concrete contextualized examples of writing *this*, their own piece. In my reworking, I do not impose my own style but strive to rewrite in the manner of the student. My goal is to complete the writing so that the students feel that the article is theirs although they know it is not entirely theirs.

In my experience – especially with non-English speaking graduate students – I may rewrite as much as 95 per cent of an MA student's first article; their third article requires a lot less change. At the end of a person's doctoral study, having worked with me on a minimum of six publications, students write quality research articles almost entirely on their own. Writing together, as with collectively collecting data sources and doing data analysis, provides opportunities for tacit and explicit modes of instruction, and for reflection on the praxis of writing.

Research methods courses

Teaching research through working closely with students is evidently easier with a small number of students in a research group, where new students also learn from more senior students and postdoctoral fellows that are part of the community. Readers may think that the model is impossible when teaching classes and seminars. But this is not entirely the case. For the past 17 years, I have been teaching introductory quantitative and qualitative research methods. Consistent with my emerging conceptual framework in cultural–historical activity theory, I introduce students to and develop their skilful engagement with research through *authentic* tasks. Students design and conduct research in groups, which, because of the possibilities for development available in collectives, also allows them to learn by doing and reflecting. More recently, I have used data from my research, analysed them with a class and we published a paper together (Roth et al., 2004).

With larger classes, I may use an existing set of data sources as the basis for asking students to collect additional data sources and to write studies that in turn contribute additional categories to describe and theorize the data. Alan Schoenfeld (1985), a mathematics professor, provides some interesting suggestions about how to allow students to learn mathematics authentically in large lecture classes – these may work too for research methods. My students have full access to the data sources and to the articles that have been written using the materials; they are asked to contribute to the further development of an understanding of relevant phenomena (Laroche and Roth, in press). In some of my classes, a slightly competitive spirit develops pushing students to be particularly innovative in their search for additional data sources and in producing well articulated and well-grounded analyses.

Engaging in research collectively and having the remainder of a class serve as a sounding board leads to learning by implicit and explicit means. It allows students to find the relevance of any statement of research – as they may read it written in a textbook or as I may articulate it during our class discussions – in their own actions. In the whole class situation, we analyse a new researcher's own practices, for example, by watching a videotape of an interview with the purpose of better understanding interview practices.

Coda

In this chapter, I have described the praxis of learning to do research by participating in research. Participation in praxis, especially when accompanied by critical reflection on praxis, allows implicit (learning by doing) and explicit modes of learning (learning by finding relevance in descriptions), and provides a forum for further development through reflection, interpretation and explanation. The approach is grounded solidly in existing practice theories, which presuppose knowledgeability as something available for assessment and training purposes only in concrete praxis. Participating in praxis, new researchers experience relevant actions in context. They experience their own actions in this context and, together with their supervisor or more experienced peers, can evaluate the appropriateness of their actions in *this* situation.

It should be evident that in this approach, one cannot supervise a large number of students, as one can only really supervise 'on condition of actually doing it along with the [student] researcher who is in charge of it' (Bourdieu, 1992, 222), including designing questionnaires, doing interviews, analysing videotapes and writing research articles. Bourdieu concludes that those who pretend to supervise large numbers of students do not really do what they claim to be doing: supervising and inducting new researchers. My own experience with a functioning research team shows that once such a group exists, individuals other than the supervisor become integral to the training process and may to some extent substitute for the supervisor.

In my approach, I do not think of the research culture as a stable entity into which a new researcher is socialized, as if the culture were a box that constrains and forms the person entering it. Rather, each new and old researcher is constitutive of the culture. That is, each shapes the culture as much as he or she is shaped by the existing possibilities to use resources and to act. By working with students to develop their own particular ways of doing research, I continually find myself developing, changing the way I do and teach research. This therefore leads to changes not only in our little research group but, through our interactions with other researchers, the research culture as a whole.

Chapter 11

The (In)effectiveness of Various Approaches to Teaching Research Methods

Terrell L. Strayhorn

Introduction

Teaching research methods is difficult and often a miscellany of approaches is used to proffer students a less than useful introduction to a wide range of concepts. In fact, a large majority of graduate students complain that their research methods courses inadequately prepared them for independent research. For example, one doctoral student remarked, 'I took classes in statistics and research methods as part of my coursework, but what I learned and was able to do on my own was insufficient for carrying out my dissertation project. I really struggled through the dissertation' (anonymous student, personal communication, 18 April 2005). Another PhD student in Business noted: 'I am struggling in graduate school. Students in my department are required to take four courses in statistics and research methods … but these classes differ in rigour and intensity. I realize now that my classes lacked the intensity, rigour, and focus needed to prepare me for my dissertation. Now I feel up the creek without a paddle' (anonymous student, personal communication, 28 September 2005). Given the fact that most graduate students in the United States have to complete independent research to earn their degree (Golde and Dore, 2001; Mitchell-Kernan, 2005), anecdotal comments such as these point to a major problem for faculty who teach such courses.

This chapter presents evidence to demonstrate the need for more information about the effectiveness of various strategies for teaching research methods at the graduate level. Briefly, the next section will highlight the problem addressed in this chapter and segue into the review of literature. In general, the purpose of this chapter is to provide a useful discussion of the (in)effectiveness of various strategies in teaching research methods. To that end, it focuses on the nexus between theoretical understandings of research methodology and practical applications of such knowledge to research problems.

The Pedagogy of Research Methods

Prior studies suggest that a limited number of strategies are used to teach research methods, particularly at the graduate level. O'Connell (2002) noted the use of four strategies including structured data analysis assignments, open-ended data analysis assignments, article reviews and annotating computer output from specific multivariate statistical packages. She defines structured data analysis assignments as exercises in which instructors pose specific questions whose answers are found through computer calculations or hand computation. Open-ended assignments provide students with an opportunity to design a hypothetical research project, develop research questions based on a data set and/or to analyse data appropriately. Article analysis is synonymous with article critique in which students are required to read an article and answer a set of related questions based on it. Output annotations provide students with detailed information or instructions on output from computer statistical packages, such as Statistical Package for the Social Sciences (SPSS).

While it is reasonable to assume that new and innovative strategies are available, all too often research methods instructors *teach the way they were taught*. This approach to teaching preserves the normative paradigm in which the teacher is all knowing and the student is an empty vessel waiting to be filled. It goes without saying that such pedagogical approaches relegate the student to a non-participant status and seem to run counter to the goals of graduate education. Other strategies are needed that empower students to participate in their own learning process and to make the connection between conceptual and procedural knowledge (O'Connell, 2002). These are a few of the desired learning outcomes associated with graduate study.

There are additional outcomes for graduate student learning and development in terms of statistics. First, students should be able to understand published research literature. Another objective is to choose appropriate statistical methods for different research situations. Students should also be able to conduct and interpret univariate and multivariate statistical analyses. Identifying and anticipating potentially confounding factors in addition to the limitations and alternatives of a study are other important outcomes for graduate level instruction on methods. Finally, to return to the point about relating theory to practice, classroom practices must reflect our instructional goals (Shepard, 2000). Instruction in research methods should allow students to apply principles to new research topics (O'Connell, 2002).

Much of the literature related to the teaching of research methods focuses on introductory courses at the undergraduate level across a number of disciplines and falls into two categories. The first line consists of studies and chapters about teaching statistics generally (Cobb, 1992; Garfield, 1993; 1995). Literature in this area has increased in recent years (Gal and Garfield, 1997). The second highlights the impact of technology on pedagogical options in research methods (Dallal, 1990; Searle, 1989). Such studies speak to the effectiveness of statistical computing packages in teaching methods. Dallal encourages the use of statistical computing packages as he believes it would be difficult, if not impossible, to write a report without interpreting the output. On the other hand, Searle warns against using statistical packages in introductory courses as students might feel that 'easy to use computing packages can be a substitute for (rather than a supplement to) a proper knowledge of statistical methodology' (p. 190).

As mentioned, much of this work focuses on introductory methods courses at the undergraduate level. A small but growing body of writings about teaching methods courses at the graduate level points to differences between undergraduate and graduate students (Strayhorn, 2005; Wagner and Okeke, Chapter 5). Most evidence suggests that understanding research methods is highly important to graduate students as success in learning enables graduate students to aspire to academic and professional careers, particularly faculty positions (Golde and Dore, 2001). Still other studies focus on the use of various strategies in teaching research methods (O'Connell, 2002). Yet, more information is needed about the effectiveness of various strategies on graduate students' statistical knowledge (conceptual) and ability (procedural).

The remainder of this chapter will present findings from an assessment project designed to measure the effectiveness of various pedagogical approaches to teaching research methods to students in education and social science fields. The last section will discuss the importance of findings and highlight implications for practice and future research.

An Investigation into the Effectiveness of Strategies

The purpose of this study was to measure students' perceptions of the effectiveness of various teaching strategies used in graduate research methods courses. Specifically, in an attempt to understand the relationship between *learning about* and *learning how to do* research. I conducted a study, using both quantitative and qualitative techniques, which was designed to measure students' perceptions of various teaching strategies. A questionnaire was developed, consisting of 32 items. Three of these elicited information about students' biographical characteristics including gender, race and age. One question asked students to indicate their rating on the Myers-Briggs Personality Type Indicator. Responses included seven categories ranging from ENTJ to ISFJ.[1]

One item asked respondents to enter the number of research methods courses that they had taken to date, while another asked them to select all teaching strategies that had been used in research methods courses noted in the previous question. Response options included lecture, textbook reading, research article reading, article critique or analysis, structured computer assignments, open-ended assignments and annotated output.

Two questions were designed for participants to self-report their level of *knowledge about* research methods and their *ability to use* methods appropriately in their own research using a Likert-type scale. Scores ranged from 1 (very low) to 5 (very high). Scores of 4 indicated that respondents felt their knowledge or

---

1   Myers-Brigg type was included on the survey to test the hypothesis that a relationship existed between personality type and preferred teaching style. No significant relationships were, in fact, established or reported.

ability was 'higher than their peers' while scores of 2 corresponded with feeling that one's knowledge was 'lower than their peers.' Overall, the instrument was deemed reliable and valid for the purposes of this research; standardized Cronbach's alpha was .71.

A convenience sample of master's and doctoral students currently enrolled at a research-extensive, public university in the United States was drawn and invited to complete the online survey. Given the small sample size (n=33), analysis was limited to descriptive statistics, correlations and comparisons across groups. Chi-square tests could not be calculated as some cells in the contingency table included fewer than five cases, thus violating the main assumptions of the test statistic (Hinkle et al., 1998).

The final sample was nearly equally mixed in terms of gender (45 per cent males, 55 per cent females). Sixty-four per cent of the sample consisted of white students while 36 per cent of the sample was black and/or African American (used interchangeably). The average age was 28 years old (SD=7.13). The average number of research methods courses taken was 2.36 (SD=1.75). For the purposes of this research, a course was defined as a single class for which three graduate credit hours were earned upon completion. Mean level of knowledge about research methods was 3.18 (SD=.75); mean level of ability to use techniques appropriately was 3.27 (SD=1.10).

Teaching strategies

Findings suggest that textbook reading is the most commonly used teaching strategy among the list of choices. Ninety-one per cent of all respondents indicated that their research methods instructors required reading from textbooks. Formal lectures and reading a research article were also frequently cited (82 per cent). Fewer instructors used article critiques as a way of teaching research methods. Less than three-quarters of the sample noted that article critiques were used in research methods courses that they had taken. Slightly more than half of the sample noted that their instructors used structured computer assignments to facilitate teaching about research.

Table 11.1   Teaching strategies used

Strategy used?	% Yes	% No
Lecture	82	18
Textbook reading	91	9
Read research article	82	18
Article critique	73	27
Structured computer task	55	45
Open-ended assignment	82	18
Annotated output	36	64

Of particular interest, a small percentage of participants (36 per cent) reported that instructors used annotated outputs as a pedagogical tool for learning research methods. By annotated output, I mean that the instructor provided detailed notes, feedback or commentary on computer-generated outputs related to an analysis or assignment. This was the least commonly used strategy. Table 11.1 summarizes these results.

Preferences

In effect, students did not discriminate much in terms of their preference for various teaching strategies. This may indicate that they do not prefer one strategy more than the other. Equally, it might also mask their preference for another strategy not measured here; there is a need for further research on this issue. In short, students in my sample preferred self-directed activities more than guided activities, such as annotated outputs and formal lectures. Self-directed activities included reading research articles, structured computer tasks and open-ended assignments. Table 11.2 summarizes these findings.

Students' preferences differed by race, though a degree of caution should be exercised in interpreting these findings given the small sample sizes. For example, more black graduate students (75 per cent) preferred textbook reading, article reading and open-ended assignments as a way of learning research methods than their white counterparts (43 per cent). This is a possible indication that black graduate students in this sample preferred self-directed activities. Given the design and sample size, it is inadvisable to make generalizations based on these data; however, this finding is interesting given that the weight of evidence suggests that students prefer collaborative or cooperative learning environments (Pascarella and Terenzini, 2005). Conversely, more white graduate students preferred structured teaching and learning exercises than black students. For example, 57 per cent of all white students preferred formal lectures compared to only 50 per cent of black students. Similarly, more white students (57 per cent) indicated their preference for article analyses. This finding, too, may be related to racial differences in learning styles, but more information is needed before such conclusions can be drawn.

Table 11.2   Strategies preferred

Strategy preferred?	% Yes	% No
Lecture	55	45
Textbook reading	55	45
Read research article	64	36
Article critique	55	45
Structured computer task	64	36
Open-ended assignment	64	36
Annotated output	36	64

Students' preferences also differed by gender. Men showed a strong preference for textbook reading and article critique (80 per cent respectively). Women, however, preferred research article reading, structured computer assignments and open-ended assignments. In short, men tended to prefer structured activities while women preferred both structured and self-directed tasks. Table 11.3 presents the results of this analysis.

Table 11.3   Preferences for teaching strategies, by gender

Strategy	% Men	% Women
Lecture	60	50
Textbook reading	80	33
Read research article	60	67
Article critique	80	33
Structured computer task	60	67
Open-ended assignment	60	67
Annotated output	60	17

Self-rated knowledge

Overall, students who were taught through textbook reading rated themselves higher on both knowledge and ability compared to those who were not taught through textbook reading. For example, students who were taught about research methods through textbook reading rated themselves 3.30 on ability to use such methods for research purposes. On the other hand, students who were not taught through textbook reading rated themselves 2.00 on ability to use such methods. See Table 11.4 for more detail.

The mean of those who were taught by lecture was higher (M=3.33, SD=.71) than those who were not taught in this way (M=2.50, SD=.71) in terms of knowledge. Students who were taught about research methods through textbook reading were also more likely to rate themselves higher in terms of knowledge than their non-textbook peers.

Table 11.4   Mean self-reported knowledge and ability levels

Outcome	Used textbook reading	Did not use
Knowledge	3.20 (.79)	2.50 (.71)
Ability	3.30 (1.16)	2.00 (1.41)

Note: Standard deviation shown in parentheses.

Other teaching strategies were associated with higher perceptions of knowledge about research methods. Reading research articles was associated with higher average scores on knowledge about methods (M=3.33, SD=.71). Yet, critiquing an article for the purpose of learning research methods yielded a slightly higher mean score about research knowledge (M=3.38, SD=.74). Both structured computer assignments (for example, running data in class) and open-ended assignments (for example, designing a hypothetical study on any topic) were associated with higher knowledge means. Those who did not learn by way of these two methods rated their knowledge of research methods at or below 3.0, while those who were taught using such strategies rated their knowledge above 3.0. Table 11.5 presents the results of this section.

Those who took more research courses (for example, four or more courses) had higher knowledge scores (M=4.00, SD=1.41) than those who took only one course (M=3.00, SD=.63).

Table 11.5   Mean knowledge level, by teaching strategy

Strategy used?	Yes	No
Lecture	3.33 (.71)	2.50 (.71)
Textbook reading	3.20 (.79)	2.50 (.71)
Read research article	3.33 (.71)	2.50 (.71)
Article critique	3.38 (.74)	2.67 (.58)
Structured computer task	3.50 (.84)	2.80 (.45)
Open-ended assignment	3.33 (.71)	2.50 (.71)
Annotated output	3.50 (1.0)	3.00 (.58)

Note: Standard deviation shown in parentheses.

Self-rated ability

The mean of those who were taught by lecture was significantly higher (M=3.56, SD=.88) than those who were not taught using a lecture format (M=2.00, SD=1.41) in terms of their ability to use methods appropriately. In fact, those who were taught using formal lecture were slightly more than one standard deviation higher on mean ability to use appropriate methods in research. This represents a large statistically significant difference between the means for these two groups.

As shown in Table 11.6, textbook reading was also associated with higher scores on ability to use methods appropriately. Students who were taught using textbook reading assignments rated themselves approximately one standard deviation higher than their non-textbook counterparts. This represents a significantly higher mean than that observed among non-textbook learners (M=2.00).

Using articles to teach research methods resulted in higher ability ratings as well. For example, those who took courses in which instructors required students to read research articles rated themselves much higher on their ability to use those methods (M=3.56, SD=.88) than those who did not have such experiences (M=2.00, SD=1.41). Still, critiquing an article seems to increase one's perceptions of one's ability to use methods appropriately more than merely reading a research article. The mean ability score of those who critiqued articles was 3.63 (SD=.92) compared to 2.33 (SD=1.16) for those who had not critiqued a research article.

Using structured computer assignments (for example, running data in class) appeared to have a positive influence on a student's perception of his or her ability to use methods appropriately. Those who learned through structured computer tasks rated themselves most highly in terms of ability to use appropriate methods (M=3.83, SD=.98). Not only is this 1.23 units above the mean for those who did not learn through such structured exercises, but it represents the highest mean ability score across all teaching strategies measured in this study.

Both open-ended assignments and annotated outputs (for example, studying notes written on SPSS or SAS output) were associated with slightly higher scores on *ability to use*. For example, students who learned through annotated outputs rated themselves 3.50, on average, compared to 3.14 for those who did not learn through an annotated output approach. Table 11.6 presents the details of this analysis.

Table 11.6   Mean ability level, by teaching strategy

Strategy used?	Yes	No
Lecture	3.56 (.88)	2.00 (1.41)
Textbook reading	3.30 (1.16)	2.00 (1.41)
Read research article	3.56 (.88)	2.00 (1.41)
Article critique	3.63 (.92)	2.33 (1.16)
Structured computer task	3.83 (.98)	2.60 (.89)
Open-ended assignment	3.56 (.88)	2.00 (1.41)
Annotated output	3.50 (1.00)	3.14 (1.22)

Note: Standard deviation shown in parentheses.

Taking more research courses was positively and moderately associated with higher ability levels (r=.40). Students who took four or more methods courses rated themselves higher (M=4.00, SD=1.41) on ability than those with one course only (M=3.00, SD=1.27).

Though rather intuitive, knowledge was found to be positively and strongly associated with ability (r=.90, p<.01). That is to say, those who reported that they had more knowledge about research methods tended to also feel that they had a higher level of ability in terms of using methods appropriately in their own research. This may provide an important impetus for developing additional strategies for teaching research methods. Moreover, it speaks to the main point at issue in this chapter – does *teaching about* lead to *ability to* do. The results of this section suggest that there is a nexus between learning about (knowledge) and learning how to (ability to/applicability).

Best Practices and Recommended Strategies

The contention that there is a relationship between pedagogy and student learning outcomes is well substantiated by Bloom's (1956) conceptual framework. Bloom identified three domains of educational activities: cognitive; affective; and psychomotor. These three categories relate to knowledge, attitudes, and skills respectively. Further, he defined six dimensions of learning for each category. For example, the cognitive domain is divided into six skills areas of increasing cognitive complexity: knowledge; comprehension; application; analysis; synthesis; and evaluation.

Bloom's taxonomy is useful for identifying teaching strategies that promote higher levels of learning and skill development in students. According to the model, knowledge and comprehension are the lowest form of cognitive development. Key terms include: recall; define; describe; and explain. These terms are often associated with activities such as formal lectures, textbook reading and article reading. Other activities that enhance one's knowledge and comprehension are fill in the blank exercises and, in class, call and response assessments. For example, instructors may encourage rote memorization or recall of facts by using prompts in class, such as: What are standard measures of central tendency? Done with repetition, this activity can eventuate general understanding of basic concepts.

Equally important – in fact, arguably more important for graduate education – are strategies that promote higher forms of cognitive development and skill acquisition. These are defined as application, analysis, synthesis and evaluation in Bloom's framework. Application refers to the use of concepts in new settings. Key words include *apply*, *compute* and *solve*. In this study, structured computer assignments were found to be highly related to this domain. Research methods instructors may consider this approach as a follow-up to a series of guided activities. While guided activities, such as in class examples, may lead to basic knowledge of statistical concepts, structured computer or handwritten exercises require a level of confidence and independence. Independence is particularly important for those graduate students who aspire to conduct their own original research.

Analysis is another more complex outcome than mere knowledge or understanding of concepts. Bloom defined this category as the point at which an individual separates material into component parts. Key concepts include analyse, compare and contrast. A good example of how this is used in teaching research methods is article critique. Interestingly, despite the quality and quantity of learning that can result from such assignments, this pedagogical tool was not commonly used according to the sample referenced in this chapter.

Research methods instructors may consider adapting current practices to include analysis activities. For example, instructors can select an article that demonstrates a particular analytical technique and ask students to critique the study focusing on its design, results and conclusions. Specific prompts might require students to identify the purpose of the study, describe the population and sample, separate independent from dependent variables and explain the study's findings in their own terms.

Synthesis and evaluation are the highest categories of cognitive development in Bloom's framework. Synthesis refers to one's ability to build patterns or relationships from diverse elements and it might be developed in research methods courses through open-ended exercises that require students to design a study of their own and to map out an abbreviated research proposal identifying the study's purpose, target sample, method, analytical technique and limitations. Synthesis may also be achieved through collaborative learning or group settings. Instructors might divide students into groups of two to three individuals and ask each group to create a research study that responds to a particular problem in education, sociology or engineering. For example, one professor of engineering divided her class into five groups of no more than three persons per group. After several lectures on the problems associated with water treatment, she asked each group to design a study that would investigate the issues highlighted in her lectures (for example, water quality, environmental health, mortality). Proposals were submitted to the instructor and evaluated on the basis of design, implementability and soundness of their approach (N. Love, personal communication, 10 January 2005).

Evaluation, in short, refers to one's ability to make judgements. Evaluation activities require students to make choices among a set of options. Open-ended assignments discussed earlier relate to this dimension of learning. For example, open-ended assignments can be designed in such a way that students have to determine a research question or hypothesis and then select the most appropriate or effective method for collecting and analysing data. As added proof of mastery, an instructor might require students to support their decision using appropriate statistical concepts and terms. In my assessment, open-ended assignments were among the most highly cited teaching strategies used in research methods courses. Interestingly, a fairly large percentage of students (64 per cent) preferred open-ended assignments to other instructional practices. Yet, even more (73 per cent) indicated that open-ended assignments were *most effective* in teaching them *how to* do research and/or analyse data.

Still other innovative teaching strategies are possible. Cobb (1992) and Garfield (1993) recommend the use of individual and group projects. The water treatment example above demonstrates how this technique might be used in teaching research methods. Poster displays are another recommended strategy (Denson, 1992) and may prove useful for students who are visual learners. Still multiple choice questionnaires (Wild et al., 1997) may be effective strategies for making students evaluate a number of competing options to select the most effective or appropriate choice. Garfield (1995) noted that learning is enhanced when students are actively involved and engaged in activities, tasks or assignments that give them an opportunity to apply newly acquired knowledge to real situations and/or data. Cooperative group tasks and computer-based problem-solving simulations may be appropriate pedagogical techniques for promoting such deep learning.

Conclusion

Several results from the present study support prior conclusions. For example, the finding that students most strongly preferred structured computer exercises and open-ended assignments confirm those of O'Connell (2002). Others, however, suggest some new and interesting conclusions. First, students also strongly preferred reading research articles, which may be a good pedagogical motivation for using articles, particularly those that highlight a number of designs and a blend of analytical techniques, including descriptive and inferential statistics. Since the mere reading of research articles is unlikely to lead to any degree of proficiency in using methods to conduct research or analyse data, instructors should link reading assignments with activities that allow students to apply concepts to 'real life' problems or sample data sets. For example, teaching students to use multiple regression techniques may be facilitated through the use of an article that demonstrates *how* a researcher used regression to investigate a question followed by in class instruction and guided examples on calculating goodness of fit measures and R-squared values. Finally, students might be expected to design a hypothetical study using variables selected from a small data set in which multiple regression is the appropriate analytical technique.

The title of this chapter reflects its central focus – to measure the effectiveness of various teaching strategies that are widely used in graduate research methods courses. The results of these studies indicate that two of the most widely used teaching strategies (lecture and textbook reading) are rated among the least effective by students. The single most commonly cited strategy – textbook reading – is also rated as the least effective. In other words, while most respondents reported that textbook reading assignments were widely used in their methods courses, only 18 per cent of them found such assignments to be effective in developing their understanding of research. This may have significant implications for pedagogical practices and future research. In short, the strategies that we use as research methods instructors may also be the least effective, according to students, in teaching them *how to* conduct research and *how to* analyse data. Strategies outlined in sections above may represent more effective ways of teaching research concepts.

The results provided data about the types of teaching strategies used in research methods courses. For example, a majority of the sample indicated that their instructors used textbook reading as a way of presenting information about research methods. However, relatively few individuals indicated that their instructors used structured computer exercises and annotations of output. Given the potential of such strategies, research methods instructors might consider the recommendations above when designing new courses and redesigning activities for existing methods courses.

It is important to note this chapter is based on two assessments with relatively small sample sizes. Therefore, it is needful to resist large generalizations. But, given the size of most graduate level methods courses – ranging from less than 10 to 25 – small samples may reflect typical classroom settings. This is particularly true when referring to advanced quantitative and qualitative methods courses in which fewer students enrol. To the extent that these findings reflect the population, results presented here may provide an introduction to the differences between instructors' use of various strategies and graduate students' preferences and perceptions of the effectiveness of such practices.

In summary, graduate school is vastly different from the undergraduate experience in college. It seems to follow that teaching strategies used in graduate school might differ, to some extent, from those used with undergraduate students. Given the purpose of graduate school – to gain in-depth understanding for the purpose of developing expertise in a topic or discipline (Ebel, no date) – teaching strategies that emphasize higher forms of thinking and learning seem to be fundamental. This chapter presents data that speak to the ineffectiveness of commonly used teaching strategies such as lecture and textbook reading in methods courses. In addition, it highlights a number of ways in which instructors can promote student learning and development at higher levels of cognitive and skill complexity. Ultimately, our efforts should be geared toward moving theoretical discussions *about* methods to practical applications and *uses* of methods in problem-solving.

Chapter 12

Teaching the Use of Technology in Research Methods

João Batista Carvalho Nunes

Scientific and technological development has transformed societal life. In addition, the field of research in humanities and social sciences, particularly in education, has benefited from technological advances. With the advent of the computer, scientific research in many diverse disciplines provides both quantitative and qualitative contributions to knowledge production. The technologies used in carrying out this research are evolving or are changing, further presenting opportunities for research and how we implement that research.

Although there is sensible difference in technological conditions between countries, states and research institutions, technological development modifies the *modus faciendi* of research. New theoretical approaches, bibliographic management, data collection, organization and analysis, and the communication of one's findings are appearing in educational research, thanks to the introduction of new technologies.

Concern about how to teach research methodology for undergraduate and postgraduate students grows. While, in the past, there was a polarization between quantitative and qualitative research, currently the integration of both approaches in research is advocated, in what is called 'mixed methods' (Johnson and Christensen, 2003). Many scientific publications stress experiences about research methods teaching (Babbie, 2003; Bell, 2004; Blank, 2004) and, in particular, about mixed methods teaching (Bazeley, 2003; Tashakkori and Teddlie, 2003).

Nevertheless, there are few studies in humanities and social sciences on the teaching of technological tools for use in research. Despite the impact of computer and Internet use on the diverse stages of research (Nunes, 2006), a culture of computer integration throughout the methodological process has not been attained yet. Jackson (2003) points out that the most popular qualitative research texts still restrict the use of software to a specific section, fortifying a disconnection between technology and research methodology. It is necessary, therefore, to stimulate the use of the computer in all research phases, integrating it into the research design. This will contribute to optimizing the available time for conducting research and to strengthening the trustworthiness of the findings from either qualitative or quantitative data.

In this text I intend to argue, from the scientific literature and my personal experience, for inclusion of the teaching of the use of technology in educational research. I will limit my argument to computer mediation, including its use as a tool to access the Internet. I will address the strategies used for working with the computer at two research stages: attainment of scientific information; and data analysis. The coverage of the complete use of computers at every stage of research is not possible in the space allotted for this chapter; thus, I will not be able to address other phases. For further discussion on the use of technology in the research process without a teaching perspective, I refer the reader to Nunes (2006).

This chapter is organized into three parts. First, I will address the teaching of technology use in obtaining scientific information. Second, I will deal with strategies used to teach data analysis with specific software. Finally, my conclusions will be shared.

Obtaining Scientific Information

The research process involves knowing what information there is about a subject that one wants to study. Developing the literature review is an important step, although it cannot be completed before the data is collected. It occurs throughout the various research stages. Further, it can be used to generate possible categories of analysis to investigate, as well as serve as a comparison source for the data and the resultant analyses (Strauss and Corbin, 1998). Some researchers, like Glaser (1992), believe that it is necessary to enter the field without being biased by the literature of a particular topic, yet they emphasize its importance during data analysis.

Although researchers still search for bibliographic material in public libraries, university libraries, research centres and other institutions, the increasing role of the Internet as an information source cannot be refuted. To illustrate this, it is estimated that, annually, there is an addition of 170 terabytes of information to the World Wide Web. This is equivalent to 17 times the 19 million books and other print collections of the Library of Congress (Swearingen et al., 2003).

There are strategies that can be used so that students learn to search scientific information on the computer connected to the Internet. Although these strategies shared in this chapter are directed to the field of education, they could be used in other areas of knowledge with appropriate adaptations. Among them, I point out such strategies as: working in pairs, which stimulates a cooperative learning process with mutual support; presenting the main sources of available scientific information in the area; compiling bibliographic material about the subject of interest and publishing the work in the course syllabus; and maintaining a personal bibliographic management software.

Working in pairs

Vygotsky's (1989) research stressed the importance of interaction in the process of learning, promoting effective student development. Recent studies demonstrate that working with small groups in the classroom contributes to improving student learning (Boud et al., 2001). In teaching research methods, this situation is not different. Although the classroom/laboratory may have sufficient computers for all students, I suggest that the professor puts everyone in pairs to enable students to learn from each other.

Placing students in pairs, however, does not guarantee more effective learning. It is necessary to stimulate dialogue between them and address such problems as they may arise, such as facilitating their joint search of new software resources, solving challenges that arise from group interaction, and negotiating concepts and procedures. Each student in the pair should have a certain level of knowledge about computer use and about research methods. In this way, the stronger student may be able to coach the weaker one and, thus, may be able to better understand the content themselves (Babbie, 2003). My emphasis in teaching must centre on student learning to aid them to fully develop their capacity to learn new technologies, new ways of doing research, and new formats for scientific publication.

Presentation of scientific information sources

The Internet has transformed into one of the main technologies that allows access to the world of information. Whereas, in the past, we utilized more traditional information sources, such as print collections (books, journals, documents, etc.), today, we can find many of these sources on the Internet and more. My objective in this text, however, is to show how to teach the use of technological tools in educational research, rather than how to search for information through the use of print sources.

When students engage in studying research methods, some already have some knowledge of scientific methodology, but they are few. In general, they possess a knowledge grounded in common sense. This situation is more improbable in postgraduates, for they typically had research experiences in college. Most students come to these classes with little experience of using technology in conducting research.

The professor can illustrate a variety of possibilities for accessing information sources using the computer. There are sources accessible via the Internet, university or college Intranet, or optical media (CD-ROM and DVD, mainly). At the same time, the teacher should stimulate the pairs to carry out their own journey into the use of these materials, testing different ideas for logical search terms, exploring other resources, arguing the potentialities of each, analysing how the various resources distinguish themselves from others and optimizing time involved in bibliographic searching.

There are many useful information sources in educational research. In the Brazilian context, there are several that are prevalent in use as sources of information for the student's literature review:

- Periodicos.CAPES portal (http://www.periodicos.capes.gov.br): 10,520 national and international scientific journals, and more than 90 databases with document summaries in all knowledge areas. In education, there are 714 national and international full scientific journals (September 2006).
- Databases: ERIC (http://www.eric.ed.gov); PsycINFO (http://www.apa.org/psycinfo); Web of Science (http://www.isinet.com/products/citation/wos); Education Full Text (http://www.hwwilson.com/Databases/educat.htm); and Sociological Abstracts (http://www.csa.com/factsheets/socioabs-set-c.php).
- Master and doctorate theses abstracts: CAPES Thesis Database (http://www.capes.gov.br/capes/portal/conteudo/10/Banco_Teses.htm), Biblioteca Digital de Teses e Dissertações – BDTD (Digital Library of Thesis and Dissertation – http://bdtd.ibict.br); Dissertation Abstract International (http://www.umi.com/umi/dissertations); TESEO (http://www.mcu.es/TESEO/).
- Sites about qualitative, quantitative and mixed methods research: QualPage (http://www.qualitativeresearch.uga.edu/QualPage); The Qualitative Report (http://www.nova.edu/ssss/QR/index.html); Quantitative Research Websites (http://library.uncfsu.edu/reference/quantitative_research_websites.htm); Bridges (http://www.fiu.edu/~bridges).
- Sites of professional associations in education: Associação Nacional de Pós-Graduação e Pesquisa em Educação – ANPEd (National Association of Postgraduation and Research in Education – http://www.anped.org.br); American Educational Research Association – AERA (http://www.aera.net); European Educational Research Association – EERA (http://www.eera.ac.uk).

Bibliographic searches and construction of the web page

In my experience, I teach basic abilities to the students to help them develop their research capabilities. A useful strategy for this objective, and simultaneously so that they learn to carry out bibliographic searches; to select materials of diverse sources; to analyse which ones are useful, is to request from the students a list of references about their potential research topic. In using the proposed student pairing, each pair will have to present an annotated list of at least 50 works about the chosen subject. The list must have the complete reference of the selected bibliography. This commentary should be short, between three and five lines, bringing one brief statement about what the work is. Students need to be encouraged to relate references from diverse information sources, including digital material or printed material from the university library.

After analysis and discussion of each list with all students in the class, they must publish their lists on the course site. They may use available resources, such as word processors (MS Word, OpenOffice.org Writer), that allow them to export a text page as a web page (HTML format) or they may create it with HTML editors.

Some institutions already have websites for courses. For the publication of the students' material on these sites, it is necessary, however, that they formally authorize this inclusion. Web publication of these lists can serve to help other individuals and future classes interested in the subjects. If this material grows, it can be organized as an annotated bibliographic database by subject.

Personal bibliographic management

All researchers constantly read material related to their area during inquiry development or when they think about research they want to carry out in the future. There is the necessity to organize this material as it is read, registering its bibliographic reference, writing its main ideas or making an abstract, classifying it by subject. In this way, it is possible to know where references that deal with specific themes are located when one needs them.

Although the use of paper cards remains a strategy used by some researchers, the computer offers many resources that facilitate the process of material organization. With the exponential growth of worldwide scientific production, the personal bibliographic management (PBM) software has given the researcher certain benefits: storing and organizing a bibliographic database, flexibility to execute searches according to useful criteria; scientific writing that is more optimized, because it facilitates the insertion of citations and bibliographic references into diverse styles of writing (ABNT, APA, Chicago, MLA, etc.); little risk of information loss; and an increase in productivity.

There are several available PBM softwares. For a comparative analysis among them, Dell'Orso (2006) can be consulted. As the PBM programs tend to possess a set of similar functions, the choice of one will depend on the researcher's analysis of their PBM needs, the computer operating system employed and the capacity to pay a user site license.[1] Even word processors, such as MS Word and OpenOffice. org Writer, may be used in lieu of specific PBM programs.

Teaching Computer-aided Data Analysis

Data analysis represents the apex of one's research. During the analysis, the researcher may work alone with the themes and categories, searching to extract from them the answers to their research questions. When searching regularities for explication or prediction of a social phenomenon or trying to understand

---

1   There are PBM programs that offer free software.

an educational context, the researcher faces decisions about which analytical techniques to choose and which softwares to adopt. Researchers are not obliged to use specific software for data analysis, but the adoption of appropriate software for quantitative or qualitative data analysis is growing.

Although I defend, like Jackson (2003), the necessity to integrate the study of computer use in data analysis during a research methods course, there still are challenges to overcome so that this integration happens (as there is limited time for its inclusion) given all that must be covered in a single course, and many professors have little experience with computer-aided analysis. Therefore, a specific course devoted to computer-aided data analysis enables the integration between technology and methodology.

Instead of limiting the study to one piece of software on quantitative or qualitative analysis, I suggest that the course include work with both statistical and qualitative analysis software. While they can be studied separately to satisfy quantitative or qualitative research, they also can be integrated to satisfy mixed methods research. Separation of quantitative and qualitative computer-aided analysis programs tends to strengthen the separation between the two research approaches instead of encouraging the use of mixed methods.

It is more effective to have a relatively small number of students, between 14 and 16 (preferably even numbers for the work in pairs), to teach computer-aided data analysis. As Blank (2004, 194) suggests, 'data analysis still requires learning by doing'. Therefore, the professor's work with bigger groups would make it impractical to give any individual assistance to each student and/or pair.

The professor must have knowledge of and experience with distinct approaches (quantitative, qualitative and mixed) and with the software employed. Several strategies can be used in these courses: work in pairs to stimulate a cooperative learning process with mutual support; use of real data for practice with the software; integrated discussion of techniques in quantitative and qualitative data analysis and data analysis software; writing of a report explaining the computer-aided data analysis; and analysis of the reports with the class.

The work in pairs is more necessary during the study of data analysis. Variables and category definitions require an intense process of negotiation between the pairs. As Blank (2004) notes about qualitative data analysis, 'two of the most difficult problems in qualitative research are the creation of coding categories and the assignment of codes to segments' (p. 193). Mutual support of the student pairs provides, on the one hand, development of better concepts and understanding of procedures, and on the other hand, more trustworthiness in defining useful variables or categories, the units of analysis assigned to the categories, and the relation between variables and categories in a study.

Data used for students should be real data. It can be secondary data from national archives, reports, websites, novels, etc. (Bazeley, 2003) or primary data from a small research project. In this case, before teaching data analysis, each pair must conduct a simple research project, that will require quantitative and qualitative data collection, using a closed questionnaire or interview guide, in consideration for the limited time afforded by the course. A professor can propose as research subjects individuals who are easily accessible, such as university students or work colleagues.

The discussion about quantitative and qualitative data analysis techniques cannot be separated from the use of the computer, as the analysis must direct how the computer is used. The professor should explore the software resources as they teach the diverse procedures of data analysis. In my case, I work with SPSS for quantitative data, N6 for qualitative data and both for mixed methods research. Other computer-aided data analysis softwares available for use include Atlas-ti, HyperResearch, NVivo, R, SAS, and others. If a professor is teaching quantitative or qualitative data organization, he or she can show the students how to enter data in SPSS, structuring the variables in columns and the cases in lines. In N6, they can illustrate the various document formats and types, choice of text unit and definitions of sections. The available space in this text does not allow for detail in elaborating the procedures, but the integration between theoretical and practical aspects of the analysis become more understandable during this process for the students.

Despite the variety of methods, teaching specific elements of both quantitative and qualitative approaches contributes to the students' understanding of the common and unique aspects of the approaches, instead of a 'total distinction' perspective. This is not an easy task. It demands that the professor plans so that he or she does not make a mistake when they teach the procedures for each approach.

In mixed methods research, I agree with Bazeley (2003, 123) that 'the employment of software for analysis becomes most significant with respect to integrated analysis methods which involve not just the addition of matched data of another format, but the conversion of data from one form to another'. Thus, I encourage students to work with the N6 resources that allow them to import a table produced for statistical programs (such as SPSS) or electronic spreadsheets (Excel, OpenOffice.org Calc, etc.). It also is possible to export qualitative data to tables in accepted format for statistical programs or electronic spreadsheets. Such conversions make it possible to trace comparisons between quantitative variables and qualitative categories. As Richards (2002, 16) reminds us: 'if your qualitative data are the open ended questions from a survey, there is probably considerable information stored in a statistical package about each case'.

To that end, the pairs can be requested to write a report. I specify the following aspects that compose the report: experience about the data analysis process; decisions that they made; negotiation between the pairs; difficulties they experienced; and course evaluation. This report is discussed later with all class members. The positive and negative points are analysed, including which elements need to be improved and what the professor must do to improve the course.

Conclusion

The use of technology, particularly the computer with Internet access, represents a key aspect in the development of the various stages of scientific research. Irrespective of the chosen paradigm, methodology or method, the researcher is confronted with the necessity to use technology to optimize available human resources, material and time and to confer greater trustworthiness to the inquiry. To conduct research today in education or other disciplines without the use of a computer in some phases is almost impossible.

Therefore, the new researchers in humanities and social sciences, particularly in education, who are being trained in our universities and research centres, need to learn to use the computer as one of their work instruments.[2] The image of the researcher, who used paper and pen to register his or her observations in a classroom or parents' meeting in the outskirts of a small town, must change to the image of the researcher with his or her handheld or smartphone, who, after one work day, will directly transmit the collected data to their notebook, where he or she will analyse them using diverse types of software.

Our students need to be prepared for this reality and others that we do not imagine yet. For that reason we professors also have to evolve as technology users. We cannot refute the computer as if it were competing with us. It is not our enemy. It is an important mediation element between the researcher and the information. We need to integrate computer use in research methods courses, not as an isolated part of the syllabus, but as a constituent aspect of it.

We cannot forget that technology use in research is not only related to teaching and methodology, but also to access. It is intimately related to the socio-economic conditions and the policies that a country has in this area. In the specific case of Brazil and other similar realities in Latin America, for example, this is a large challenge to overcome, given the precarious conditions that many of the public universities still face to fully carry out teaching and research activities.

Moreover, instead of relying on either a quantitative or qualitative perspective, we must look at the increasing complexity of the world and begin to search for other methods and techniques to answer the problems in our field of study. Perhaps some of them demand a more quantitative methodological design, others, more qualitative; however, a significant number of them will very probably benefit from the integration of qualitative and quantitative approaches, and our students have the right to learn about all of these possibilities.

---

2   The instrument is understood in Vygotsky's (1989) socio-historic perspective as mediator of the main activity in the world; therefore, it is an element of great meaning in the construction of the person.

Chapter 13

Best Practice in Research Methods Assessment: Opportunities to Enhance Student Learning

Erica L. James, Bernadette M. Ward, Virginia A. Dickson-Swift, Sandra A. Kippen and Pamela C. Snow

It is well recognized that assessment has an important role in the teaching and learning process. In this chapter we consider the role of assessment in the undergraduate training of health practitioners, in the fields of nursing, health promotion and environmental health, but our comments apply equally to most social science courses. Research assessment can be a valuable tool in enhancing student motivation and consolidating student learning. Innovative assessment not only assists in student learning, it can also guide teachers in continually refining a curriculum that is relevant to the professional competencies recognized as essential components of practitioner training. Employing a variety of assessment tasks provides students with a rigorous framework from which to learn, use, practise and evaluate health research.

This chapter outlines how assessment can be used to set clear expectations that result in effective student learning and achieve best practice in teaching research methods. The six areas discussed are:

1. using competencies to design research curriculum and assessment tasks,
2. balancing theory and practical assessments,
3. using multiple assessments tasks,
4. developing assessment that builds on previous knowledge,
5. balancing group and individual projects, and
6. providing and receiving feedback.

In each of these six sections, we outline the relevant theory that informs practice and provide practical examples to demonstrate how this can be achieved. The series of research subjects in the Bachelor of Public Health programme is used to illustrate these concepts and provide examples of positively evaluated assessment tasks.

The Bachelor of Public Health (BPH) is a three-year undergraduate degree that provides public health education and training in a regional setting to build the capacity of the Australian public health workforce. Students major either in Health Promotion/Health Education or Environmental Health. A four-year Bachelor of Nursing/Bachelor of Public Health programme is also offered. Graduates are employed in diverse public health roles, including project officers, community workers, environmental health officers and research officers.

The BPH programme teaches public health practice with an emphasis on the social model of health and the socioecological foundations of health inequalities. Core research subjects include Public Health Research A, Public Health Research B and Epidemiology, and these are sequenced over the three-year degree. These subjects are based on the philosophy that public health practitioners need to be able to understand, critique and conduct rigorous research. The teaching materials are based on practical examples and highlight the importance of public health practice being evidence-based. In the first year (Public Health Research A) students examine the basic activities involved in conducting research relevant to public health. Topics include formulation of a research question, literature searches and reviews, critical appraisal and foundation qualitative and quantitative analysis. In the second year of the programme (Public Health Research B) students develop a questionnaire based on qualitative data they have collected and analysed, examine ethics in health research and design a research project in the format required for a grant application. Building on these two subjects, in the third year (Epidemiology), students are introduced to the concepts of population statistics and the measurement of disease and health-related states in a given population.

Using Competencies to Design Research Curriculum and Assessment Tasks

The content of education programmes should be based on research about the knowledge and skills required for practice, rather than on intuition or tradition (James et al., 2006; Talbot et al., 2007). Utilizing professional competencies provides a practical and evidence-informed process when designing research subjects (Greenhalgh et al., 2003; Howat et al., 2000). Matching research-related professional competencies to subject objectives is also a useful strategy to enhance student motivation since students who recognize a topic to be highly relevant and useful are more likely to feel motivated to learn (Ramsden, 2003).

In the BPH programme we used the relevant Australian Health Promotion Workforce Competencies (Shilton et al., 2002) and the Environmental Health Professional Literacies (AIEH, 2004) to develop the three consecutive research subjects. In each subject outline we listed the objectives as they aligned with the professional competencies and explained this process to students in the introductory session. This process could easily be replicated in other countries and for other professional groups, such as nurses, psychologists and teachers.

Our evaluations of these subjects demonstrate that the students clearly see them as relevant and as providing important skills for their professional practice. For example, between 2000 and 2005, 80 per cent of student responses (n=474) in

Public Health Research A, B and Epidemiology rated the content of the subject as 'highly relevant' or 'very relevant' for their professional practice.

Assessment should be an integral component of effective teaching and learning processes. However, all too often assessment tasks are set as a final consideration in isolation from curriculum content. This is in contrast with the fact that students often work 'backwards' through the outline focusing firstly on how they will be assessed and how they will be required to demonstrate what they have learned. We find this to be common among students undertaking research subjects where the levels of anxiety in relation to assessment performance are relatively high. Ramsden (2003, 182) has observed 'from our students' point of view assessment always defines the actual curriculum', so, selection of assessment tasks is important not only in assessing student learning, but also in facilitating student motivation to learn specific topics and tasks (Crooks, 1988). The role of assessment has been emphasized by Crooks (1988, 2) who stated, 'Work which is assessed, and particularly work which counts towards a final grade, often is undertaken more seriously and diligently than work which is not assessed.'

To address these issues, we place student assessment at the centre of the teaching and learning process. At the beginning of each session, expected outcomes and course content are discussed in the context of assessment.

Our department assessment policy promotes congruency between subject aims and objectives which in turn are reflected in content and teaching strategies and assessment (Biggs, 2003). The more important aims and objectives are more thoroughly covered, while those of lesser importance are emphasized less. In addition, we link these to the relevant research competencies. For example, in Epidemiology the assessment focuses on practical skills that are essential for health promotion practice and address a range of the health promotion workforce competencies such as:

1. identifying and sourcing data on the health needs of individuals/communities/populations,
2. determining priorities for health promotion from available evidence,
3. using regional, state and national data,
4. applying and interpreting statistical methods/analyses, and
5. using the Internet as a work tool.

In this subject the students undertake two projects: one requiring the use of the Internet to access epidemiological data and a second requiring the analysis and interpretation of real data (for example, from a source such as the Australian Institute of Health and Welfare).

Balancing Theory and Practical Assessments

The ultimate goal in our research teaching is to produce graduates with competencies that allow them to make a smooth transition into the workforce. This is best served by a balance of theoretically grounded framework, conceptual understanding and practical skills (Fraser and Greenhalgh, 2001) which should be clearly reflected in the set assessment tasks.

Both skills and knowledge in research are recognized as core requirements in professional workforce competencies documents relevant to the BPH. It is essential that both these aspects of the research component in these courses should be appropriately supported and given high priority. In the health professions, students with hands on experience of research are highly valued. However, the ability to elaborate in an essay the finer points of in-depth interviewing or how to design a questionnaire is not necessarily an indicator of the ability to translate such concepts into practice in real life situations. Therefore, in the first unit (Public Health Research A) students are asked to:

*   thematically code a piece of transcribed data,
*   carry out inter-rater reliability checks to a level where they obtain 80 per cent agreement (Miles and Huberman, 1994) with other students' codes,
*   cluster their themes together and put them into a 'mind-map' format which demonstrates pictorially the links between the themes,
*   answer questions and write a short summary, or 'story' about the data.

In the past we added to the level of difficulty by asking students to transcribe from handwritten data, but in recent times we have bowed to the electronic age, where the skill of reading handwriting is debatably becoming less relevant in workforce competencies. The students submit for assessment the hard copy of the transcribed data with coding and reflective comments entered, the coding map and a written explanation of the codes.

In the following year's research subject, students are required to conduct a one to one in-depth interview to generate ideas and themes, from which they develop and pilot a questionnaire. They must submit for assessment a tape recording and hard copy transcription of the interview, coded and analysed, and the resulting questionnaire. These activities are preceded by the development of an information sheet and consent form for their interview participants, which provides a practical application of health research ethics.

Although the students are given a thorough grounding (through both subjects) in the concepts relating to these tasks, they are very often surprised at the intricacies of putting that conceptual understanding into practice. Their reflections, shared with the class, range through such mundane issues as difficulties with recording equipment, to being lost for words in a sensitive situation or finding it challenging to activate what they had been taught about closing an interview. The exercise of transcribing the interview, although a somewhat onerous task, gives them some insight into the importance of immersing themselves in their data. The development of the questionnaire requires the drawing of a coding map and the pulling together of themes, followed by decisions about which questions to ask and how to phrase them, the order of the questions and the overall presentation of the questionnaire. Through these steps the students gain a sense of increased satisfaction and confidence in having attained a skill level that will serve them well in the workforce.

Using Multiple Assessment Tasks

Research methods subjects should employ multiple assessment tasks. Our experience is that first year students, who are still undergoing the school-to-university transition, prefer assessment in a series of small tasks. It is important that no individual project appears too daunting and that students receive regular and early grades and comments, giving them feedback on their progress.

Other small assessment tasks used in our first year subject include:

- a data retrieval exercise using library databases on a topic of the students' choice,
- a critical appraisal of a published research paper,
- collection, entry and analysis of quantitative data using Microsoft Excel.

At the beginning of the course, such assessments provide an overview of skills that will stand students in good stead throughout their research career and that will be reinforced in subsequent research methods subjects. The variety of the tasks maintains interest, as does the careful selection of content relevant to the student group and, in some assessments, the flexibility for students to choose the topic to be investigated. In our programme, the later subjects also include multiple tasks, but they are fewer in number and more complex than those required in the introductory subject.

A note of caution must be sounded here. Considerable care needs to be taken with multiple assessments if they are to be effective teaching tools. Multiple assessments can work counterproductively. They can overload the students, overload staff and be difficult to weight fairly.

The first potential concern can be addressed through considering the timing, spacing, variety and interest of the assessment, with regular submission dates that take account of assignments in other, unrelated subjects. For a number of the assessment tasks, the workload of students can be reduced through preliminary work undertaken in class and by ensuring that students have both lecturer and peer input to clarify task requirements and build up their confidence in their ability to succeed.

Overloading of staff can result from both the increased workload associated with student consultation, as well as having to mark five or six assessments per semester per student, even when the total word count (or equivalent) is the same as that required in two 1,000–2,000 word essays. One way to deal with this is to allocate particular assignments to particular staff, so that the flow of work coming in is not continuous and can be planned for. We have also found it useful to place assignments in an order such that those requiring more intense marking alternate with those that can be marked relatively quickly.

Then comes the question of how to weight the allocated marks for assignments. This is of particular importance where there are multiple assessments, as weighting can advantage or disadvantage students with different learning styles. It is important to differentiate between 'essentials' and 'optional extras' (Crooks, 1988). The former are closely linked to the objectives and students are made aware of their importance. They do not allow for any significant flexibility and are heavily weighted in the assessment. The optional extras, on the other hand, add depth and richness to the learning process, but can be flexible in both content and the way they are assessed. For example, we believe that all students must be able to write an information sheet and consent form that meets human research ethics committee requirements. To achieve this, we require that all students meet with the lecturer to discuss and refine their information sheet and consent form prior to collecting data. Students do not proceed with data collection unless they have carried out this task to a satisfactory level. In contrast, the development of a questionnaire is a very complex task and needs to be assessed on the basis that this is an introduction to questionnaire development. Reliability and validity analysis is considered to be beyond the scope of the unit objectives at this level.

Developing Assessment that Builds on Previous Knowledge

Building on previous knowledge is a core principle of adult learning (Knight, 2002) and fosters deep, rather than surface, learning (Biggs, 2003). Säljö (as cited in Ramsden, 2003) described five different understandings among adult learners of what constitutes learning. They include learning as:

1. a quantitative increase in knowledge,
2. memorizing,
3. acquiring facts, skills and methods that can be retained,
4. making meaning, and
5. interpreting and understanding.

When students are relatively new to research, it is vital that the learning is concrete and practical, that it fosters an understanding of research and assists with the acquisition of some research skills. In our research subjects we use a range of assessment tasks that directly relate to the different levels of learning and build on previous knowledge. At the lower levels, only surface learning (Biggs, 2003) can take place, whereby students are able to memorize and 'regurgitate' material without any understanding of what that material might mean. Many students are attracted to learning by memorizing facts and figures in research subjects, but do not develop higher order skills (deep learning) required in research, such as synthesis, interpretation and understanding. Variety in assessment offers opportunities for reinforcement, as well as building on knowledge from previous subjects.

Balancing Group and Individual Projects

Group projects are a useful strategy to enhance the quality of learning through peer learning and support (Ramsden, 2003). Students can develop a range of valuable skills including: teamwork; analytical and cognitive skills; collaboration; organizational abilities; and time management. Group projects can enable students to learn from each other and to test their knowledge against that of their peers and are useful in giving students confidence (James et al., 2002). There are, however, some potential difficulties. Assessment of group work is often a source of concern for students due to anxiety about fair assessment of unequal individual contributions; assessment may not reflect a given individual's work (James et al., 2002). It is vital, therefore, that group management processes and clear assessment guidelines are in place. Some useful strategies are to ensure that: group membership is specified at the outset; roles and responsibilities are set; assessment is based on both process and product; and the assessment criteria are clear (James et al., 2002).

A range of adult learning activities which actively engage students with research (Edwards and Thatcher, 2004) includes:

• incorporating strategies such as cooperative and collaborative small group activities,
• class discussions,
• case studies,
• role plays, and
• brainstorming activities.

The aim is greater depth of understanding and retention, active involvement of students, development of higher order skills (such as critical analysis), and an increase in student motivation and enthusiasm while promoting both individual initiative and the ability to work in a team. Assessing both group and individual projects helps to take account of a range of different learning styles.

While there are many advantages of using group work, it does not allow us to develop an understanding of the quality of an individual student's learning (Rowntree, 1987). Continuous assessment (using both individual and group tasks) allows both lecturers and students to gain an understanding of the learning outcomes gained by particular students. Assessment in this way ensures not only that students develop knowledge of the core material, but also that they can understand and apply that knowledge.

Assessments need to be flexible so that a wide range of learning styles can be accounted for. Teaching staff might consider working closely with the access and equity unit based at the university to ensure that students with different learning needs are supported throughout the course. Lecturers should be aware of and able to devise assessments that meet individual students' needs.

Providing and Receiving Feedback

The final point, and one that is often neglected, is the feedback cycle. This cycle is bidirectional. That is, lecturers give feedback to students and vice versa. At the beginning of each subject, when outcomes in the context of assessment are being discussed, we provide students with information about marking guides, summary answer sheets and informal feedback that will be given. Students are encouraged to provide feedback to the teaching staff both via the university quality assurance (QA) process and informally. While students' verbal feedback is encouraged, students are often apprehensive about this, so specifically targeting questions in the anonymous QA process provides an opportunity for students to have input into improving the assessment process.

Our QA and evaluation of teaching data collection forms include explicit items regarding the appropriateness of assessment items in research subjects (see Table 13.1 for samples of such items). Our research subjects have been continually refined following student feedback, for example, changing a focus group activity to a one to one interview and changing the computer program used to teach statistics from SPSS to Excel. We report such changes from previous QA activities on our department website.

Table 13.1   Examples of items for QA or evaluation of teaching regarding the appropriateness of assessment items (designed for a Likert-type response scale)

Assessment in this subject is based more on testing what you have memorised that what you have understood.
The feedback on assessments in this subject were useful in helping you learn.
The assessment requirements for this subject were clear.
Marked assignments and other work was handed back promptly.
The grading of work was fair.
I have had enough opportunity to demonstrate what I have learned in this subject.
There is too much emphasis on practical assignment work.
There is too much emphasis on formal examinations.
There were too many assignments.
The assignments encouraged understanding.

Effective feedback from staff to students needs to be explicit, informative (identifying areas of strength and weakness), constructive and timely (Crooks, 1988). Students often find the language of research 'mysterious' and 'divorced' from their professional practice. All assessment marking guides need to make the criteria as clear and defensible as possible and should be provided to students at the outset (Crooks, 1988). Considerable effort needs to be devoted to defining and systematically applying the criteria. Marking guides are an invaluable tool in improving the effectiveness of the assessment task, but in research units they are often underutilized. Prior to each assessment task we provide a copy of the marking guide that will be used (see Table 13.2 for example of the marking guide used in Public Health Research B for the proposal writing task). These marking guides include an indication of expectations for the various sections of the assessment, along with a breakdown of how marks/grades will be allocated.

Table 13.2   Sample of the marking guide used in Public Health Research B for the proposal writing task

Marking Guide Public Health Research B Research Proposal Name:	
SYNOPSIS *Introduction* Has the issue to be researched been clearly identified? Has the public health significance of the problem been presented?	/5
Literature Review Have the relevant previous studies been identified? Have the studies been critiqued? Is the literature review presented as a logical argument? Does the literature review progress towards providing a clear rationale for the study?	/15
STUDY AIM AND/OR RESEARCH QUESTION Are there clear statements of the aims and/or research question(s)? Is a hypothesis included (if appropriate)?	/5
Study Design Is the research paradigm clear? Has the study design been clearly identified? Has an adequate rationale been given for the use of this study design? Have the strengths and limitations of the study been identified?	/10
Sampling Has the sample frame been identified? Have the sampling strategies been described and are they appropriate?	/10

Table 13.2 continued   **Sample of the marking guide used in Public Health Research B for the proposal writing task**

Data Collection Tools Have the data collection tools (e.g. interview guide(s), surveys, other) been presented and justified? Have these been included in the Appendices? Are these tools appropriate?	/10
Analyses Have details of the analyses been given and justified? (e.g. descriptive statistics, thematic analyses) Are the analyses appropriate?	/5
LOGISTICS Have the logistics been thought through and the budget fully justified? Have possible sources of funding been provided? Is the timetable reasonable and does it include all necessary phases?	/15
Ethics Have ethical considerations been thought through? Has a copy of the relevant documents been developed and included in the Appendices? Do these documents address the ethical concerns?	/10
Overall Presentation Is the proposal set out in a logical manner? Is there clarity in the research proposal?	/5
References Has Harvard referencing been used? Are the references appropriate? (e.g. number, peer reviewed, dates etc.)	/5
Total: /100 Grade: Comments: Signed:	

Formative assessment is an important component of deep learning in research methods and so written feedback needs to be provided to allow the return of each piece of assessment prior to the due date of the next item. Class wide feedback sheets that summarize the main areas where students did well or poorly are particularly important in the more theoretical areas of research that students often find challenging. For example, students sometimes have difficulty in providing the theoretical framework for an interview guide. In this case, the class summary sheet provides some model answers demonstrating some common theories and how they have been used in developing interview questions. The written individual and class summary sheets are reinforced by oral feedback that is provided to the whole group.

Providing students with access to relevant examples of assessment tasks is also a useful strategy, and provision of model answers and examples of best practice from previous years is very well received by students. In Public Health Research B, for example, we have kept the best questionnaire design assignments and research proposals from the past five years in a library of 'exemplars'. This is particularly important in research subjects where students are not expected to demonstrate expertise in research skills. We find that students often see textbook examples of research tasks and then expect that they are required to perform at the same level. Providing example answers from previous years helps allay student fears.

Conclusion

Carefully constructed assessment tasks that are cognisant of the issues discussed in this chapter can play an integral part in the teaching and learning process that enhances student motivation and consolidates learning in research methods. This chapter has outlined ways in which assessment can be used to set clear expectations that promote effective student learning. We have provided a theoretically grounded framework (see Kawulich, Chapter 3) and some practical examples of assessment that we believe can serve as a basis for designing and continually refining research curricula that achieve best practice in assessing research methods.

PART IV
Approaches to Teaching Particular Methods

Chapter 14

Researcher Know Thyself! Emerging Pedagogies for Participatory Research

Peter Taylor

Introduction

The choice and application of research methodologies are determined by a wide range of factors, including personal ideological perspectives as well as more pragmatic decisions linked to research questions or hypotheses, and the conditions and context in which the research will be carried out. Guba and Lincoln (2005) present a range of research paradigms that include positivism, postpositivism, critical theory, constructivism–interpretivism and participatory research, each having distinct ontological, epistemological and methodological bases, but acknowledging also that the boundaries between these paradigms are shifting constantly.

There is continued interest in the relationship and relative value of all these different paradigms, but this chapter focuses particularly on *participatory research.* Although much contested, the notion of participatory research attracts the attention of many practitioners and professionals working in development contexts, as well as enthusiasm and concern, probably in equal measures, among students of education programmes that fall within the broad category of 'development studies'. This interest has undoubtedly been aroused in part because of the observed and reported dissatisfaction among some communities with the kind of research that might be described as 'traditional' (Brown, 2002; Stoecker, 2005). In particular there have long been concerns about the value of positivist research with communities in which hypotheses are generated externally in advance, tested, and an analysis and conclusions generated far from the community itself. In effect, this means the entire process of knowledge production is removed from the ownership of the community. 'Community' may be interpreted quite widely to include not only civil society and non-governmental organizations, but other forms of organization, including governmental, public service and educational institutions.

A recognition of the limitations and, as some might see it, the dubious morality of such a research approach in community contexts has encouraged the emergence of research that is purposeful and empowering of communities in which the research takes place. Participatory research, which may be considered as a research approach encompassing a wide range of methods, has the potential to take those engaged in the research process beyond the realm of 'finding out' and actually 'make a difference' to the lives, expectations and opportunities of community members. As Mikkelson (2005) writes, research approaches are participatory when 'staff, partners, people affected (stakeholders) by an intervention or piece of work, and others involved with the work participate directly in planning and carrying out a study ...' (p. 348).

This understanding of the concept and practice of participatory research has significant implications for how it is learned and how it is taught. This chapter outlines firstly some key principles that underpin participatory research, as well as its particular characteristics. It then goes on to describe the implications of this for an emerging pedagogy of participatory research and describes several examples of how participatory research has been taught. It ends with a series of questions and issues that arise through reflection on the growing body of experience of learning and teaching participatory research.

Participatory Research – Principles and Characteristics

Participatory research starts from the premise that people know and are capable of identifying and sharing issues (life situations), analysing and learning from their analysis and thus developing strategies and action for addressing their situations. It has a rich and complex history, well elaborated by a number of authors (Chambers, 1997; Cornwall and Jewkes, 1995). Hall (2005) traces its emergence over a 35-year period, starting with its use in Tanzania in 1970 as a means of describing a variety of community-based approaches to the creation of knowledge. Since then, participatory research has gradually become more visible within the field of adult education, especially in the work of Paulo Freire (1972), through the work of non-governmental organizations, social movements and most recently being acknowledged as a legitimate research approach within the practice and teaching of universities. As Hall suggests, 'participatory research has come "in from the cold", that it has come in from the margins to become an accepted member of the academic family' (2005, 2).

Participatory research has emerged in part as a response to research approaches in the arena of community development that have been extractive, with data generated through the research process remaining in the hands of external researchers, even when those being 'researched' have been involved in generating questions and articulating problems that provide the research focus. This has resulted in information being taken from the local context, analysed and used by researchers for their particular purpose, with local people becoming 'objects' of the research. Participatory research aims to counter such perceptions and is underpinned by a number of principles (Caldwell et al., 2003):

- A defined methodology complemented by a systemic learning process is followed, within which all those involved (possibly including a wide range of groups of people, with different amounts of power, including the exploited, the poor, the oppressed, the marginal) learn together.

- The subject of the research originates in the community itself and the problem is defined, analysed and solved by the community.
- Multiple perspectives are described and valued; reaching consensus is not always necessary.
- Group learning processes vary, but are based on dialogue, and can utilize different inputs.
- Context determines the approach – there is no blueprint.
- Facilitation is key to the process.
- The research process can create a greater awareness in people about their own resources and mobilize them for self-reliant development.
- Since change in the perspectives or worldviews of those engaged in the research process may often be of a quite radical nature, capacity development may be required in order to address learning needs that emerge as a consequence of their engagement.
- The researcher is a committed, engaged participant and learner in the process, often needing to make choices about his allegiances and positionality, for example, to other stakeholders or institutions with whom he or she interacts through the research process.

These guiding principles are important since they provide an underpinning for a broad family of participatory research approaches, which aim to foster a wider process of learning, change or transformation within the community than might be considered through more traditional positivist research. This may leave participatory research open to criticism, however, by those who perceive it to be more a form of political action than a 'scientific' approach. There has also been concern from those who believe that it is not the most appropriate research approach for all situations and who observe also that it is sometimes misused and abused (Cooke and Kothari, 2001). This mirrors the wider debate on 'participation' which has emerged within development processes, not only as a means of promoting inclusion, but as a means of recognizing and shifting power structures, and ultimately contributing to social change and transformation.

Learning and change are common outcomes of participatory research approaches. A researcher engaged in participatory research may be, in effect, at the service of the community and act as a facilitator of community learning. In other cases, the researcher may become a joint or collaborative learner with members of the community, in which case roles and responsibilities become different. Not all research processes that lead to change are participatory, however. 'Action research', for example, may not address questions over *whose* solutions, suggestions and actions are involved (Reason and Bradbury, 2001).

Implications for a Pedagogy of Participatory Research

The continuation of the critical debate on participation, which currently is witnessing a shift from a view of participation as 'tyranny' (Cooke and Kothari, 2001) to that of 'transformation' (Hickey and Mohan, 2004), has valuable lessons for participatory research, since it contributes a constructive and critical edge to the very notion of participation that has for some time been viewed as problematic. This is helpful for those engaged in developing a pedagogy for participatory research that can guide the learning and teaching process.

A pedagogy that guides innovative and imaginative teaching and learning of participatory research is needed urgently, because of the inherent risks and challenges associated with this research approach and the potential damage that may be caused within communities through its misuse. There are cases, for example, where researchers enter the practice of participatory research with little or no training and with little theoretical understanding, even if they are guided by personal beliefs, convictions and sets of values which support participation for development and social change. There are many incidents, especially in recent years, in which a rapid growth in 'participation' has been seen, such as participatory rural appraisal (PRA), participatory appraisal (PA) or participatory research (PR) (versions of the last are spreading very rapidly in the UK, for example), but which in practice may be perceived to be either a tokenist gesture or a limited application of a set of tools without a sound conceptual base.

It is vital, therefore, that researchers acquire a solid grounding in participatory research concepts, approaches and methods, and are able, as a result, to be open and transparent about expectations, contributions, roles and responsibilities and use of outcomes from those with whom they engage. For example, the researcher may have particular needs and expectations from his or her involvement in the research that are different from those of other community members: the need to publish in academic journals; to gain a qualification; or to satisfy other forms of institutional accountability. Recognition that these are real concerns for many researchers has led to approaches that draw strongly on participatory research, but are more collaborative than purely community-led. One such approach has been called 'Practitioner–Researcher Engagement' (PRE) which seeks to promote engagement among civil society practitioners and researchers, thus making a contract 'between "activist scholars" and "reflective activists" in the service of better understanding complex political, economic and social problems' (Brown, 2002, 9).

It is vital also that the researcher learns to develop a personal, ethical position on the rigour with which he applies his chosen approach and underpins it with principles that encompass trustworthiness and authenticity. This has particular implications for awareness of power relations between the researcher and other co-learners and links to concerns that the nature or form of participation taking place is often not considered in sufficient depth and without enough attention given to power (Veneklasen and Miller, 2006). Participation may be approached unproblematically, based more on deference to fashion than upon an acknowledgement and understanding of theory and principles.

Another crucial issue relates to knowledge and epistemology, and the growing interest in paradigm inquiry within the field of social knowledge. The time has passed when the validity of research which could be understood as non-positivist would be seen as beyond debate by those frustrated by positivist paradigms in the context of research with communities. As Guba and Lincoln (2005) point out:

> Critical theorists, constructivists, and participatory/cooperative enquirers take their primary field of interest to be precisely that subjective and intersubjective social knowledge and the active construction and co-creation of such knowledge by human agents that is produced by human consciousness. Further, new-paradigm enquirers take to the social knowledge field with zest, informed by a variety of social, intellectual and theoretical explorations (p. 203).

In learning participatory research, therefore, the learner needs to grapple with a very complex and intertwined series of paradigms and perspectives viewed in relation to the specific context of the research. In participatory research, knowledge is interpreted as an extended epistemology, with practical knowledge and critical subjectivity given primacy. Knowledge is considered living and created as a result of negotiated processes or discourse among participants, the nature of this discourse being determined by power relations.

These complexities present real challenges for those who aim to 'teach' participatory research to others. How are learners expected to acquire attributes such as flexibility, commitment to aspirations and dreams of a better world, facilitation of processes, and not least, to learn the meaning and practice of participation for themselves and for others? How can they be encouraged to construct perspectives and meanings of knowledge that are commensurate with the principles and practice of participatory research? How can they develop their capacities for reflective practice, and understand and develop a sense of their own identity (determining how they perceive their own values, knowledge and worldviews) and positionality in relation to the research process they are engaged in?

Developing a Pedagogy for Participatory Research – Reflections on Experience

In my roles as both researcher and teacher, working within universities but also for a non-governmental organization and in attempting to develop my own approach as a reflective practitioner, which is itself in keeping with the principles of participatory research, I have engaged with and felt challenged by questions such as these. Two particular experiences of facilitating learning of participatory research at the Institute of Development Studies (IDS) at the University of Sussex in the UK have provided opportunities for much personal reflection.

Teaching a short course on participatory research methods within a broader
Social Science Research Methods programme

As part of the MSc in Social Science Research Methods offered by the University of Sussex, students may select an optional course in participatory research methods. Some students choose this option in order to master the method for use in their own projects. Others, however, are interested in the academic debate on participation, and see this course as an opportunity to learn more about the participation debate mentioned earlier in this chapter. As a result, the course must attempt to develop students' understanding of the evolution of participatory research within the historical context of development, while also giving an opportunity to discuss principles, concepts and methods, and even providing the possibility for students to practise specific tools.

The course has two components: a half-day introduction to history, concepts and principles, followed by a full-day workshop on methods and tools. To facilitate the learning process and in keeping with a participatory ethos, the co-conveners contact all students who have selected the course in advance, and ask them to share information on why they have chosen this option, what they hope to gain from it and how they see it relating to any research they intend to carry out. Most students respond to this request, and often express appreciation and surprise at being asked for their views. The half-day discussion session is usually very lively, with some critical debate relating to participation and participatory approaches in general. Students are asked to write a short paper on the relevance and potential application of participatory research methods in their own research and to suggest specific research tools, or groups of methods, that they are interested in experiencing in the full-day workshop. This feedback is returned to the co-conveners, and is very helpful in planning the workshop, which provides students with an opportunity to apply what they are learning practically. Typical tools used include: developing timelines; institutional analysis (Venn diagrams); ranking exercises; mapping; and interviews. These are, of course, a small array of a much larger family of methods, but the opportunity to practise even a few provides rich experience for further critical reflection. The students practise using one of the instruments with one another, but first identify an issue of common concern into which they can inquire; this avoids the problem of treating the tool entirely in the abstract.

On occasions, students are encouraged to go out into the institute and engage with staff and students (who are requested in advance to be prepared to give a little time for this purpose) around a question of common interest. This has led to some very interesting learning outcomes, not only for the students, but also for the wider institutional community. For example, one student group used the process as a means of articulating concerns about wider organizational issues relating to the MSc programme, based on the outcomes of a matrix-ranking exercise to rank issues and concerns arising from the programme against a series of criteria (including capacity for short, medium and longer term change, and extent of student engagement in action). The students in the course shared their findings with a wider student body and then built a successful case for needed change which they presented to the relevant university authorities. This provided them not only with the experience of practising participatory methods, tools and techniques, but the opportunity to see for themselves how participatory approaches in research might lead to real engagement in a change process – in this instance, with actual change taking place as a result.

The course ends with the students carrying out a short participatory evaluation of the course itself and also providing written feedback in a standard university evaluation format. This approach is again a valuable part of the learning process, since evaluation and feedback methods are very important in the wider array of participatory research tools.

Teaching participatory research as an integral component of a longer-term postgraduate programme

In 2004, a new MA in Participation, Power and Social Change was introduced at IDS, which aims to meet learning needs of practitioners experienced in the use of participatory approaches who wish to develop and deepen their conceptual understanding. The MA is constructed around an iterative cycle of critical reflection on experience, linked with opportunities for practice and application in a work-based context. It is formed of three parts; first part, students spend ten weeks at the institute engaged in study of theories and concepts of participation, as well as learning a range of skills that enable them to undertake a process of action learning within a work-based context. Complemented by the preparation of an analytical paper, each student develops a learning plan that will guide his or her action learning during the second part of the programme of nine months duration. During part two, students may apply the concepts and skills that they have developed in a 'real life' situation and are encouraged to reflect critically on their learning, aided by a supervisor who provides distance support. Finally, students return to the IDS for part three, in which they present a reflective essay on their experience over the nine months, accompanied by a portfolio which provides evidence for their learning claims. This may be evidence of personal learning or of learning emerging from the context in which they carried out their research. They then complete the programme, with several presentations and further study of specific topics, finally preparing a paper that synthesizes their learning overall.

The different action learning processes undertaken by students have provided a wealth of learning material, in a range of different countries (for example, India, Nigeria, South Africa, Surinam, Tonga, the UK and the US) and in different development contexts (including education, health, community development, citizen engagement with the state, agriculture, organizational development, environmental conservation). Power issues have been a key element encountered by most students, and they have needed to question their own roles and identities as 'students', 'researchers', 'managers', 'administrators' or even 'change agents'. Confidence, expectations, decision-making roles and responsibilities have all been identified by them as areas of challenge, and also for those engaged with students as teachers/co-learners and for colleagues with whom they interact professionally.

An important area of focus in the MA programme has been reflective practice. The opportunity to develop an understanding of what this means as well as a range of reflective practitioner skills can help prepare students for the challenges they face while undertaking action research, as well as helping them to seize opportunities which may arise as they proceed. Teaching participatory research, therefore, requires careful consideration of the relationships between teachers and students. As a co-convener of the programme wrote:

> A transformative educative process involves reflection and self-awareness for all involved while also promoting meaningful, and meaning-making, engagement with the curriculum itself. Horizontal, egalitarian relations between individuals facilitate transformative learning where impersonal, hierarchical relationships tend to impede it (Pettit, 2006, 25).

Other issues have emerged also through these experiences of teaching and learning. Undertaking participatory research in situations where conflict is endemic poses particular dangers, and indeed most students discover that they need to deal with high levels of complexity within the context in which they work. Students have faced challenges in the act of writing about their action learning; expectations of traditional academic writing may differ from the actual need to express personal and subjective reflections on individual learning and experience, for example, through the use of learning journals or reflective essays. There have been questions over what can be deemed as acceptable writing for different audiences, for the student personally, for the course requirement or for partners and collaborators with whom the student–researcher has engaged in collective research and learning processes. For example, should the writing follow the somewhat 'removed', third-person style commonly associated with dissertations and theses or should students have an audience in mind that is different from the academic institution, such as a development agency or community group with whom they undertook their research?

Questions Emerging for a Pedagogy of Participatory Research

This book aims to stimulate a pedagogical culture in the field of teaching research methods. As the above discussion and experiences demonstrate, there are particular challenges for teaching participatory research. Narrow skill sets and limited conceptual frameworks are insufficient preparation for the participatory research practitioner, who may need to draw on a wide range of attributes, determined by the requirements of a particular context. As well as addressing methodological and theoretical issues, learning participatory research is about development of the whole person and relationships with others. It addresses in learners the capacity to empathize, to communicate, to observe, listen, and to support others in doing the same, and to be more aware of the importance of attitudes, values and beliefs about the nature of society, power and change. This is certainly challenging, but also a wonderful opportunity for researchers to engage more fully in the world, and to learn about themselves and the world as they contribute, systemically and methodologically, to the learning of others.

A key challenge in developing a pedagogy for participatory research is to build a conceptual base for learning itself, providing a foundation for the particular characteristics of participatory research. This raises many questions for those intending to design, deliver and evaluate teaching and learning of participatory research. For example:

- Are we clear about the knowledge, principles, values and ethics that underpin our teaching of participatory research?
- How can we teach participatory research when resources and time are limited, especially if we wish students to gain real experience within a community/organizational context?
- How can we build greater participation in the classroom when teaching participatory research? (For example, by inviting community or organizational members to contribute to teaching.)
- How can we avoid problems of tokenistic participation or accusations of superficiality when teaching participatory research in a classroom context, and how should we achieve real and enabling linkages with a community to support the learning of participatory research by our students?
- What kinds of support and mentoring are needed from supervisors and tutors for students undertaking participatory research?
- Who is the researcher (the 'I') in a participatory research process, and how do we address issues of identity and positionality of both teacher and student?

Such questions emerging within the search for a pedagogy of participatory research are extremely difficult to address, and they have been shared with a wider group of people concerned with learning and teaching participation; much has been learned through the ensuing dialogue. The Learning and Teaching for Transformation (LTT) initiative, convened by the IDS, since 2002, has sought to deepen thinking about pedagogical approaches within higher learning. A key aim of this has been to challenge potentially influential development actors, such as major donors and international development agencies, to adopt participatory inclusive and pro-poor decision-making processes in shaping development agendas. The dialogue shows that LTT participants are united by some unease with established concepts and practices of teaching and learning, and a conviction that there are alternatives which can be shared and adapted. They recognize the need to attend to the personal, reflective and relational dimensions of practice and have an understanding that process and content cannot be separated, with ways of working being as vital as content. They appreciate also that knowledge and learning are constructive processes, and hold a respect for the inherent worth and dignity of learners as individual beings, with agency for transforming themselves and their societies (Stackpool-Moore et al., 2005).

The dialogue has helped, in particular, to raise attention to the importance of integrating theory and practice in learning and teaching programmes: 'learning about' participatory research is not sufficient. If real learning is to take place, students need to learn how to practise participatory research methods by developing a link between their application in a real context and an adequate theoretical or conceptual base.

Conclusions

Learning participatory research can be intrinsically motivating, providing more than the purely extrinsic satisfaction of meeting demands set by teachers and examiners. It allows engagement with people and real issues; it demands involvement in actual change processes. It addresses real problems and, hence, is useful to a wide range of stakeholders who may engage in the research process.

There are dangers, however, that the teacher of research methods may fail to make adequate connections between the conceptual framework and practice in relation to a real area of students' concern. Students undertaking participatory research who take short cuts or try to apply blueprint methodologies may do direct harm to others involved within the context of the research, and also may serve to reinforce the mistrust in this form of research by those who doubt its validity and legitimacy. For these reasons, researchers needs to develop and ideally to articulate an understanding of their identity and positionality, as well as acquiring a range of attributes that enable them to engage as a co-learner, facilitator and collaborator within the research process. In short, research students need to learn to know themselves, a learning outcome that is ambitious, even for a university level education programme. It is a challenge for educators, as well as for those who wish to learn participatory research, to develop a pedagogy that supports the learning of such attributes in a systemic and structured way, but it is one that we would do well to meet.

Chapter 15

Teaching Research Methods to Trainee Practitioners

Tuyen D. Nguyen and Brian T. Lam

The teaching of research methods to trainee practitioners is a challenging task. The traditional utilization of the 'subjective' knowledge or practice model (Klein and Bloom, 1995), reflects a lack of interest in 'objective' knowledge or empirical model in students pursuing careers in social work and human services. Because research is perceived to be technical and not relevant to practitioners' needs as compared to other courses in the major, students may be entering the classroom with trepidation and/or a lack of enthusiasm from the very beginning of the semester.

With a heavy emphasis on skills applications, social work and human services professions are perceived as places that teach practitioners how to utilize knowledge to solve problems in practice settings. Rein and White (1981) reported that historically 'social work called attention to the importance of context and resisted rigid classification, process rather than formal structure, and the reciprocity of means and ends which blurred the boundary separating purposes and procedures' (p. 6). With this philosophical assumption, practitioner's roles might have been conceptualized as the expression of the arts and humanities (Goldstein, 1992). Consequently, trainee practitioners are drawn to courses that teach them about human behaviour and clinical techniques. The majority of the prospective trainee practitioners do not know that they have to take research methods as part of their academic training. Some are confused once they find out that they have to take a research methods course, needing a detailed explanation from an academic advisor about the reason why they are required to take the course. Many trainee practitioners argue that they will never do research, so why should they be required to take research methods?

Understanding the mentality of trainee practitioners is a crucial component in teaching them research methods effectively. In this chapter, the authors will provide an overview of typical students in social work and human services majors; delineate differences between effective and ineffective research methods teaching techniques; and offer guidelines and suggestions to improve one's teaching of research methods courses to trainee practitioners.

Overview of Social Work and Human Services Students

Social work and human services students are unique and different from one another in their gifts, talents and capabilities. However, there are commonalities among these students; for example, they work well with people, which draws them to the same profession: the helping profession. In the United States, there is not one educational or governmental entity that collects and maintains information on a typical profile of students in these majors (for example, gender, age, standardized test scores); the authors, however, have researched four major universities' websites in the country to acquire the information. The authors selected these universities to reflect the geographical areas of the country: 1) the University of California at Los Angeles for the western region; 2) the University of Michigan at Ann Arbor for the midwestern region; 3) Columbia University for the eastern region; and 4) the University of Texas at Austin for the southern region.

Data from the above universities show that entering students are individuals with varying ages and work experience, and are mainly females from various ethnic backgrounds. With respect to standardized test scores, the undergraduates have to achieve an acceptable score, for example, on the Scholastic Achievement Test (SAT) at the university level if they apply for admission directly after high school. Other undergraduates who have gone to a community college can transfer their credit units without having to take a standardized test. At the graduate level (master's level), of the four universities listed above, University of Michigan and Columbia University do not require the standardized test Graduate Record Examination (GRE). And across the United States, taking the GRE is not a requirement for admission into the master's programme in social work and human services. In short, a master's in social work (MSW) is considered a terminal licensable practice degree that attracts individuals who are most interested in working and helping others, not conducting research *per se*.

Student career aspiration

People entering the fields of social work and human services are individuals '… who care about people, who want to make things better, and who want to relieve suffering' (NASW, 2005, 1). Within the field of social work, for example, there are various specialties which one can choose to practice (for example, case management, clinical social work, administration and management, and research). The majority of social work professionals work directly with clients on a daily basis and are competent in what they do. According to the National Association of Social Workers (NASW) (2005, 10), 'many researchers begin their careers in direct services and program development, then return to a university to get a doctoral degree to pursue a research career'. In short, it is evidenced that students majoring in social work or human services generally have a mindset of working with people in direct practice once they obtain their degrees, not conducting research. Following are students' anecdotal statements, reflecting their career aspiration in the helping profession:

- The reason I decided to major in Human Services is because I am a people person and I have always been comfortable with people. People show me love and I show them love back. It feels good to feel wanted and needed. I am serving a purpose in this world is how I feel about being in this profession (Faye, Human Services undergraduate student).
- Any major pertaining to servicing other people is for me. Human services major sparks interest in me because it deals with people who are suffering and hurt in many ways. I want to be the instrument that eases people's pain as much as possible (Verna, Human Services undergraduate student).
- Although I'm currently a real estate agent, my Human Services Degree will afford me the opportunity to work with people and I believe that's what the field is all about. An aspiration that I have in this helping profession is that it would be a stepping stone for me to work for the county or a non-profit organization that deals with some aspects of the law. Lately, there's been debate about the enforcement of immigration law and human trafficking, which reflects one of the concerns of the field of Human Services (Lydia, Human Services undergraduate student).

From the above statements, as articulated by trainee practitioners, their aspiration for majoring in the helping profession is serving others through various career paths in the human service field. However, the primary interest for trainee practitioners resonates the dominant view of social work and human services as an embodiment of a set of skills.

Student mindset regarding research

Students majoring in social work and human services are interested in skills of 'know-how' rather than 'know why' (Rein and White, 1981). Social work and human services practitioners are often involved in the exploration for meaning of events or behaviours in contexts. As a result, courses that are technical and statistical in nature are perceived by students to be uninteresting and somewhat irrelevant to what they want to do in their careers. Some students are even surprised that they have to take research courses, when all they want to do is direct practice with clients in the future, for example, being a therapist. Furthermore, some students in these disciplines have switched their majors from psychology and sociology because of the heavy emphasis on research in these fields. Following are students' anecdotal statements, reflecting their views on research methods courses in general:

- I don't think that this research class should be a requirement for the human services major. I feel that the subject matter is very dry, dull and drawn out. I would benefit a lot more in another class; one that enhances my knowledge effectively for my future (Lynn, Human Services undergraduate student).

- I was surprised to find out that I had to take a research class as a social work major. My interest is in helping people through being a psychotherapist in the future. If I didn't have to take a research class, I would take something more to my interest (Edward, Social Work graduate student).

As the above two statements suggest, trainee practitioners in general view research methods courses as dull and irrelevant to their career aspirations in the helping profession. Consequently, trainee practitioners may have a tough time in research methods courses, not necessarily because they do not understand the content, but their understanding of the worth of research and its application may be hindered due to their career aspirations at the time. Therefore, the role of the instructor is extremely important in teaching the course because it determines how the students will respond to the subject in general. There are both effective and ineffective styles of teaching research methods courses to trainee practitioners, as evidenced by student evaluations and comments. Ineffective styles will be examined first, then the effective styles.

Ineffective Styles in Teaching Research Methods to Trainee Practitioners

The authors find that the quickest way to lose students' interest in a research methods class is to lecture continuously on methodologies and statistics without any periodic reference to everyday living or real life direct practice situations. The instructor in these instances would continue lecturing impersonally on the methodological materials at a theoretical level without making connections between theory and practice. Wilensky (1997) defined 'epistemological anxiety' as 'a feeling, often in the background, that one does not comprehend the meanings, purposes, sources or legitimacy of the mathematical objects one is manipulating and using', as the key source of statistical anxiety (p. 172). Lalonde and Gardner (1993) proposed that learning methodologies and statistics is like learning a second language which requires immersion, guided by an instructor, step by step to ease the student's anxiety. When students do not comprehend the materials and their implications in a research class, they often become anxious and lose confidence in themselves, the course and the instructor. The instructor who may have understood the materials already would not feel the need to break it down to a level that is comprehensible to students. The class, as a whole, may be feeling anxious about the subject matter due to the foreignness of the technical language spoken in research methods that may have nothing or very little to do with human beings' issues. And once students do not understand certain basic elements of research, they rarely ask questions once the class progresses to a more difficult subject matter throughout the course of the semester. As some students lament:

- Professor M. did not even realize and/or care that the class had trouble understanding his lectures. He went on and lectured for almost three hours per class session without asking if we understood. We had to get a tutor to help us understand research (Sam, Social Work graduate student).
- Sometimes it was hard to keep up with Professor P.'s lectures. I found the class material a bit dull, way too dry to keep students interested (Pam, Human Services undergraduate student).

The second most ineffective way to teach research methods to trainee practitioners is the instructor's omission in emphasizing again and again the worth and application of research methodologies in practice situations. Often trainee practitioners find research lectures to be impersonal, in spite of the instructor's best intentions, simply because students have a difficult time understanding the worth and application of research methodologies for their future careers. Students rationalize that they will not be conducting research in the future; therefore, research is an obstacle to overcome: that is the bottom line. Below are some comments made by students, reflecting the frustration they had while taking research methods courses:

- Sometimes when we asked questions about research applications, Professor G. had difficulty explaining it in a non-technical way. He would just pour a lot of information on us. Every class there was something new to learn. We learned the materials to pass the class; it was very overwhelming and frustrating (Cindy, Social Work undergraduate student).
- Sometimes I felt the instructor did not quite understand the questions we were asking and where we were coming from in terms of the value of the subject, so he had a hard time responding. I would get even more confused (Rachel, Social Work undergraduate student).

As one can see, instructors who are ineffective in their teaching of research methods to trainee practitioners do not understand their students' mentality and needs. As a result, these instructors would pour technical information on to their students without breaking it down to a level that is comprehensible by the students, which leaves them overwhelmed and frustrated. Furthermore, these instructors do not help trainee practitioners to see the value of research methods in the course of the semester.

Effective Styles in Teaching Research Methods to Trainee Practitioners

An examination of the instructors who received high student ratings in research courses reveals some commonalities among these individuals in the way they teach research methods (Onwuegbuzie, 1998). First, these instructors create a learning environment that is personal, yet academically rigorous. To do so, they constantly invite students to provide feedback to decrease their fear of the instructor and to ask for help in general (Onwuegbuzie, 1997). From the very beginning of the semester, the instructor would spend some time getting to know each student's academic background, strengths as well as weaknesses, and allow the students to verbalize their perceptions, fears and doubts about research in general. The instructor would ease the students' uneasiness about research through pointing out how it has benefited their daily life (for example, presidential polls, consumer surveys, university questionnaires, etc.).

A very ambitious and positive climate is necessary in the classroom to keep students on a productive level. An objective grading system, a demanding curriculum and consistent enforcement of high expectations are all essential to providing a positive and challenging learning environment. This climate can only enhance the rapport between students and teacher – a rapport that is an essential element in the learning process which can be promoted only by a caring and sincere instructor. In short, creating a 'safe', personal, approachable learning environment that is conducive to open discussion and feedback is a trait of an effective instructor in teaching research methods to trainee practitioners:

- I learned a lot in Dr. K.'s class because she created a learning environment that was flexible, compassionate and giving. Thank you! (Tony, Human Services graduate student).
- The classroom environment was like a group setting where people processed with one another in learning the materials. Everyone was at ease in learning the contents of the course (Tom, Human Services graduate student).

Second, effective instructors are practical in their usage of research. They always have real life examples ready to be told in class, examples that are related to any new complex methodological concept being introduced to the students for the first time. These instructors are great storytellers who know there is a need to 'emphasize connections to the learner's knowledge that make the transition to new knowledge both safer and more meaningful' (Wilensky, 1997, 178):

- I believe Professor E. reached the class very well and made the material interesting with real life examples (Jill, Human Services graduate student).
- Dr. F. was great. He always had real life stories to help the class understand the materials before moving on to different topics (Randy, Human Services graduate student).

Instructors who are effective in teaching research methods to trainee practitioners understand the mentality of their students and their needs and meet them in a creative manner that fosters learning. These instructors know the importance of creating a non-intimidating learning environment, having a rigorous curriculum and at the same time emphasizing the connections of research methods to real life practice situations. In short, these instructors know what it takes to reach their students with the subject that is initially perceived by them as technical, impersonal, dull, difficult and irrelevant to their careers in the helping profession.

Implications and Ideas for More Effective Teaching of Research Methods

Despite the difficult task of teaching research methods to trainee practitioners, there are things that an instructor can do to increase the effectiveness of his or her teaching of the course. Based on student feedback, instructors who are effective in teaching research methods implement an interactive teaching style that requires serious and thought-provoking participation among all the students in the classroom. They have a distinctive ability to promote challenging ideas to the students while offering and extending necessary and constructive feedback that encourages self-reflection on the part of the students. To improve their teaching performance, these instructors study and analyse both quantitative and qualitative data from each of the student evaluations; based on the student evaluations, they regularly make adjustments in their teaching style.

Following are some suggestions that an instructor can incorporate into his or her curriculum in teaching research methods to trainee practitioners. This proposed model, Personal Practice Models (Mullen, 1983), is built on the integration between experience, theory and research. This process consists of six stages:

Stage 1: Students begin their study by performing critical analyses of review articles. At this stage, students learn to be cognizant of various relevant sources, including their own experiences. This stage challenges students to apply their newly acquired research methods knowledge and to use it to critique others' research that has been done in the past. This stage requires an integration of library and field inquiries. Subsequently, students are also able to recognize the consistency (or not) in research and field findings.

Stage 2: Students are required to provide summary generalizations which provide consensus or the lack thereof regarding information reviewed. This summary includes: substantive generalization (the examination of the nature of the relationship between study variables); limiting generalization (the examination of relevant environmental, organizational, client conditions); and quality of evidence generalization (soundness of the research). In class exercises can be used to accomplish this goal. The aim here is for students to be able to codify, retrieve information, provide generalizations about what they have learned and personalize their newly acquired research methods knowledge. Using in-class activities in research methods classes has been documented to be effective in assisting students in understanding course objectives and achieving their own learning goals (Mill et al., 1994; Onwuegbuzie, 1998).

Stage 3: Practice guidelines can be drafted as the result of the consensus in Stage 2. The implementation can be risky. Therefore, pilot testing in a controlled setting is strongly recommended. In this stage, students will learn how to acquire skills to implement the intervention and monitor and evaluate guidelines.

Stage 4: Field implementation of practice guidelines provides the opportunity to test assumptions of practice guidelines in actual clinical conditions. A group proposal is advisable. Two to three students can work together in class and out of class during the course of the semester. (The proposal is like a scholarly research project with the data collection.)

Stages 5 and 6: Soundness of practice guidelines is monitored and evaluated. Guidelines might be revised. Feedback is considered for ongoing evaluation of practice. General application for practice might be generated.

The following example illustrates the proposed process in a practice situation. In Stage 1, the instructor requires students to perform a literature search in the area of assessment and treatment of depression. Students are encouraged to search for review articles which provide a comprehensive assessment of the strengths and weaknesses of various perspectives in this area. Sources can be research-based or can be practice wisdom-based. For instance, students might find a large body of literature supporting the role of cognitive functioning in depression. They then are asked to record the operational definition of depression, which leads to dimensions of assessment and treatment. Subsequently, students locate several experts (practice wisdom) in this area and document the contrasting perspectives. They can also report some field interviews with experts in this area.

In Stage 2, using information from both research and practice wisdom, students are asked to provide a summary of: 1) elements of assessment for depression and treatment priorities (substantive generalizations); 2) disadvantages and advantages of the uses of specific assessments and interventions (limiting generalizations); and 3) quality of the evidence of the studies (in term of the methodology, design, sample size, instruments used). Experience can be used as a source of evidence. The final outcome of this stage is the template of different areas of assessment of depression, including the screening instruments for depression, and evidence-based treatment. In the area of depression, depression was measured by affect, interpersonal relationship and somatic expression. In addition to the screening tool, students might find additional risk and protective factors for depression evidenced in literature and in the practice experience. In stage 3, this template is then pilot tested with a small group to assess further the consensus about the treatment and assessment. Stages 4–6 are implementation stages and refinement via a series of pretests and post tests to assess the soundness of the template for assessment and treatment of depression.

In conclusion, learning research methods or any subject matter in general is a continuous, everyday process, and that education is a multifaceted stimulus in the progress of life. Learning takes place between students and teachers, as well as between teachers and students – in other words, it is a process that occurs between all of us. We learn and grow from experiences and from each other, and the constant interaction between people offers continuous opportunities for learning at all levels. Generally speaking, everyone is a teacher and everyone is a learner at different stages of life. Therefore, people need each other to help bring to the surface what they already know and then to broaden and refine those ideas and concepts to become significant individuals who can offer special attributes that positively influence our own daily lives as well as society.

Chapter 16

How to do Case Study Research

Donna M. Zucker

Introduction

There are multiple definitions and understandings of the case study. According to Bromley (1990), it is a 'systematic inquiry into an event or a set of related events which aims to describe and explain the phenomenon of interest' (p. 302). The unit of analysis can vary from an individual to a corporation. While there is utility in applying this method retrospectively, it is most often used prospectively. Data come largely from documentation, archival records, interviews, direct observations, participant observation and physical artifacts (Yin, 1994).

The terms 'case study', 'case review' and 'case report' are used loosely in the scientific and professional literature. The key features of a 'case study' are its scientific credentials and its evidence base for professional applications. A 'case review' might emphasize a critical reappraisal of a case. A 'case report' might refer to a summary of a case or to the document reporting a case, as in case law or medicine. Case studies of individuals in health care research (to take one example) often involve in-depth interviews with participants and key informants, review of the medical records, observation, and excerpts from patients' personal writings and diaries. Case studies in nursing, for example, have a practical function in that they can be immediately applicable to the participant's diagnosis or treatment.

Case study as a research method is often indexed in most undergraduate research textbooks as neither quantitative nor qualitative. Little attention is paid to the usefulness of this method, with an average of two pages devoted to this research approach (Burns and Grove, 1999). This chapter will provide a step by step guide to this research method. The goal of this chapter is to translate this step wise approach into a 'curriculum' for teaching case study method.

In Preparation

Case study method is indexed in many introductory research textbooks and is often taught in qualitative research methods courses that discuss a variety of methods. These may include grounded theory, phenomenology, discourse analysis and case study, for example. Reasonable goals for the learner would be to explore and understand the philosophical and aesthetic paradigms that are foundational to qualitative research methods, compare and contrast the distinctions among selected methods, evaluate traditional and emerging qualitative designs within their disciplinary area, and to apply methods and techniques. Using a step wise approach students will learn how to design studies, generate data, analyse and interpret the data and disseminate findings. The teacher creates a teaching and learning environment to meet those outcomes.

Pedagogical approaches commonly blend learning and doing: these include seminar participation wherein students are responsible for researching and presenting a didactic lesson; discussing and critiquing qualitative research reports; engaging in field work activities; presenting findings to their class; and writing a report. In most cases generating a proposal for the review of human subjects and obtaining university approval for the field experience is required.

Prior to Beginning

Students should form a list of possible methods in their mind when reviewing their research question and ask how can I get the information I am looking for? There are many considerations prior to embarking on case study methods but at the onset it should be clear that no other descriptive method is possible or will get the level of description the researcher is looking for, except case study methods. Time in the field, lengthy interviews and transcription and analysis are all factors that should be thought out well in advance of engaging with participants.

In teaching case study method a primary aim is to define what case study is and what it is not. Various authors of case study methods discuss and demonstrate a variety of paradigmatic perspectives. I will discuss the most commonly cited perspectives. According to Yin (1994) the case study design must have five components: the research question(s); its propositions; its unit(s) of analysis; a determination of how the data are linked to the propositions; and criteria to interpret the findings. Yin concluded that operationally defining the unit of analysis assists with replication and efforts at case comparison.

Stake (1995) emphasized that the number and type of case studies depends upon the purpose of the inquiry: an instrumental case study is used to provide insight into an issue; an intrinsic case study is undertaken to gain a deeper understanding of the case; and the collective case study is the study of a number of cases in order to inquire into a particular phenomenon. Stake recognizes that there are many other types of case studies based on their specific purpose, such as the teaching case study or the biography. Feigin et al. (1991) state that, irrespective of the purpose, unit of analysis or design, rigour is a central concern. They suggest that, while proponents of multiple case studies may argue for replication, using more than one case may dilute the importance and meaning of the single case. Yin (1994) points out that case studies are the preferred strategy when 'how' and 'why' questions are posed.

Guba and Lincoln (1981) describe case study 'types'. These types are factual, interpretative and evaluative. Each case study must outline the purpose, then depending on the type of case study and the actions proposed by the researcher, the researcher could determine the possible products of the study. For example, research undertaken to describe men's experience in living with chronic coronary heart disease (CHD) could be placed in both factual and interpretative categories (Zucker, 2001). The researcher's actions include recording, constructing and presenting, and producing a chronicle, a profile or facts. Additionally the researcher is construing, synthesizing and clarifying, and producing a history, meanings and understandings. A student's understanding of such activities helps him or her form the stages of the case study method.

In summary the purposes of case study research may be exploratory, descriptive, interpretive and explanatory (Mariano, 2000). Articulating the purpose of the research will inform the remainder of the case study design.

Strategies

In order for students to develop some confidence and competence in learning case study methods a variety of tools are made available for student examination, use and critique. Yin (1994) offers a very straightforward protocol approach for case study emphasizing field procedures, case study questions and a guide for the final write up. This 'tool' is intended to: 1) assist the researcher to carry out the case study; and 2) increase reliability of the research. Similarly Stake (1995) has proposed a series of necessary steps for completing the case method, including posing research questions, gathering data, data analysis and interpretation. A remarkable distinction is Stakes' emphasis on a more naturalistic approach, the importance of the philosophical underpinnings of case method, and the importance of the description of contexts. Developing a protocol will serve as a frame of operation and include all the necessary elements in the proper conduct of students' research. The following list illustrates a common case study protocol that guides the researcher's methodology:

- Purpose and rationale for case study;
    - significance of the phenomena of interest,
    - research questions.
- Design based on the unit of analysis and research purpose.
- Data collection and management techniques;
    - field methods,
    - transcribed notes and interviews,
    - mapping of major concepts,
    - building typologies,
    - member checking.
- Describe the full case.
- Focus the analysis built on themes linked to purpose and unit of analysis.

- Analyse findings based on the purpose, rationale and research questions;
    - case perspective,
    - disciplinary perspective,
    - cross-case comparison,
    - write-up the case from an emic perspective,
    - biography, autobiography, narratives.
- Establishing rigor;
    - credibility,
    - transferability,
    - dependability,
    - confirmability.

Developing a protocol will serve as a frame of operation and include all the necessary elements in the proper conduct of students' research.

Sample

Another important component in teaching case study method is to emphasize unit of analysis and description of the sample. When the unit of analysis is an individual, for example, an important concept to consider is life history. Bromley states, 'The case study emphasizes the proximal causes of the behaviour and circumstances, whereas life history emphasizes the remote origins, and the continuities and discontinuities in the organization of behaviour over a relatively long period of time' (1991, 86). According to Stake (1995) the case study researcher may be somewhat of a biographer focused on a phase or segment of the life of an individual. Various reports in psychology (Bromley, 1986), sociology (Creswell, 1998; Yin, 1984; 1994) and education (Stake, 1978; 1995) have studied the individual as the unit of analysis, and have used the case study method to develop rich and comprehensive understandings about people. Yin (1994) describes single and multiple case designs. One rationale for these designs is to identify an extreme or unique case. The single case may focus on/employ a single unit of analysis or multiple units of analysis. This contrasts to multiple (comparative) case studies, which Yin describes as analogous to multiple experiments; they follow a 'replication logic'. The 'logic' underlying the use of multiple case studies is: each case must be selected so that it either 1) predicts similar results (a *literal replication*); or 2) produces contrasting results but for predictable reasons (a *theoretical replication*) (Lee, 2006).

Methods and Analysis: Iterative Processes

An important component of teaching case method is to allow students an opportunity to move in and out of the literature before, during and after the case study has begun. It is important for students to understand that method and analysis occur simultaneously in case study research. For the remainder of this discussion this example will focus the reader on the following three stages to illustrate this process:

- Stage 1 – describing experience,
- Stage 2 – describing meaning,
- Stage 3 – focus of the analysis.

Stage 1 – Describing experience

In this stage the researcher creates interview questions prior to the first interview, which serve as a script for moving the interviewer closer to eliciting experience and meaning from participants in each succeeding interview. The questions should be broad and loosely structured, following the intent of the research questions. Using techniques suggested by Schatzman and Strauss (1973) journals and logs are kept to track methodological, observational and theoretical field notes during data collection.

Next, the interview questions are accompanied by a list of possible sources of data. Using the example of describing the experience of living with chronic CHD across 10 to 15 years, a list of potential sources was made that included the participant, his spouse, physicians and nurses, and other possible significant key informants. The medical records in at least three settings had to be located: hospital archives; doctors' offices and outpatient rehabilitation centres; and clinics. The medical and nursing literature can be a rich source of information on patient experiences in the form of standards of practice, most of them in classic texts that are updated every one to three years. Additional standards were found in published discipline-specific guidelines. Because experience across time was an important feature of this study, the researcher had to be mindful of advances in cardiac interventions after 1985. Experts were consulted from nursing and medicine to validate the current standard of care.

Finally, the literature was reviewed for definitions of experience, particularly as they related to chronic CHD. For example, Strauss and colleagues (1984) and Miller (1992) referred to patients' illness experiences as their illness trajectory. Literature from the disciplines of nursing and medicine revealed a common trajectory for patients with CHD. The literature was revisited between interviews to gain a better understanding of new data. Clear conceptualizations assisted in taking definitions into the study and combined with the other sources of data, comprised the mass of data available to study the phenomenon of interest. Thinking in metaphors and creating simplistic models and thematic maps were essential activities in data management.

Mapping the data from multiple data sources is an important task. In this study, principal data were derived from two to three lengthy interviews lasting from two hours to two and a half hours. Assembling tables, charts and grids assisted with clustering of concepts. For example, after the first two interviews it became clear that

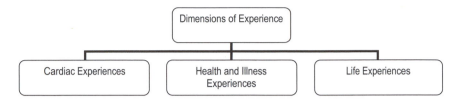

Figure 16.1   Early model of summarized interview transcript

acute cardiac experiences did not occur in isolation, rather three large dimensions of experience emerged. Experience was coded by colour in the transcripts; for example, red for cardiac experiences, green for health and illness experiences and blue for life experiences. Various perspectives were bolded (spouse) or underlined (nurse or doctor) to distinguish them from those of the patients (normal typeface). Finally all of these data sources were read, summarized and organized. Interviews were transcribed by a professional transcriptionist. Early models, such as the one seen in Figure 16.1, were constructed to assist in conceptualizing dimensions and ideas that clustered together.

Experiences were further categorized as physiological, sociological and psychological within each dimension. Colour codes, taxonomies and chronological ordering were used to manage the data that were assembled in large tables first on newsprint, then in the word processor.

Stage 2 – Describing meaning

In this stage the researcher consults the literature and links the research questions and methods to the philosophical framework. Because the meaning of experience was also central to this study, the literature on meaning that had the most relevance for this population was reviewed. Multiple perspectives were reviewed from social constructionism, medical sociology, existential analysis and symbolic interactionism. Processes similar to those used to explore and describe experience were used to study the importance of the concept of meaning. Burbank (1988) studied the meaning in life of older adults from a symbolic interaction perspective and described a hierarchical model of meaning. The first level is labelled 'meaning of signs and symbols' and represents a micro level perspective on meaning. This level is considered a foundation or beginning of creating meaning. For patients with CHD this may refer to what they see and read in print or in the visual inspection of persons with known heart disease. Powerful words such as 'CPR', 'Chest pain' or 'MI' are a few that convey meanings about absolute life and death.

The second level is 'meaning of people, things and events in a person's life'. This 'mid-level' of meaning builds on the first and assumes that 'a variety of things may be meaningful in varying degrees to different people' (Burbank, 1988, 13). Meaning in life for patients with CHD may correspond to the crises or episodes of illness, significant others before, during or after the illness, and quality of life issues which include work, intimacy and freedom to live according to one's own desires. Examples of events or treatments include angioplasty, stents and heart surgery.

The final level of meaning is an abstract, macro level, labelled 'the meaning of life as a whole'. Individuals may have no conscious awareness of this level of meaning, but rather function within a set of values and beliefs about life's meaning. This existential or cosmic meaning differs from the query, 'What is the meaning of my own life?' which reflects one's need to have purpose in living. The latter may assist the patient with CHD to plan for the future given his current physical and psychological circumstances. Burbank equates 'meaning of life' as a whole, as interrelated to the other two levels and is seen as one's worldview. In conclusion these levels of meaning may encompass humankind's capacity to find importance in the experiences of living.

In the study of CHD patients' experiences, the mid-level of meaning was most helpful due to the preponderance of participants' events and situations noted in the transcripts, archives and medical records, as well as interactions with others and self. Burbank's model was not fully supported in this study, as there were periods when no meaning could be found in either of the cases. Again the use of a simple model assists in pulling together data from the case study and tying it to meaning making. In this instance support from existential analysis was helpful. See Figure 16.2 for a basic model of meaning based on Burbank's work.

Interestingly, in the case study of the experience and meaning of men living with chronic CHD, two cases emerged that differed widely, one being the more 'textbook' case, the other the more idiosyncratic. Rather than following a traditional approach to case analysis using replication logic (Yin, 1994), efforts were focused on drawing comparisons between the two cases. Prior to analysing instances of meaning from these cases, the original transcripts were once again reviewed and marked with a small 'm' for each instance of meaning. Particular words, sentences and passages were noted in a separate journal. Interpretations of what patients were thinking, doing and feeling added to an understanding of the meaning of their experiences. This experience of reading and rereading, refining the methodology as data is received as an important set of activities in case study research.

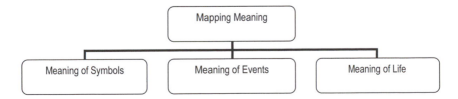

Figure 16.2   Basic model based on Burbank's work

Stage 3 – Focus of the analysis

Generalization of case study findings is limited to the case itself or types of cases. However, attention to selected details enhances the analysis and increases clarity of reasoning. Some general techniques are mentioned that have been useful in focusing the analysis of the example used here. According to Yin (1994) analysis hinges on linking the data to the propositions and explicating the criteria by which findings are to be interpreted. While generalization limits the use of case study method by some social scientists, Yin (1984) argues that theoretical generalization is to the domain of case study what statistical generalization is to the true experiment. An important technique used to incorporate rigour into the study design is the use of the negative case to serve as a study 'control'. The use of the extreme case, the deviant case and the normal case are helpful for making points of comparison.

The stand taken by Stake (1978) focuses on context-specific or 'naturalistic' generalization. Such an approach resonates with readers' tacit knowledge, which helps people make connections and associations without the benefit of words. It is believed that people have the capacity for this kind of knowledge and from it they build understandings.

In the example of the experience and meaning of men with chronic CHD, major themes identified with the use of maps and typologies emerged as focal areas of the analysis. The metaphor 'journey' became a central organizing concept and was linked to a variety of sub-concepts, and relationships among them were sought. Two complete cases were reviewed. Each case was analysed separately with an eye toward describing experience and meaning. According to the description by Feigin et al. (1991), one appeared as a 'normal' case and one an 'extreme' case. The strategy was to focus the analysis on the journey, by concentrating on how it: 1) was tied to a physiologic state; 2) carried consequences; and 3) compared with the typical health/illness trajectory.

Examining Rigour

It is the role of the case study researcher to test and confirm his or her findings in order to indicate the findings are valid and the procedures are rigorous. Rigour is built into this process by focusing the strategies used to generate meaning from the qualitative data. See Table 16.1 for these strategies. Those strategies in italics were selected for the example case study.

Investigators within a constructivist paradigm, such as that used by case study research, attempt to reconstruct participants' understanding of the social world (Denzin and Lincoln, 2000). Thus, traditional criteria of internal and external validity are replaced by such terms as trustworthiness and authenticity. Guba and Lincoln (1981) suggest an alternate view of establishing rigour based on a critical realist paradigm that is juxtaposed to a more traditional view. In this case

Table 16.1   Strategies used to generate meaning

What Goes with What?	Integration Among Diverse Pieces of Data
Noting Patterns *Clustering* Seeing Plausibility	*Making Metaphors*
What's There?	Sharpen our Understanding
Counting	*Making Comparisons* Partitioning Variables
See Things and Their Relationships More Abstractly	Assemble a Coherent Understanding of the Data
Subsuming Particulars Into the General Factoring *Noting Relations Between Variables* Finding Intervening Variables	*Building a Logical Chain of Evidence* *Making Conceptual/Theoretical* *Coherence*

Note: Strategies in italics were selected for the example case study.

Source: Miles and Huberman, 1994.

reliability is contrasted with dependability or auditability. In this sense we are asking if the researcher's processes were consistent and reasonably stable over time and across researchers and methods. Internal validity can be contrasted with credibility or authenticity. Here we aim to answer the questions, do the findings of the study make sense? Are they credible to the people we study themselves or others? Finally we want to know if our conclusions are transferable to other contexts? How far can they be generalized? Here we contrast external validity to transferability or fittingness (Miles and Huberman, 1994).

Quality standards for case studies in psychology, for example, have been developed emphasizing the scientific and professional benefits to other disciplines. Fishman (1999) describes such standards, outlining quality of knowledge issues across three paradigms: the positivist model; the pragmatic model; and the hermeneutic model. Procedural guidelines for fulfilling these criteria rely heavily on methodological arguments and techniques – sampling diversity, triangulation or agreement and monitoring bias. Lincoln (1995) argues that quality also involves ethics. The researcher's decision whether to embark upon the research must be considered in relation to the risk of harm to participants or their families. Using an outside auditor is required to check each step as the case study is developing. Thus attention to quality control must be incorporated into the case study protocol.

Writing-up the case

There are some suggestions new case study researchers may find useful prior to writing up their findings. The first is to spend some time at the outset reading 'good' case studies. Course assignments should include adequate time and support for students to complete pilot studies and practise writing, both excellent ways to develop the 'artistic' expertise required of such writing. Other strategies include joining a writing group, participating in writing retreats and soliciting English or literature experts to begin reading one's writing. Decisions about writing style will become clearer as the intent of one's audience is determined. For example, a narrative, biographical or autobiographical approach may be useful for dramatic effect, while a full description may be well suited to an organization. In any event, the goal is to tell the story and its findings clearly separated from conclusions or interpretations.

In the example of the experience and meaning of men living with chronic CHD, the writing began with a review of the stages of analysis. The first stage defined the typical trajectory and mapped the cases' experiences. Definitions came from the literature, experience and nursing practice. Patient interviews and other sources of information revealed three phases of experiences common to patients with CHD. Exploration of interview data and medical records uncovered three dimensions of experience and three categories of experience that could be viewed within each dimension. This analytic stage also ordered the data chronologically and placed them within the frame of reference of the data source.

The second stage of analysis focused on mapping meaning. Here theoretical support came from a model based on the symbolic interaction perspective. This model assisted in mapping the meaning demonstrated in the transcripts across the three phases of the trajectory and across the levels of meaning. The third stage focused the analysis on three important notions: how experience was tied to a physiologic state; how it carried consequences; and how it compared with the typical illness trajectory. Both case studies included in-depth descriptions of individuals whose adult lives had been significantly impacted by CHD. Physiological processes, while central to experience, were only a portion of that experience. This level of analysis assisted in bringing together the notions of experience and meaning as seen within the context of life. Putting all the pieces together helped create a beginning model that informed the trajectory of living with chronic CHD. This process assisted in developing a logical chain of factors contributing to the understanding of the data. The result was a series of maps and typologies representing perspectives about the meaning of experience, from all data sources. A beginning model emerged describing the trajectory of chronic coronary heart disease (see Figure 16.3).

The 'style' of the manuscript in this case was biographical using a chronological flow. Participants' own language was used whenever possible throughout the manuscript in an effort to retain the integrity of their stories and meanings.

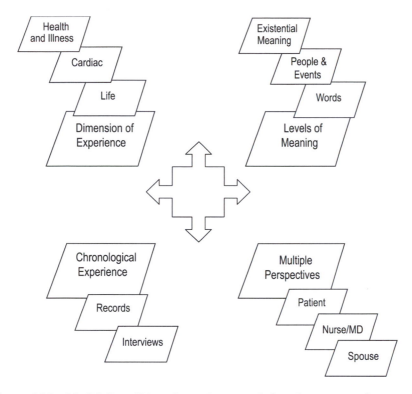

Figure 16.3 Model describing the trajectory of chronic coronary heart disease

Conclusion

Case study method can be a creative alternative to traditional approaches to description (quantitative descriptive and descriptive correlational descriptive designs) emphasizing the participant's perspective as central to the process. In the example used here the value of the case study was the findings. Theoretical implications informed nursing practice directly. Case study conclusions created opportunities for nurses to adapt their model of care to incorporate all three phases of the chronic illness trajectory. For example, changes in history taking and follow-up as well as ongoing provision of support to the patient and family were emphasized. At the organizational level such findings require resources and administrative action for implementing a transitional model of care. Other implications, no less important, include the impact of the method itself on moving description of a phenomenon to intervention. Finally the utility of a case study is that it encourages educators to consider additional steps in a caring educational curriculum that emphasizes communication and relationships between human beings (Scott, 2005).

Chapter 17

Symmetries and Asymmetries between Curriculum and Pedagogy in Teaching Critical Ethnography

Shijuan Liu and Phil Francis Carspecken

Introduction

Critical ethnography, or critical qualitative research, has been developed as a research methodology from the tradition of critical theory. There are different versions of critical ethnography but the one we are familiar with is based on Habermas's critical theory.

There are unique challenges and opportunities in teaching this methodology. To understand the opportunities and challenges encountered some of its basic principles should first be explained. Although it is not easy to provide a comprehensive view of critical ethnography in a few short paragraphs, we will do the best we can by drawing attention to the word 'critical'. Readers who are interested to familiarize themselves with this method can find more from Carspecken (1996; 1999; 2003).

The word 'critical' in critical theory and critical ethnography is used with the sense Immanuel Kant originally gave to it in his 'critical philosophy'. For Kant, certain types of knowledge can be found only through the disciplined use of reflection which he called 'transcendental argumentation'. Empirical knowledge, for example, depends upon experience but experience depends upon conditions that are not themselves revealed through observations.

The 'critical' in critical ethnography also entails the idea of reflection. People living their lives within various cultural groups and contexts have interpretations of their world and their experiences ready at hand. But they are often not aware of the cultural conditions for their own interpretative schemes, conditions that are not easily captured – 'interpreted' – by these interpretative schemes themselves. Although people in everyday life continuously employ reflection as a normal part of communication, it takes heightened forms of reflection aided by some theory to bring the deepest structures of a culture to light.

In critical ethnography the researcher first gains access to the cultural world of those he or she is interested in by acquiring an insider, or emic, position to the highest extent possible. With an emic perspective the researcher is able to interpret the world and other subjects close to the way their participants do. Then implicit features of this culture are raised into explicit formulation producing an ethnology

– a description of a culture from an insider's perspective. Finally, cultural forms that are now understood more clearly through the process of explicitation can be critiqued, not simply nor essentially by the researcher, but by the participants in a study themselves.

Reflection and critique are permanent features of everyday life but they are heightened in critical ethnography. In everyday communicative practices people reflect in order to repair misunderstandings, to defend what they say or do when challenged, and to demonstrate themselves as moral agents who are able to separate themselves from their actions in the form of taking responsibility for them and being capable of self-critique. These normal processes, however, operate within conditions of constraint. Reflection is related to a person's quest for autonomy, freedom and self-actualization, such that one can feel one is the author of one's own life and yet goes beyond it in that one takes responsibility for it and can change. Wherever social relationships and cultural forms limit the ability of a person to be the author of his or her own life we have a form of power. This power can be very subtle, such that one may feel constrained but in ways one initially consents to, based on challengeable beliefs that remain implicit – outside critique. Critical ethnography as we teach and practise it aims at bringing subtle constraints of this nature to explicit awareness, so that those affected by them are able to fully consider them in order either to consent or to object, and thus to become more empowered and free. Critical ethnography is practised by establishing relationships as free of power distortions as possible, facilitating the growth in awareness through reflection of both the researcher and researched. We teach a five stage method (see details from Carspecken, 1996) to this end, along with the theory that makes sense of reflection and its core position in human life as well as this research methodology.

The connection between critical ethnography, human growth, consciousness raising and freedom provides the opportunity to help students find a special connection between things that are most precious and of intrinsic interest to them – who they are, why they are as they are, how their relationships with others are structured and what they can possibly become in their lives. They learn how to understand and analyse social interactions in subtle ways, which means that all interactions in the classroom will become more and more transparent to them. Students learn about the way in which identity claims inhabit all meaningful acts and also gain heightened awareness of how important identity is to all human beings, how vulnerable people can be with respect to it, and how identity is intertwined with relations of power from the very gross to the very subtle levels. The invariable presence of interlinked values, norms, power and identity in all social actions are taught to students as part of the course content such that opportunities and challenges exist for the instructor regarding the relationship between what they teach and how they teach it.

Symmetries between Curriculum and Pedagogy

This idea of 'symmetry' between curriculum and pedagogy is of course an empirical issue insofar as different instructors will establish different relations between what they teach and how they teach it. But our concern is to explore something like the 'limits and possibilities to symmetry' that are entailed with this particular subject matter. The idea is to reveal the intrinsic relations between the course contents of critical ethnography and any pedagogic approach that could be used to teach it. The result will be an elucidation of boundaries that instructors can negotiate as they best see fit.

We begin with intrinsic symmetries that individual instructors can use as resources for their pedagogy in any number of ways. We have found six such intrinsic symmetries: value related; power related; relationship related; awareness related; design related; and reflection related. The distinctions we make to put forth precisely these six symmetries will be clear from our analysis but it should also be clear that these relationships we discuss are not isolated from one another but arise together. The distinctions are analytic and heuristic rather than substantive.

Value-related symmetries

Critical researchers are concerned with social inequality, and aim to help make positive social changes. For critical researchers, the contributions of a critical study are not only to produce empirical-descriptive information, but also to help deepen the understanding of such social theoretical concepts as power, culture and structure (Carspecken, 1996; Carspecken and Apple, 1992). Factors associated with inequality typically include social status, gender, culture and language, etc. Some groups are found to have more power than other groups in specifiable ways, and social relationships within groups will display power disparities. Power need not be a bad thing in itself, but where it needs to be contested is where subordinates do not consent to their subordinate status, or would not do so were they fully aware of it.

The value orientation of the critical ethnographer is therefore one that objects to inequalities in social life that are not understood and consented to by those affected. Participants in a study must be highly respected and their own views of their lives honoured. At the same time the critical researcher is to facilitate consciousness-raising and thus not simply to accept what people say about their lives initially, in order to bring the conditions underlying such statements into explicit articulation and then discussion.

When teaching this research method, instructors need to inform their students of the value orientation associated with it as part of the curriculum content. Clearly, then, a symmetry should be sought between classroom dynamics and these values that object to oppression and affirm deep respect for all others, including their life experiences and interpretations. Instructors must act according to these values in the classroom and challenge instances in the classroom where students bridge the values in their treatment of each other. Consciously or unconsciously, instructors convey their values to students through their teaching, no matter what subject is being taught. As McKeachie (2002) notes, '[o]ur choices of content, our choices of teaching methods, our very ways of conducting classes reveal our values and influence our students' reactions' (p. 292). In the case of teaching critical ethnography where part of the curriculum is mastering skills for spotting subtle distortions in communication due to power relationships, the relation between classroom dynamics and curriculum will be all the more obvious to everyone and in fact something to use for instructional purposes. This symmetry is therefore a must in teaching critical ethnography. Failure to maintain this symmetry will produce a contradiction between pedagogy and curriculum that students will quickly notice.

Power-related symmetries

As critical researchers note, power is prevalent in culture, education, in fact all areas of social life. Power, as we have said, is not always a bad thing, but those who have power must keep it open to critique by those affected, have their consent to use it, and use it with great care.

Generally speaking, researchers have more resources for power than those being researched in conducting research. They come to the field with explicit forms of knowledge that their participants do not have. Researchers also possess the means for representing their interpretations of others to a larger public, which these others cannot counter by seeking their own publication outlets. In this sense, the researcher could consciously or unconsciously distort communicative processes with participants and could affect the lives of the participants much more than the participants could affect the life of the researcher.

This situation is mirrored in the classroom. Instructors have more knowledge than their students, and this can result in students deferring to them and silencing their own views. Instructors have the power to decide the course schedule and the assignments, and to assign final grades that students may or may not agree with.

Researchers are cautioned not to abuse the power that they have in doing research, not only for ethical reasons, but for reasons of validity as well. Critical qualitative researchers must equalize their relations with participants as much as possible. Only in this way will participants articulate perceptions and interpretations and engage in full discussions of the analysis. These are purely validity issues that require the equalization of power where possible, as much as possible, and the responsible use of power when equality cannot be established.

The same principles apply to classroom instruction. Power should be shared with students to the highest extent possible. Instructors of critical ethnography are in a better position than many educators for spotting very subtle forms of power at play, and they should articulate such things when they are spotted, including self-critique at appropriate times. There are various ways to reduce the power differential between the instructor and the students. The instructor can ask students to choose the topic of the research project that is of interest to them, so as to give students more control over their learning process. It is worth noting that giving learners more control of the educational process has been urged in the literature on teaching and learning since at least the 1970s. Some scholars advocate a paradigm shift from teacher-centredness to learner-centredness (Reigeluth, 1999). Two major advantages of empowering students can be identified. First, the ultimate purpose of education is to help students learn. What counts more, ultimately, is not what teachers teach, but what students learn (Lowman, 1995). Empowering students by giving them input with respect to the pace, specific contents, and even evaluation system of the course helps achieve the educational purpose and simultaneously illustrates values and principles of critical ethnography.

Second, students who take an active role are found to be more motivated in their learning process and are more likely to achieve better learning outcomes (Prosser and Trigwell, 1999). And third, in the case of critical ethnography, relationships between instructor and students can be explicitly discussed, both in order to illustrate course contents and to show how relationships change when awareness is raised about them. Do some students get more attention than others from the instructor? Do students feel it is harder to talk when certain other people are present or when the instructor takes on a certain kind of role? Instructors should look for and, where it would not be too threatening, articulate and analyse such things.

Relationship-related symmetries

Intertwined with the power-related symmetries are the symmetric relationships between the researcher and those being researched in conducting critical ethnographic research, and between the instructor and students in teaching this research method. Critical research aims to be a collaborative endeavour untaken by both the researcher and the participants to the highest extent possible (Carspecken and Apple, 1992; Carspecken and MacGillivray, 1998). A researcher reconstructs meanings ultimately with the help of participants by engaging them in discussions requiring caring, respect and openness as well as democratic procedures in the production of research reports. To achieve this, researchers are advised to build trust and rapport with their research participants.

Symmetrically, from the pedagogical view, instructors need to be caring and open, and engage students in the instructional activities if they want to be successful as well as ethical (Keller, 1983; Noddings, 1998). Based on his studies on some exemplary university instructors as well as related literature, Lowman (1995) develops a two-dimension model of effective college teaching: intellectual excitement and interpersonal rapport. According to him, students highly value those instructors who are extremely warm and open, highly student-centred and predictable. In critical ethnography instruction, the relationships in the classroom should also provide content for intellectual stimulation.

In both the research field and the classroom, participants should be enabled to feel comfortable in challenging the researcher/instructor. Trust-building is essential in both arenas.

Awareness-related symmetries

Critical ethnographic methodology is designed to bring what is implicit and tacit into explicit, discursive formulation (Carspecken, 1996; 1999). A central goal in teaching critical ethnography is to increase the awareness of all participants in the class, including the instructor. The self of the teacher has to be engaged and at times put at risk in the teaching process, just as the self of a critical ethnographer must be put at risk and continuously engaged during a field project.

Validity claims that constitute meaningful action are primarily implicit and tacit in nature. People understand them intuitively but often not clearly enough to subject them to critique. This is one of the ways that power can work: people take many of the validity claims that exist as themes in their culture for granted, as part of common sense. Making them explicit relativizes them and opens them up for critique. At the same time, identities serve as the ground for many validity claims, particularly those of the normative type, and also for holistic, worldview-like structures within which all validity claims are implicitly cast. Criticizing claims to which many identities are attached risks causing pain, fear and insecurity in the subjects of one's study. The same thing happens in classrooms where these skills at articulating the implicit into explicit discourse are taught.

Design-related symmetries

To conduct any kind of research it is necessary initially to produce a research design. In qualitative research such designs are important but they must also be flexible. Symmetrically, in one's teaching, the instructor needs to develop a well-planned curriculum with flexibility included. According to Lowman (1995), good planning, clear presentations and well-organized classes are inseparable elements for excellent teaching.

We have found one effective way for teaching critical ethnographic concepts to be the following. First, provide a classroom exercise that challenges students to understand something from real life with respect to concepts they already use, at least tacitly, in making sense of such things. Next, work with students to develop theory components from the exercise. This requires students to make ideas, with which they are already implicitly familiar, more explicit and to refine them in the process. Next, present a fully worked out theory that is in accord with critical ethnography, such as a theory of meaning, of the self, of power and many other things. Here is where flexibility must be artfully employed. The theory as it is already articulated for the instructor must not be presented in a way that simply negates what students have come up with in the exercise. Rather, the instructor must notice and make use of opportunities to link the formal theory with themes that came from the students. Finally, conduct another small group exercise to apply what was learned theoretically back to real life. The best way to do this is often to pass around field notes and to have students analyse them in relation to the theory just presented. Sometimes having students spontaneously act out a skit with others taking notes will provide the material desired for practising theory application. As the semester proceeds, classes may be effectively commenced with exercises to refresh the memory of concepts and ideas already learned. Exercises that help students understand internal connections between concepts already learned and new concepts will also be illustrated with examples.

Like critical qualitative researchers, instructors need to be ready to make necessary changes to their curricular plans at all times to make better use of spontaneous opportunities. This is crucial for teaching this research method to postgraduate students, as the students are usually from diverse backgrounds and have different research interests.

Reflection-related symmetries

Of course, critical qualitative researchers need to be reflective – we have already explained that critical and reflective are related concepts. Now we shall become just a little more specific. Meaning always has both implicit and explicit features to it. It is conditioned culturally in ways of which actors are frequently unaware. Critical ethnography is partly the art of deeply reflecting, with the aid of theory, to articulate these submerged portions of culture. Furthermore, reflection helps researchers become more aware of their own biases in observing, interviewing the participants, analysing the data and so on, thereby improving the quality of the study (Carspecken, 1996). Finally, being reflective helps researchers to become more cautious of the aforementioned unfair advantage they have over those being studied, thereby helping to achieve one of the ultimate goals for conducting critical research, that is, fostering heightened and shared awareness that is empowering.

Symmetrically, instructors teaching this method need to be reflective as well. As previously indicated, one purpose of teaching critical ethnographic methodology is to increase the awareness of all participants including the instructors themselves. Being reflective is necessary for the instructor to become more aware of his or her own assumptions – conditions underlying his or her own actions including those in the classroom. Instructors in all fields are always at risk of inadvertently causing pain, fear and insecurity for students but the more reflective we are when teaching, the less often this is likely to happen. Such self-reflection should be modelled continuously when teaching by being explicit about it where appropriate. When students demonstrate reflection in their classroom participation this should be pointed out and affirmed.

As with doing critical research, there are other benefits for being reflective in teaching this research method, such as modelling reflection to students so that they will practise it more and more themselves, becoming more empowered in the process. Reflective teaching improves teaching in all subject areas (Light and Cox, 2001), and it is particularly crucial for teaching critical ethnography, given the fact that course content includes theories about reflection.

Asymmetries between Curriculum and Pedagogy

Only two asymmetric relationships are found between the curriculum of critical qualitative research and the pedagogy of teaching it.

Learning versus the teaching process

A qualitative researcher will usually play many and various roles when doing fieldwork. For instance, in a study Laurie MacGillivray conducted on elementary school children, sometimes she played the role of an adult teacher to the children, sometimes of a fellow 'kid' who played with the children and sometimes she simply observed from a distance. Researchers' roles will vary during a single study, based on a large variety of factors (Carspecken and MacGillivray, 1998). Different roles involve different power relations between researchers and participants.

However, the master role that the researcher plays in a critical research study, as Creswell (1998) notes for qualitative approaches in general, is like that of an active learner, in that the researcher seeks to understand and represent things from the participants' view. A qualitative researcher will wish to avoid the role of an expert who passes judgement on participants. Correspondingly, though research designs vary according to situation and research questions, the research process is usually primarily a learning process for researchers and their role is that of a learner in relation to the participants who 'teach'.

In contrast, when teaching this research method to students, the master role that the instructor plays is that of an expert who educates. Although once again we find roles changing flexibly, with the teacher often willing to learn from students in such things as the group exercises we described above, the instructor has the master status of an expert who knows, more than the students, what it is they need to learn.

This asymmetry between master roles to take in the classroom compared to those taken in the field can be further illustrated by the flow of feedback given in the learning versus the teaching process. Specifically, for the researchers, the process is a learning process. Researchers seek feedback from the participants to determine whether they have understood the participants' perspective accurately or not. In classrooms, the instructor provides feedback to students for the same purpose.

This asymmetry is general in form. In both the field site and the classroom critical ethnographers must be careful in revealing all they think they know to their participants and students. A balance between openness and only sharing knowledge that will be constructive to those with whom they share it is necessary in both contexts. But in the field the researcher seeks to build understanding and trust to the point where full openness is possible without causing harm. There is enough time to do this because the length of a project should be chosen so as to ensure that this happens. In the classroom, however, time is constrained to one semester or term. Usually instructors will never reach a degree of trust and rapport sufficient to fully share everything they interpret of the interactions with their students.

Conceptual order

When conducting a qualitative research project, concepts necessary for data analysis must be already mastered to a certain degree by the researcher. Data analysis, for example, consists primarily of coding data. But to code data properly many concepts must be understood in advance. So, although coding is what one begins with to analyse data, it is one of the last things taught in class.

Additionally, a qualitative researcher will gain initial impressions of the meaning and significance of the social phenomena studied holistically. Single acts of meaning are not often of significance in themselves, but rather in the full sequences of interaction in which they emerge. The analysis of qualitative data will usually consist of noticing whole chunks of activity that have an internal dynamic or pattern to them, or whole chunks of an interview that have a narrative structure to them. Then analysis becomes more detail-oriented: looking more precisely at particular acts within a sequence of action and so on.

By contrast, teaching concepts of meaning, action, interactive sequences, roles and forms of power seems best done in reverse order. The small units are first explained theoretically – the nature and internal structures of a meaningful act, the array of validity claims that constitute a singular claim to meaning and so forth. From these small units we build up toward larger ones – entire roles, instead of mere single acts; entire action sequences; entire narrative forms instead of singular statements within an interview.

This asymmetry should be explained to students at the very start of a course on critical ethnography, and students should be reminded of it repeatedly as the course continues. We have found that failure to make clear this difference in conceptual direction between the data analysis done for a real research project and the analysis done in the classroom to learn concepts can lead to misunderstandings. Students have been known to begin analysis of their data for a dissertation project by taking it act by act, analysing each one sequentially, which is a needless and ultimately impossible task.

Conclusion

In this chapter, beginning with a brief and partial introduction to critical ethnography, we explored the relationships between the curriculum of conducting this type of study and the pedagogy of teaching this research methodology. Six symmetric relationships and two asymmetrical ones were identified. Some of the symmetries between the curriculum and pedagogy we drew attention to are not limited to teaching this research methodology, but exist between curriculum and pedagogy in general. However, in most cases critical ethnography has a unique status, insofar as what is taught cannot differ from how it is taught without producing actual contradictions. In many respects, for critical ethnography, the pedagogy is the curriculum.

PART V
Approaches to Teaching Non-traditional Students

Chapter 18

Learning Research Together: Reciprocal Benefits for Individuals With and Without Disabilities

Annabelle L. Grundy and Michelle K. McGinn

Individuals with disabilities are important members of the research community. Through self-study and auto-ethnographic research, they can contribute to the field of disability studies by raising awareness about the world of disabilities and diminishing the risks of objectifying people with disabilities in research (Oliver, 1992; Zarb, 1992). Furthermore, their contributions to research are not limited to the field of disability studies, but inform all fields. The research community learns by bringing different perspectives to bear on the phenomena under investigation, so research in any field that is undertaken by researchers with disabilities can generate new understandings that are unavailable to scholars without disabilities (Grundy et al., 2005). For example, Colligan (2001) learned about the openness required in the Karaite religion as a result of the openness about her own body dictated by her need for assistance with showering and personal grooming during her fieldwork. It is important for the scholarly community to provide opportunities for individuals with disabilities to be educated as researchers (Parker and Baldwin, 1992).

This chapter focuses on the first-hand learning experiences of the two authors as the first author (Annabelle) undertook a research-based Master of Education programme under the supervision of the second author (Michelle). Annabelle is hard of hearing. She has a severe to profound sensorineural hearing loss in both ears, uses an FM amplification system in conjunction with personal hearing aids and speech-reads. Michelle has no identified disabilities. After meeting in a research methods course, Michelle hired Annabelle as a research assistant and later became her thesis supervisor. In this chapter, we document our ongoing attempts to identify suitable accommodations to compensate for Annabelle's disability as she developed as a researcher through her coursework, research assistantships and thesis research. We focus in particular upon four experiences that became learning moments for both of us. In this way, our considerations about teaching and learning research methods are not confined to research methods courses, but extend into other research learning experiences as student, assistant and academic supervisor. While we draw specifically upon our own experiences, the purpose of the chapter is to highlight the learning potential for both parties when an instructor works with a student with a disability.

A Situated Learning Perspective

Learning is a situated activity that is realized through participation and self-identity (Lave and Wenger, 1991; Wenger, 1998). Doing research, knowing research and being a researcher are inherently intertwined processes that take place in social settings (see Garner and Sercombe, Chapter 7). By working together on research tasks, individuals learn research skills and construct their identities as researchers. This is true for students like Annabelle who are engaged in their first research project, and it is true for seasoned researchers like Michelle who have conducted numerous research projects. Education as a researcher is an ongoing process that continues over career and life cycles as individuals interact with others and explore new research areas. Teaching and learning research methods involve much more than unidirectional relationships from instructors to students and are not confined to research methods courses.

Learning Research Together: The Context

Consistent with the situated learning perspective outlined above and the apprenticeship models described elsewhere in this text (see Preissle and Roulston, Chapter 1; Roth, Chapter 10), Michelle organizes her research methods courses to provide multiple opportunities for students to collaborate in actual research activities. These research activities provide opportunities for students to apply material from course readings and discussions, and to implement technological tools as appropriate (Nunes, Chapter 12). Most assignments require students to act as researchers by collecting, analysing and reporting data, thereby engaging in a praxis of research (Garner and Sercombe, Chapter 7; Roth, Chapter 10).

In the introductory research methods course, Michelle set assignments that were focused upon the research and experiences of other graduate students enrolled in the Master of Education programme. The main assignments in the course required students to: write critical analyses of completed theses and projects; perform statistical analyses of numeric data gleaned from the theses and projects; interview a student or recent graduate about their experiences conducting research in the programme; and transcribe and analyse the interview according to a self-selected qualitative research tradition. The focus on gathering and analysing data specific to the graduate programme in which the students are enrolled was intended to provide valuable models and strategies that students could use to facilitate their own research plans. The assignments were intended to help students build a repertoire of conceptual and practical research skills as a foundation for the design and implementation of an independent thesis or project, which was to be completed at the end of the programme under the supervision of an academic staff member.

Building upon the foundation provided in the required introductory research methods course, students who are planning to undertake qualitative research studies are encouraged also to take a qualitative research course. When Annabelle enrolled in this course with Michelle, students engaged in a sequence of activities that provided experiences with the most common data collection activities in qualitative research: analysing a thesis or project; observing in a public setting, constructing a fieldnote, and analysing the resulting data; and completing an ethics review application, conducting an interview, transcribing an audiotaped record of the interview and analysing the resulting data. With the grounding from the first course, students in this second course self-selected the focus for each assignment, which allowed them to conduct pilot studies for their planned thesis or project. In this way, Michelle attempted to avoid the disconnection that students often feel between research methods courses and degree requirements to conduct independent research (Roth, Chapter 10).

By participating in these research activities in the supportive setting of the two research methods courses, Annabelle (like other students in the programme) gained experience with a range of research activities. These coursework experiences were complemented by the work that Annabelle undertook as a research assistant working on faculty-led research projects (including one project with Michelle) where she: conducted literature searches; created database libraries; digitally scanned visual images; created electronic presentations; designed brochures; presented at conferences and workshops; conducted qualitative and visual analyses; edited papers; co-wrote papers for publication; and communicated with editorial staff (Grundy, 2004; Chapter 7).

Drawing upon her experiences in the two research methods courses and the various research assistantships, Annabelle identified the topic and methods to be used in her independent thesis research and asked Michelle to serve as her supervisor. Our interactions across these settings provided multiple opportunities for each of us to learn about research and about suitable accommodations for Annabelle's hearing disability.

Accommodations as Reciprocal Learning Moments

During our interactions over the course of the three years that Annabelle spent as a Master of Education student, we both learned a great deal about research. Individually and collectively, we continued to develop in our overlapping roles as learners, teachers and researchers. For the purposes of this chapter, we have selected four specific learning moments that exemplify the potential for reciprocal benefits for individuals with and without disabilities who undertake research together.

An Interview Assignment Prompts a New Methodological Breakthrough

As described above, the final assignment for the introductory research methods course involved conducting, transcribing and analysing a semi-structured interview with a student in the Master of Education programme. Due to her hearing disability, Annabelle is unable to work with audio materials. Rather than shy away from interview-based research or appoint an external transcriptionist, we collaborated to develop a new technique in which research participants transcribe their own interview tapes. Annabelle used the same technique for the interview assignment in the qualitative research course. In both courses, the technique worked well for Annabelle and met with the approval of the research participants.

The participant in the second interview was also a student in the research methods courses with Annabelle, and this naturally led to group conversations about the participant-as-transcriptionist technique and its potential uses for a broader range of researchers. The technique provided a suitable accommodation for Annabelle and seemed appropriate for other researchers who are unable to transcribe audiotapes. Preissle and Roulston (Chapter 1) argue for the value of adapting and creating the kinds of research practices that are culturally sensitive to the ethnic or national origins of student researchers. The participant-as-transcriptionist technique is a research practice that is culturally sensitive to researchers with disabilities. We also discovered that there is the potential for participants to become actively involved in the research process when they transcribe their own interview tapes. The technique eliminates third party transcriptionists, increases confidentiality and provides opportunities for participants to extend their transcripts beyond the initial comments made during interviews. Based upon our experience with the technique in the two courses, we worked with the second interview participant to present papers at national and international conferences, and subsequently published a journal article about the technique (Grundy et al., 2003).

Our collaboration increased our understanding of working as an inclusive research team (Grundy et al., 2005). During face to face meetings in which we worked on the first paper about the participant-as-transcriptionist technique, the hearing authors ensured that Annabelle could see their faces to speech-read, and they also took written notes that were photocopied and distributed as an external record of each meeting. We structured many research meetings as email dialogues in order to accommodate Annabelle's hearing abilities and organized our conference presentations to support her strengths and to ensure that she was fully involved in all sessions. At the conferences, we worked together to raise awareness about Annabelle's needs as a conference delegate and to engage other delegates in the process of creating an inclusive learning environment. We made commitments to educate the broader scholarly community about ways to be more inclusive to researchers with disabilities. The impetus for these learning opportunities began in the research methods courses, but our commitments and learning extend far beyond the courses.

Participating in practical research assignments not only allowed Annabelle to experiment with research methods and find ways to overcome the challenges of interview-based research, but also provided opportunities for her to discuss her difficulties and engage with others in trouble shooting new ways to do research. Beyond the courses, we worked together to document the technique and our experiences of attempting to be an inclusive research team. In this way, the courses led to Annabelle's full participation in the research community.

A Thesis Idea is Abandoned because the Student Lacks Sufficient Control

During her graduate studies, Annabelle chose to work as a research assistant on three different faculty-led research projects because she believed that these experiences would help her to learn more about research and better prepare her to undertake thesis research. For example, in her second term in the Master of Education programme, she was invited to participate in a large-scale research project that related to her interests and experience. Initially, she envisioned that this project would provide a suitable context for her master's thesis.

Many academics, institutions and funding agencies recognize mutually beneficial outcomes when graduate students undertake a component of a larger research study as a thesis. Student supervision is embedded in the academic's research programme and not an additional task that must be undertaken. Students devote time and effort to the project, thereby providing labour that is needed to complete the research. Students complete programme requirements and are often paid as well. The benefits of such an approach to graduate student participation in ongoing faculty research are clearly evident in Roth's chapter (Chapter 10).

Excited by the potential of the research project, Annabelle planned a related thesis and began the preliminary work. However, as her research plans took shape, she felt an increasing lack of control over the direction of her thesis. Independence and self-sufficiency are important traits for Annabelle, which she was unwilling to compromise for the research. The project supervisor encouraged Annabelle to follow the original plan for the research project and Annabelle felt pressure to undertake research tasks that emphasized her weaknesses rather than her emerging strengths as a researcher. For example, the project supervisor suggested that Annabelle conduct focus group interviews in restaurants where research participants would be gathered. Noisy, crowded, dimly lit restaurants interfere with Annabelle's personal hearing aids and her speech-reading ability. This suggested research technique was a sharp contrast to the participant-as-transcriptionist technique in which Annabelle was able to focus upon and extend her existing research skills rather than face shortcomings as a result of her hearing. The mismatch between her emerging skills as a researcher and the approach suggested by the project supervisor eventually led Annabelle to abandon this first thesis idea. Participation in this research project, along with other experiences as a research assistant, led her to make research assistantships the focus for her thesis (Grundy, 2004).

Taylor (Chapter 14) advocates the importance of research that is purposeful and empowering for the communities in which the research is undertaken. This learning moment reminds us that the research must also be purposeful and empowering for the student, and that the research practices must be culturally sensitive. Sensitivity is needed not only towards national or ethnic cultures, but also towards culture as defined by disability status. For some students and in some instances, that research may be undertaken in conjunction with a faculty-led project, but the potential pitfalls of faculty-led projects must be avoided. There can be synergy between students' research ideas and such projects, but students need to feel a sense of ownership and control in order to maximize their learning. Student ownership provides opportunities for students to generate new ideas and demonstrate flair.

Hiring an Assistant can be a Disability Accommodation and a Methodological Decision

Throughout her second year in the Master of Education programme, Annabelle focused on her new thesis idea. She conducted four case studies of learning and identity development for research assistants in our department (Grundy, 2004). One of these case studies documents her own experiences as a research assistant. This revised thesis plan allowed Annabelle to focus on her emerging strengths as a researcher and to apply the participant-as-transcriptionist technique. The technique prompted us to think carefully about the ethical issues related to compensation for transcription work.

Through the courses, Annabelle had experience with the institutional ethics review process and was cognisant of the importance of ethical thinking, not just form completion. This background proved invaluable when she was planning her thesis research. She planned to invite participants to transcribe audiotapes of the interviews for her thesis. She was able to compensate participants for their transcription time through a bursary to support students who have expenses related to disabilities. However, the set rate for transcription could be construed as enticement to participate in the research, so we had to think through the ethics of payment.

There were two sets of interviews for each participant. We decided not to mention compensation when we initially invited research assistants to participate in the first interview. After the first interview, Annabelle then informed participants that she would require assistance with transcription and gave them the option of transcribing themselves or appointing an external transcriptionist. In this way, the decision to participate in the research study was separated from the decision to transcribe the interviews and no potential participants could be tempted to participate in exchange for money. This approach was accepted without question by the institutional ethics review board and fully supported by the research participants.

One component of the thesis involved a self-study of Annabelle's own learning during her research assistantships (Grundy, 2004; Chapter 7). Clearly, Annabelle was unable to serve as a participant-transcriptionist for her own interviews, so she hired someone to interview and transcribe for her. This led to our discussions about what constituted a disability accommodation and what constituted a methodological choice. The bursary fund could be used for transcription services, but Annabelle's decision to hire an interviewer was a methodological choice that was unrelated to her hearing disability. As a result, she used the bursary money to compensate her assistant for transcribing, but found other means to compensate this individual for interviewing.

Annabelle's thesis plan required her to establish dual roles with research participants who were interview participants and transcriptionists, and with her assistant who was an interviewer and transcriptionist. Garner and Sercombe (Chapter 7) emphasize the importance of new researchers learning about the social relations that are integral to the conduct of research and the different relationships that researchers develop with research participants, assistants and the research community. By conducting interviews using the participant-as-transcriptionist technique in the research methods courses, Annabelle already had practice navigating these complex and changing social relations, which facilitated her thesis research.

The Thesis Defence Demands some Accommodations

Annabelle completed her thesis during her third year in the programme. As a final step, she was required to present publicly and defend the written thesis at an oral hearing that was also attended by: her thesis supervisor (Michelle); two committee members who had provided formative feedback while the research was in progress; an external examiner from another institution; a chairperson; and a few student colleagues. To prepare for this task, Annabelle attended other thesis defences to experience the kinds of questions that examiners ask. She recognized that she might face challenges being able to speech-read the examiners' questions. One solution could have been to use a real time captionist to capture the dialogue of the examiners. However, Annabelle could foresee problems with trying to hear and understand the context of the questions without a way to keep the examiners on track. Together, we identified a suitable accommodation involving simple cue cards. Examiners wrote their questions on cue cards and when their turn came to ask a question, they passed the card to Annabelle and asked the question. The cue cards worked well for Annabelle because they facilitated her understanding of the oral questions and also prompted the examiners to be succinct in phrasing their questions.

We evaluated the technology, natural supports and multi-modal communication strategies for the defence, and provided the examiners with clear expectations in advance. Not only did these measures offer a framework from which Annabelle could succeed, but they also set a precedent from which other academics, students and support personnel could plan other possible accommodations for thesis defences.

Concluding Remarks

Researchers regularly encounter new challenges: research is a continual learning process. New researchers who have disabilities may face particular physical or sensory challenges, as well as attitudinal barriers. Colligan (2001), for example, described the 'friendly advice' that she received as a new PhD student: an instructor advised her not to attempt field research because she would face prejudice as someone with a disability. Like Colligan, Annabelle designed and implemented her own research project despite warnings she received and challenges she faced. Together, we were able to engage in research practices that were culturally sensitive for a researcher with a hearing disability. By developing culturally sensitive research methods, Annabelle had opportunities to demonstrate flair and innovation. The push towards participatory and emancipatory approaches to disability studies research (Barnes, 2003; Kitchin, 2000; Oliver, 1992), combined with the contributions of researchers with disabilities across a broad range of research fields (Grundy et al., 2005), has led to greater recognition of the need to educate people with disabilities as social researchers.

In this chapter, we illustrated the thought processes behind some accommodations that could be considered for researchers with hearing disabilities and articulated the reciprocal learning potential that accrues for individuals with and without disabilities who engage in research together. Graduate education and researcher development extend far beyond research methods classrooms, so we advocate the importance of facilitating conditions for all researchers that are enabling rather than disabling. We found that doing research together was a mutually rewarding learning experience. The time invested in reflecting on the research process and exploring alternative ways of doing research was invaluable. We offer the following recommendations to others involved in research education as they strive to include student researchers with disabilities.

First, student researchers with disabilities must be encouraged and supported to engage fully in research activities. It is imperative that they gain access to the tools and insights that will contribute to their successful degree completion and possible future careers as academics. Course assignments, independent research requirements and research assistant opportunities must be fully accessible to all students.

Second, instructors should create learning situations that are authentic and provide students with opportunities to participate in the research process. Building awareness about how research could be conducted and becoming open-minded to new ways of performing research will provide those with disabilities with a chance to focus on their strengths instead of their weaknesses.

Third, instructors need to invite students to communicate their needs, strengths and weaknesses with regards to participating in research activities. Students may need help to identify matches and mismatches between their individual strengths and weaknesses and the demands of various research approaches.

Fourth, instructors should encourage learning experiences that allow students to collaborate on research. These learning experiences might occur through group assignments in courses or through opportunities for students to collaborate on research projects outside formal course assignments. The ensuing conversations about research are educationally beneficial for students with disabilities and for their collaborators.

Fifth, as instructors and students identify suitable disability accommodations, these ideas should be documented and shared with disability support personnel to build a repertoire of possible options for subsequent students.

Principles of universal instructional design advocate classrooms that are accessible to all students (Scott et al., 2003). Consistent with these principles, our recommendations emphasize proactive steps to design instruction that is inclusive of a broad range of learning needs, but we also recognize that individual accommodations may still be required.

Authors' Notes

The two authors contributed equally to the production of this chapter. We wish to thank our colleagues Dawn Pollon, Kelly Powick and Kimberley Gunning for their contributions to the projects described in this chapter and their commitments to building an inclusive research community.

Chapter 19

Bridging Gaps: The Quest for Culturally Responsive Pedagogies in Collaborative Research Methods

José Antonio Flores Farfán, Mark Garner and Barbara Kawulich

Introduction: The Diversification of Cultures within Higher Education

As recently as the last couple of decades, the student body in many university social science courses was presumed (with some justification) to be more or less culturally homogeneous, and the content and orientation of the curriculum reflected this presumption. There was little perceived need to provide a basic general grounding in research methods, since students entering the courses would have at some earlier stage in their education (it was assumed, with perhaps less justification) become familiar with the basic principles of Western research traditions. Any more detailed understanding they needed could be picked up from the research literature. Today, however, a large and ever increasing proportion of students come from a wide variety of social and cultural backgrounds. Whatever grounds there were, a generation or two ago, for assuming cultural homogeneity are clearly no longer valid. Although this applies to most, if not all, non-traditional students (including those from regional and socio-economic subcultures; disabled students; mature-age students; and the like), in this chapter our concern is with national and ethnic cultural groups. As mentioned in the Introduction to this book, the rapid diversification of the student body is one of the motivations for the contemporary emphasis in virtually all major universities on the explicit and systematic teaching of research methods.

Broadly speaking, two main groups from non-Western cultural backgrounds can be identified. One is the 'international' students. These include those from large, rapidly developing regions (such as China, the Indian subcontinent and some Middle Eastern countries), as well as groups on study abroad sessions as part of their home country degree programmes. They typically have achieved a substantial education in their own countries (although the quality of that education varies considerably) and are to be found in many universities in large numbers. They may form a sizeable cultural bloc in a class. There are also international students from smaller and/or poorer developing countries. They tend to study abroad as individuals or in very small groups, taking advantage of an opportunity to gain an education that is seen as superior to that available in their countries of origin.

The other main group comprises members of minority cultural communities within the dominant mainstream society. Governments are increasingly encouraging such students to undertake higher education within their home countries. Typically, such students have completed a substantial portion of their pre-tertiary education in the language of instruction of the university at which they are studying. Although they have a distinctive home culture, they are often relatively assimilated into the mainstream culture, which, as we discuss below, can bring its own intellectual and personal problems.

Thus the teacher is confronted with many challenges. If (as discussed in the Introduction) there are the makings of a rudimentary consensus in research methods teaching, very little of it relates to the sort of cross-cultural classroom that is today becoming the norm rather than the exception. The lack of an explicitly culturally responsive tradition of conducting research within many of the social sciences, and consequently within the teaching of research methods, means that there is not yet even a body of documented, illustrative examples on the basis of which a pedagogy can be constructed. In this chapter we aim to make a small contribution towards an illustrative literature on the topic by raising three cross-cultural issues. They are to be seen in the context of one of the wider goals of this book, which is the development of culturally sensitive pedagogies of research methods.

This is an emergent endeavour and our approach is to start with personal reflections. We touch on a few particular examples of cross-cultural encounters from our own teaching experience and draw from them some general observations that may have a wider resonance for the many other teachers of culturally diverse student bodies. Many more such reflective studies are needed before cross-cultural research methods pedagogy can be built on a solid foundation. We hope to stimulate interest in this field, which is a rich one for educational research and pedagogical innovation.

Several other authors (see Roth, Chapter 10) advocate teaching and learning collaboratively with students about research. We believe this is the only way to achieve real learning within most, if not all, facets of research methods, particularly where significantly different cultural perspectives are present in the class. In the field of methodology there is no equivalent to a body of received knowledge of the kind that underpins the pedagogy of a number of other disciplines. Not only so, but the conduct of social science research tends to involve a degree of investment of the self in theorizing and planning, as well as entering into a range of social relations, that makes high personal demands, emotionally as well as intellectually. In working with students from the outset of their learning, we are helping them to prepare for these demands.

There are many implications for practice when such co-constructed learning involves students with significantly different cultural perspectives. Our interest is in how to appropriate the possibilities of epistemologies, worldviews and communicative competencies that differ from those of the Western cultural bases of mainstream social science. In other words, an aim of this chapter is to outline some difficulties and opportunities of doing research with, and not about, indigenous people, in which the student investigates as much as the researcher, exchanging and sometimes reversing the roles of the teacher and student. It should be noted that, although we concentrate on students from distinct ethnic, religious and national backgrounds, some of the issues we discuss are probably equally relevant to, for example, class or regional subgroups within the mainstream community. The sort of pedagogical research we are advocating would include such groups in the definition of 'cross-cultural'.

Culture and Research

This chapter is not about doing cross-cultural research in the received sense of the word. That is to say, it is not about research from an outsider's perspective on other people's languages and cultures. Nor is it primarily concerned with teaching students how to undertake research that is culturally relevant or responsive. Our aim is, rather, by reflecting on various issues that have arisen in our teaching of people with very different cultural backgrounds, including speakers of minority and endangered languages, to show a possible way forward in developing what might be styled a culturally receptive pedagogy.

Cultural assumptions, which are highly complex, are particularly significant for the social sciences, as they crucially affect the planning, conduct, outcomes and applications of investigation. In a short, exploratory chapter of this type, a degree of generalization and simplification is unavoidable, but it is essential to try to avoid simply trafficking in cultural stereotypes. Both Western and non-Western traditions are able to contribute new and profound insights to the research process; both are susceptible to intellectual conservatism and sclerosis. Furthermore, individual students vary widely. Some readily adapt to Western educational values; others find them puzzling or alien. Some have, or develop through their studies, a sense of the originality and power of their own cultural backgrounds; others have or develop a sense of their shortcomings.

It is a legitimate and important goal of research methods to introduce students to the richness of Western educational values and research traditions. Indeed, some international students are funded by their home governments with precisely that outcome in mind. Nonetheless, a culturally receptive pedagogy does not simply cater to students who are able to embrace those values and traditions, in the hope that any who cannot will at least conform enough to fulfil the requirements of the course. Instead, it seeks to utilize creatively the potential of a multiplicity of viewpoints to enrich research outcomes both theoretically and methodologically. The challenges for the teacher – and, through the teacher, the whole student body – include that of developing more flexible ways of thinking to come to terms with the sometimes fundamentally different values which play a decisive role in research. The opportunities include developing innovative research methods that face the intellectual and ethical dilemmas posed by the negotiation of identities and power. If such opportunities can be grasped, research methods can become not only more widely accessible, but also more sophisticated and comprehensive.

It is important to point out that the need for a culturally receptive pedagogy is not, of course, limited to courses in research methods. There would be few teachers of any subject, in Western universities at least, who have not had students from a variety of cultural backgrounds in their classes. Particularly at postgraduate level, where the teaching is likely to be relatively intensive, interactional and personal, problems of communication can arise. It is not a question of learning *about* every culture that might be represented in the class (which would be impossible, anyway), but of being constantly sensitive to cultural referents and norms as they arise in the course of interactions, often in quite unpredictable ways.

To give one simple example, Barbara Kawulich was teaching night classes of working adults, most of them Westerners, but including one Japanese woman (MW). In the first class, as an icebreaker and to find out how much time they might have for homework, Barbara asked them to share with the class a little about themselves, such as their name, their programme of study and whether they were married or had children. When it was her turn, MW responded, 'In my country, it is impolite to ask personal questions like these.' She did, however, say she would share her personal information with the teacher after class. Sensing how MW was nervous about her language skills, Barbara patted her shoulder and said, 'Honey, don't you worry, we'll help you get through this.' This made things worse: 'In my country, we don't touch each other,' MW responded. In the break, MW had asked another student if Barbara was a lesbian, since she had called her 'honey'. With the best of intentions, the teacher had pried into the student's personal business and infringed on her personal space. Many teachers could give similar examples of the challenges of cross-cultural teaching and the pitfalls awaiting the unwary.

When it comes to teaching students research methods, the challenges are even more complex, since not only the classroom interactions but also the content of the course is heavily dependent on cultural perspectives. All aspects of the research process must be culturally receptive, but space allows us to consider only three here:

- choice of topic,
- methodology,
- dissemination of findings.

Choice of Topic

Cultural issues influence the choice of topics for research in at least three ways. First, all cultures have deep-seated values, beyond simple propriety or good taste, that determine some topics to be appropriate and others inappropriate. From whatever background they come, students tend to talk, if at all, almost exclusively about their own communities and language. Certain topics may be regarded as inappropriate for research: for example, they may be too sacred or too profane. Others topics may be so much taken for granted that researching them may be seen as entirely unnecessary. Kawulich taught an American student, married to a Marshall Islander, who wanted to do research to increase knowledge of Marshallese culture among islanders living in the US. He found it very difficult to find people in the Marshall Islands who were willing to participate. They all wanted him to address how to deal with the issue of interacting with Americans in the Marshall Islands and, ultimately, get them out, so that the Marshallese people might be self-governing.

Second, epistemology makes some topics not so much improper or unnecessary as invisible. The interest in race among Western researchers, for example, can seem surprising and largely irrelevant to a student from a relatively homogeneous community. Finally, the political context, both current and historical, can prioritize one field of research over another. A question that urgently requires an answer in one community may scarcely arise in another: African students, for example, are often much more interested in research that will enable them to develop infrastructure in their home villages than in issues with more global or national salience.

Such cultural considerations need not be accepted as absolutely definitive, but challenging them effectively requires pedagogical astuteness and personal sensitivity. A series of studies of perceptions of identity among international students at a British university was conducted, using postgraduate students as research assistants (see Garner and Sercombe, Chapter 7, for discussion of one of the studies). In one methods class, the 15 students found it very difficult to come to grips with the literature relating to theories of identity, without which they could not begin the fieldwork.

The problem was that for these students, all of them from China, the construct of identity was quite foreign. As one student put it, 'In China, people are just people, they are all the same – they don't have an identity.' It was decided to suspend reviewing the literature until the students could integrate the concept into their thinking. Over a period of four weeks, the students introspected how they thought of themselves and tried to imagine how other people might see them. They then used scrapbooks and talks to present (but not describe or explain) both of these perceptions to the class. Many of them remarked on what a revelation it was to them to realize that British people treated their being Chinese as the primary defining characteristic. By the end of the course, although the research project had not proceeded as planned and very little observational fieldwork had been undertaken, these students had achieved a sound and (as they themselves expressed it) an exciting grasp of social identity. As this experience shows, it is possible to transcend some cultural barriers to understanding, but one must be prepared to be highly flexible with one's teaching plans.

There are benefits to be derived from cultural diversity among the students. The teacher has available in the class a range of cultural orientations, which he or she can draw on to enrich the teaching and learning experiences of all students. Non-traditional students of all kinds do not only offer alternative perceptions of the processes of learning and doing research (see also Grundy and McGinn, Chapter 18). They often actually see different research problems, particularly those relating to issues from their own distinctive backgrounds, of which members of other groups are quite unaware. For mainstream students, research topics can sometimes be of purely academic interest; for students from other cultures, they are more often of considerable practical importance. Some of these students have expressed to us a desire to learn about research methods in order to solve these problems. To give a few examples, some of our own students have undertaken research to:

- develop materials for teaching an endangered language,
- improve the delivery of basic health care to jungle villages,
- establish an employment advice centre for a disadvantaged indigenous community,
- raise the standards of language teaching in their home country,
- establish an English/French/Spanish immersion school in their home country,
- create a village cooperative to establish funding for children's schooling,
- bring potable water supply pipelines to a rural community,
- gain access to a better position within the educational system.

Although these hopes are not infrequently unrealistically ambitious, they can help inspire the teaching and learning in our classes by imbuing them with a touch of idealism.

Methodology

Culture has implications, too, for methodological choices. Research that deals with community members as part of the collective, rather than as individuals, may be better conducted quantitatively because this does not demand involvement of the researcher with the individual subjects. Where a qualitative study is necessary, the researcher must establish a rapport with the participants and engender the sort of trust that facilitates confidential disclosures. The approaches complement and strengthen each other, and this indeed might constitute a discovery for students, particularly for those students from cultures (for example, in some east Asian communities) that tend to value relatively anonymous quantitative surveys over qualitative investigations which are seen as prying into areas of purely private concern.

It is this search for rapport and deep engagement with the students that led Flores Farfán to adopt autobiographical reflection as the basis of his research methods course in the two-year MA in Indoamerican Linguistics (*Maestría en Lingüística Indoamericana: MLI*) in Mexico. The MLI is organized in two streams, descriptive linguistics and sociolinguistics. In the former stream, students are expected to learn and reproduce orthodox descriptive methods and conceptions of language. The latter stream aims to develop a critical conception of language which stresses the inextricable link of language and society, for instance, in the relationships between linguistic variation and power. The teacher of research methods in this stream faces the dilemma of introducing students to a canonical body of knowledge while at the same time developing a critical approach to research involving indigenous languages and cultures. Most of the sociolinguistics students are themselves practising teachers who bring to their studies divergent expectations of the appropriate methods for research pedagogy.

Given the chequered history of indigenous minorities in the Americas, many emotional and micro-political dilemmas, paradoxes and contradictions arise in the course of the programme. Research methodology cannot be simply handed down to the students as received wisdom. Research involves all parties in complex and emergent social relations (see, for example, Garner and Sercombe, Chapter 7).

In the first year, students evince a strong expectation regarding the role of the teacher. They are the repository of ultimate 'truth', able to pronounce the definitive word on any problematic issue. When teachers strive to stimulate discussion on a number of topics, such as the descriptive categories of linguistics, participation is usually limited to urban, middle-class, Spanish-speaking students. Students from indigenous minorities are not very responsive to direct questioning (Briggs 1986; Milroy 1987) or reflexive thinking. Unlike their Spanish-background peers, they never use the familiar *tú* (you) with the teacher, preferring the respect pronoun *usted*. This reflects the status of elders and mentors in indigenous communities and the appropriate manner of speaking in school. One does not interrupt an elder who is telling a story or a teacher giving a class. It is only later in the programme that the possibility emerges among them of discussing specific issues from a more open, critical perspective.

One key pedagogical issue for methods courses is the role of research in not simply extending students' knowledge, but relativizing and questioning it. For example, in the MLI, the teaching is aimed at raising awareness among all students, from both indigenous and Spanish backgrounds, about the stigmatized and often endangered status of the indigenous languages which the majority of students speak. This runs counter to many of their assumptions: in many cases, while the teacher encourages the students to talk about their knowledge of contact varieties,[1] the students refuse to see them as in any way a legitimate focus of study, owing to a very pervasive purist ideology, which is commonplace in many indigenous communities.

Exploring research methods is a challenge not only for the students. The roles and expectations of student and teacher have to be negotiated frankly and sincerely. For instance, from the outset of the MLI the teacher tended to see it as training for cultural and linguistic activists who would return, empowered, to their home communities. Many of the indigenous students, in particular, however, saw

---

1   'Mixed' forms of language that arise from the mutual influence of two or more languages spoken within a community.

it as an opportunity for upward social mobility; they wanted to live in the city and had no intention of transmitting the indigenous language to their children. Whose view should prevail? If research is to be genuinely engaged, rather than merely a means of satisfying course requirements, the teacher–student relationship must always be open to questioning and complementary perspectives, pursuing to solve these types of conflicts.

As a preliminary to undertaking their research, students talk about, write down and evaluate their own autobiographies, including their experiences of the socio-political setting in which they have grown up. The autobiographies become the driving force for the research. They are not necessarily the object of research (although this may happen) but provide the intellectual context and personal motivation for it; they also guide the focus of its application. As the students write and discuss their autobiographies, the teacher's role is to draw out their experiences and evaluations of ethical and micro-political dilemmas. Their own experiences and evaluations are also made available for students to comment on. It is fundamental that all participants learn to show interest in and respect for others' life histories and even learn where to stop for the sake of privacy.

A number of issues that had previously been taken for granted become the focus of questioning, as students face personal dilemmas at the heart of their experiences of the shift from their first language to Spanish. One student realized that when he entered the MLI he had perceived himself to be monolingual in Spanish, denying his bilingual competence. Studying linguistics represented the opportunity of overcoming the discrimination and racism linked to speaking an indigenous language, vindicating its value in mainstream society. He was emotionally stirred by his re-evaluation of the indigenous language in the course of his research. In response, for the first time in the MLI history, the teacher together with the student decided to organize his MA defence in the student's first language, Mexicano (Nahuatl). This in turn heightened other students' (and teachers') perceptions of the language. It proved, first, that academic discussion can be conducted in Mexicano and, second, that the different dialectal varieties used by the members of the jury are equally suited to intellectual endeavour and communicative adjustment. Thus several aspects of the research pedagogy, from deciding on the topic to undertaking the fieldwork and assessing the dissertation, contributed to bridging the gap between research and intervention. The student went on to undertake doctoral research in ways of empowering Mexicano language speakers. He collaborated with his teacher in the production of Mexicano books for children, which are disseminated as part of a language revitalization project in which both are involved, considering themselves co-authors (Flores Farfán, 2006).

Another student was a young Mapundungun (Mapuche) woman from Chile, who had grown-up with deeply ambivalent feelings towards her ethnicity. She had denied it in her childhood and youth when, during Pinochet's dictatorship, indigenous peoples suffered repression, since speaking their languages was treated as subversion. Through her studies, she rediscovered a sense of pride during adulthood. As a descendant of a deceased shaman, she had been expected to assume his mantle but was unable to bring herself to do so, owing to linguistic insecurity as part of the lack of intergenerational transmission.

Enrolling in the MLI was a step towards reconnecting with her native language and culture. As she reflected on her life experiences, she began to fully acknowledge a profound sense of responsibility towards her home community. She learned to distinguish between the 'subjective' and 'objective' forces underlying linguistic and cultural shift. She had, for example, to disengage herself from essentialist images of the 'pure' Mapuche speaker. These ideological images tend to develop in response to, and as an obverse of, systemic racism. As she described and evaluated her autobiographical experiences, she became aware of the fluidity of Mapuche identity, comprising multiple and contradictory, context dependent identities. She realized how community leaders contribute to ambivalence of identity as they negotiate power within and outside the community in their efforts to gain access to material resources. She discovered, too, that other students experience the same sort of uncertainties, which are characteristic of the compensatory and alienating forces at work within endangered speech communities.

The student gradually became aware of an inextricable relationship between linguistic repertoires and identity. She was able to link her refusal of the role of shaman to the development of linguistic and cultural insecurity, the shift from Mapundungun, and the growth of confusion over her social and personal identity. She began to develop a sense of her place in both Mapundungun and Chilean society, and position herself along a continuum from active to pseudo-speakers of her native language. Today she is working as a Mapuche activist in the field of intercultural education, working, among other things, in the production of materials in Mapundungun with her former teacher. This brings us to the following point.

Dissemination of Findings

Cultural differences are evident in the dissemination of findings; what is perceived as appropriate for various audiences should be considered for discussion here. The dissemination of findings is an issue that has been quite extensively discussed in the anthropological literature (Fixico, 1996; Smith, 1999), but less so in other disciplines. Kawulich undertook a study of indigenous Muscogee (Creek) women in the central United States. She investigated how they learned about dating, male/female relationships and intimacy. The women were willing to share their stories (several had, for example, grown-up on farms and recalled being hustled away from a barnyard mating by their mothers). But Muscogee women are modest, and it is inappropriate to discuss bodies or intimacy in mixed company. It became clear in the course of the study that, while the women trusted the researcher to protect their confidentiality, they were unclear about how she could write about intimacy, when the readership included males. This problem proved insoluble, and in the end the study had to remain unpublished (for general problems on intercultural communication, see Scollon and Scollon, 1995).

Interactions with indigenous peoples and students with different cultural referents have led all three authors to emphasize collaborative, participatory approaches that are more conducive to conducting research in indigenous or non-Western communities. This approach is highly influenced by feminism, in that the emphasis is on working with participants, not subjects, in a collaborative manner (shifting from 'them' to 'we'). This approach also emphasizes the use of the emic perspective of the insider, rather than the etic perspective of the outsider (Marshall and Batten, 2004).

In attempting to achieve cultural responsiveness, the methods teacher plays three broad roles. These are, first, to develop a researching orientation. Students frame a personally significant question and suggest means of answering that question through systematic investigation. Prior learning experiences, formal and informal, are elicited and jointly evaluated. Second, the teacher provides input from his or her expertise and experience for the student to evaluate in terms of its contribution to answering the question. Finally, the teacher assists the students to frame a methodology for their own future learning through research, such as developing auto-biographies or life histories.

Some Further Questions

This chapter has hardly scratched the surface of the challenges and opportunities of developing a culturally responsive pedagogy for research methods. We have noted and exemplified three areas of interest, each of which would repay rigorous investigation in its own right. Other questions, both theoretically interesting and practically important, are yet to be addressed, for example:

1) Good research

- Can good research be judged by universal criteria or are all criteria culturally relative? Or should we combine both?
- What counts as valid data and what standards of rigour should be applied to their interpretation?
- Are some research methods more congenial or relevant to one culture than another?
- What can we learn from other cultures' methods of investigation and what can they learn from ours?

2) Research methods pedagogy

- How can we validly assess research methods students from different cultural backgrounds?

- A teacher can never have a native-like understanding of the cultural background of every student. How can the different cultural assumptions and epistemologies be incorporated into teaching methods?
- Should these cultural perspectives be used as stepping stones to Western methodology or as building blocks of a new approach?

Conclusion

We cannot attempt to answer all these questions. But what we can be sure of is that opening a more dialogical approach, posing questions such as these together with students, is an important first step to finding good answers to well formulated and better understood questions. These in turn will allow for a more in-depth comprehensive understanding of what research is suitable for.

Afterword

Mark Garner, Claire Wagner and Barbara Kawulich

As we stated in the Introduction, methodology courses are, by and large, designed and delivered by teachers working in regrettable isolation. It is clear that, as in all fields of academic endeavour, considerable benefits will accrue if the isolation can be overcome. It is easier than ever before to make contacts and form networks in order to learn from one another's experiences, as well as to engage in a continuing debate about the goals of methods education and how they can be realized. The aim of this collection is to begin that process by stimulating the exchange of ideas and encouraging further investigation, analysis and discussion – in other words, a pedagogical culture – in relation to a subject that is increasingly becoming an essential element of education and training within institutions of higher education.

There are two broad characteristics of a pedagogical culture. One is the sharing of experiences: what has been tried and whether it works. There are innumerable courses throughout the world, varying in their level, length, content, emphasis and orientation. A wide range of teaching approaches, techniques, forms of assessment and related issues can be conceived of, and probably most have been tried somewhere. There is thus a potentially rich resource of practical knowledge and experience waiting to be shared. By bringing together contributions from academics who teach on a range of undergraduate and postgraduate courses, in different social science disciplines and in various countries, the book provides the first survey, albeit a preliminary and partial one, of what is going on in the field. We hope it will be a source of encouragement to the many academics involved in attempting to develop research skills among students, and in particular to those who are in the early stages of their careers and who, thrown in the deep end of research methods teaching, feel they are at best treading water and at worst in danger of drowning.

In accordance with the aim of encouraging this sort of sharing, a few chapters have been included that focus on describing actual courses being conducted in various countries. Although we did not want the book to be a mere compilation of course descriptors, there is some value learning about how others in the field view key issues in methodology and how they are taught in different contexts. As well as being informative, it can also be heartening to discover that the challenges, strengths and weaknesses of one's own practice are not unique. As in all teaching, there is a place to reflect from time to time on what we do, why we do it, and how successfully the students learn what we set out to achieve. There are as yet, however, too few opportunities for sharing experiences and problems in research pedagogy, and this was why we have included personal and reflective contributions alongside those of a more explicitly theoretical orientation. We encouraged all authors, nonetheless, to go beyond merely giving information by discussing the thinking behind, for example, the curricular organization and pedagogical approach, as well as evaluating learning outcomes. We hope that, as interest in the field grows, the emphasis in the academic literature will increasingly be on conceptualization of both research methods themselves and the pedagogical frames within which they are communicated to students. The important role of providing information about specific courses and practical teaching suggestions, as well as the sharing of experiences, can be most appropriately undertaken by formal or informal professional groups, through media, such as interactive websites, teaching guides and workshops. We very much hope that, by drawing attention to the need for and possibilities of sharing, we will provide an impetus to forming such groups.

The second characteristic of a pedagogical culture is a concern with the theoretical foundations of practice. It is clear from the foregoing chapters that some excellent work, in theorizing both the bases of research and its educational implications, is being done in a number places throughout the world. As we indicated in the Introduction, in the attempt to canvas such a diverse and uncohesive field, some issues have inevitably been dealt with only in passing, or not at all. Nonetheless, all contributors have in common a concern with the interrelationship between theory and practice. In one way or another, all could be said to address three questions which are fundamental to articulating a systematic research methods pedagogy:

- What are the characteristics of good research methodology?
- What do students need to learn in order to conduct good research?
- How can this learning be facilitated?

The first question is the primary focus of the chapters in Part II. The second is addressed, from several different perspectives, by those in Part III and, to an extent, in Part IV. These more conceptual issues are consistently canvassed in the light of their implications for curriculum design and classroom practice. The last question is foremost in other chapters in Part IV and those in Part V. Furthermore, there is a clear pedagogical theme running through the collection as a whole: learning to do research necessitates the active, collaborative involvement of the students with one another and with the teacher. Whichever of these questions is the specific concern of particular authors, all are conducive to the view that the outcome of a research methods course must be evaluated in the light of whether students learn how to do research, rather than simply learning about it. According to this criterion, in our own experience, many courses are less than optimal, and when praxis, rather than purely theoretical knowledge, becomes the universal standard by which outcomes are judged, research pedagogy will have made considerable progress. A form of structured apprenticeship (of which Roth gives a thorough outline) is probably the ideal. Limited contact time and large classes, however, probably make this impracticable for the majority of courses, but as a number of the writers argue, it is possible to enhance participative learning even when circumstances are not conducive to close, one to one collaboration.

An important criterion for including any given article was whether we editors felt it has the capacity to act as a stimulus and a paradigm for further thinking and development. For example, Peden and Carroll's examination of historical trends in psychology in the United States could be very usefully replicated for other discipline areas and other national and educational contexts. Further, although several specific research methods are discussed, many other methods deserve similarly careful pedagogical examination in future. Such studies not only will inform the teaching of the methods themselves, but will enable comparisons and contrasts to be drawn. In particular, they will help us to engage in the debate (scarcely touched upon in this book) about the relative merits of generic and specific courses.

As a final note, both the publishers and a number of colleagues have appealed for further publications to follow this initial collection of writings. There is a demand for two types of works. One is a collection of practical exercises that have been found useful in methods courses. The other is a comprehensive look at all aspects of research methods education, including a systematic model for pedagogy that could serve as a baseline and framework for future research and discussion. We ourselves are taking up the challenge, and also encourage colleagues around the world to make their own contributions to developing a substantial literature in this underdeveloped field of enquiry.

Bibliography

Aaron, J., Bauer, E., Commeyras, M., Cox, S., Daniell, B., Elrick, E., Fecho, B., Hermann-Wilmarth, J., Hogan, B., Pintaone-Hernandez, A., Roulston, K., Siegel, A. and Vaughn, H. (2006) *No Deposit, No Return: Enriching Literacy Teaching and Learning Through Critical Inquiry Pedagogy*. Newark, DE: International Reading Association.

Agar, M. (1980) *The Professional Stranger*. New York: Academic Press.

AIEH (Australian Institute of Environmental Health) (2004) *Course Accreditation Policy 2005*. Brisbane, Australia: AIEH.

Aita, M. and Richer, M.C. (2005) Essentials of Research Ethics for Healthcare Professionals. *Nursing and Health Sciences*, 7: 119–5.

Anfara, V.A. Jr. and Mertz, N.T. (eds) (2006) *Theoretical Frameworks in Qualitative Research*. Thousand Oaks, CA: Sage.

APA (American Psychological Association) (2007) *APA Guidelines for the Undergraduate Psychology Major*. Washington, DC: Author. Retrieved 11 December 2007 (available online at www.apa.org/ed/resources.html).

Argyle, M. and Henderson, M. (1985) *The Anatomy of Relationships*. Harmondsworth, UK: Penguin.

Ashworth, P. (1995) Qualitative Methods in Psychology (Book Review). *Psychology Teaching Review* 4: 79–82.

Ayer, A. (1946) *Language, Truth and Logic* (2nd edn). London: Gollancz.

Babbie, E. (2001) *The Practice of Social Research* (9th edn). Belmont, CA: Wadsworth Thomson Learning.

Babbie, E. (2003) Lessons Learned from Teaching Quantitative Methods (Special Issue). *Qualitative Research Journal*, pp. 12–23. Retrieved on 28 January 2008 (available online at http://www.latrobe.edu.au/aqr/journal/special_AQR2003. pdf).

Babbie, E. and Mouton, J. (2001) *The Practice of Social Research*. Cape Town, South Africa: Oxford University Press.

Bamforth, D.B. (1999) Theory and Influence in Plains Archaeology. *Plains Archaeologist*, 44(169): 209–29.

Barnes, C. (2003) What a Difference a Decade Makes: Reflections on Doing 'Emancipatory' Disability Research. *Disability and Society*, 18(1): 3–17.

Bazeley, P. (2003) Teaching Mixed Methods (Special Issue). *Qualitative Research Journal*, pp. 117–26. Retrieved on 28 January 2008 (available online at http://www.latrobe.edu.au/aqr/journal/special_AQR2003.pdf).

Bell, C. (2004) Doing Sociological Research: The Genre of 'Owning Up'. *International Journal of Social Research Methodology*, 7(1): 29–33.

Bergman, M.M. and Coxon, A.P.M. (2005) The Quality in Qualitative Methods. *Forum Qualitative Sozialforschung/Forum: Qualitative Social Research*, 6(2): Article 34. Retrieved on 25 November 2005 (available online at http://www. qualitative-research.net/fqs-texte/2-05/05-2-34-e.htm).

Bernard, H.R. (1994) *Research Methods in Anthropology: Qualitative and Quantitative Approaches*. Walnut Creek, CA: Sage.

Bhaskar, R. (1975) *A Realist Theory of Science*. Atlantic Highlands, NJ: Humanities Press.

Bhaskar, R. (1979) *The Possibility of Naturalism: A Philosophical Critique of the Contemporary Human Sciences*. Atlantic Highlands, NJ: Humanities Press.

Bhaskar, R. (1998) *The Possibility of Naturalism: A Philosophical Critique of the Contemporary Human Sciences* (3rd edn). London: Routledge.

Biggs, J. (2003) *Teaching for Quality Learning at University. What the Student Does*. Buckingham, UK: The Society for Research into Higher Education and Open University Press.

Bishop, R. (2005) Freeing Ourselves from Neocolonial Domination in Research: A Kaupapa Maori Approach to Creating Knowledge. In N. Denzin and Y.S. Lincoln (eds) *The Sage Handbook of Qualitative Research* (3rd edn) pp. 109–38. Thousand Oaks: Sage.

Blank, G. (2004) Teaching Qualitative Data Analysis to Graduate Students. *Social Science Computer Review*, 22(2): 187–96.

Bloom, B.S. (1956) Taxonomy of Educational Objectives. *Handbook 1: The Cognitive Domain*. New York: David McKay.

Bohman, J. (1999) Habermas, Marxism and Social Theory: The Case for Pluralism in Critical Social Science. In P. Dews (ed.) *Habermas: A Critical Reader*, pp. 53–86. Oxford, UK: Blackwell.

Bond, T.G. and Fox, C.M. (2001) *Applying the Rasch Model: Fundamental Measurement in the Human Sciences*. Mahwah, NJ: L. Erlbaum.

Boud, D., Cohen, R. and Sampson, J. (eds) (2001) *Peer Learning in Higher Education: Learning From and With Each Other*. London: Falmer Press.

Bourdieu, P. (1992) The Practice of Reflexive Sociology (The Paris workshop). In P. Bourdieu and Loïc J.D. Wacquant (eds) *An Invitation to Reflexive Sociology*, pp. 216–60. Chicago: University of Chicago Press.

Brannen, J. (2005) Mixing Methods: The Entry of Qualitative and Quantitative Approaches Into the Research Process. *International Journal of Social Research Methodology*, 8(3): 173–84.

Brew, A. (2003) Teaching and Research: New Relationships and their Implications for Inquiry-Based Teaching and Learning in Higher Education. *Higher Education Research and Development*, 22(1): 3–18.

Brewer, C.L. (1997) Undergraduate Education in Psychology: Will the Mermaids Sing? *American Psychologist*, 52: 434–41.

Briggs, C. (1986) *Learning How to Ask*. Cambridge, MA: Cambridge University Press.

Brink, H. (1991) Quantitative and Qualitative Research. *Nursing RSA Verpleging*, 6(1): 14–18.

Bromley, D.B. (1986) *The Case-Study Method in Psychology and Related Disciplines*. Chichester: John Wiley and Sons.

Bromley, D.B. (1990) Academic Contributions to Psychological Counselling: 1. A Philosophy of Science for the Study of Individual Cases. *Counselling Psychology Quarterly*, 3(3): 299–307.

Bromley, D.B. (1991) Academic Contributions to Psychological Counselling. 2. Discourse Analysis and the Formulation of Case Reports. *Counselling Psychology Quarterly*, 4(1): 75–89.

Brown, L.D. (ed.) (2002) *Practice-Research Engagement and Civil Society in a Globalizing World*. Cambridge, MA: Hauser Center/CIVICUS.

Brown, S.R. (1993) Q Methodology. Retrieved on 10 March 2006 (available online at http://www.qmethod.org/Tutorials/Primer).

Brown, S.R. (1996) Q Methodology and Qualitative Research. *Qualitative Health Research*, 6(4): 561–7.

Burbank, P. (1988) *Meaning in Life Among Older Adults*. Unpublished doctoral dissertation, Boston University, Boston.

Burns, N. and Grove, S.K. (1999) *Understanding Nursing Research*. Philadelphia: W.B. Saunders.

Burr, V. (1995) *An Introduction to Social Constructionism*. London: Routledge.

Buxton, C.E., Cofer, C.N., Gustad, J.W., MacLeod, R.B., McKeachie, W.J. and Wolfle, D. (1952) *Improving Undergraduate Instruction in Psychology*. New York: Macmillan.

Caldwell, C., McCann, G., Flower, C. and Howie, J. (2003) *Have You Been PA'd? Using Participatory Appraisal to Shape Local Services*. Glasgow: Oxfam GB.

Callahan, L., Maldonado, M. and Efinger, J. (2003) Bridge Over Troubled Waters: End-of-Life (EOL) Decision. A qualitative case study. *The Qualitative Report*, 8(1). Retrieved on 31 March 2004 (available online at http://www.nova.edu/QR/QR8-1/callahan.html).

Carney, J.H., Joiner, J.F. and Tragou, H. (1997) Categorizing, Coding and Manipulating Qualitative Data Using the Word-Perfect, Word Processor. *The Qualitative Report*, 3(1). Retrieved on 8 December 2001 (available online at http://www.nova.edu/ssss/qr/qr3-1/carney.html).

Carr, L.T. (1994) The Strengths and Weaknesses of Quantitative and Qualitative Research: What Method for Nursing? *Journal of Advanced Nursing*, 20: 716–21.

Carspecken, P.F. (1996) *Critical Ethnography in Educational Research*. New York: Routledge.

Carspecken, P.F. (1999) There is No Such Thing as 'Critical Ethnography': A Historical Discussion. In A. Massey and G. Walford (eds) *Studies in Educational Ethnography: Explorations in Methodology*, pp. 29–56. Stamford, CT: JAI Press.

Carspecken, P.F. (2003) Ocularcentrism, Phonocentrism and the Counter Enlightenment Problematic: Clarifying Contested Terrain in Our Schools of Education. *Teachers College Record*, 105(6): 978–1047.

Carspecken, P.F. and Apple, M. (1992) Critical Qualitative Research: Theory, Method, and Practice. In M. LeCompte, W. Millroy and J. Preissle (eds) *Handbook of Qualitative Research in Education*, pp. 507–33. San Diego, CA: Academic Press.

Carspecken, P.F. and MacGillivray, L. (1998) Raising Consciousness About Reflection, Validity, and Meaning. In G. Shacklock and J. Smyth (eds) *Being Reflective in Critical Educational and Social Research*, pp. 171–90. London: Falmer Press.

Chamberlain, K. (2000) Methodolatry and Qualitative Health Research. *Journal of Health Psychology*, 5(3): 285–96.

Chambers, R. (1997) *Whose Reality Counts? Putting the First Last*. London: IT.

Chin, J.L. and Russo, N.F. (1997) Feminist Curriculum Development: Principles and Resources. In J. Worell and N.G. Johnson (eds) *Shaping the Future of Feminist Psychology. Education, Research, and Practice*, pp. 93–120. Washington, DC: American Psychological Association.

Clandinin, D.J. and Connelly, F.M. (2000) *Narrative Inquiry: Experience and Story in Qualitative Research*. San Francisco: Jossey-Bass.

Cobb, G. (1992) Teaching Statistics. In L. Steen (ed.) *Heeding the Call for Change: Suggestions for Curricular Action*, 22: 3–43. Washington, DC: Mathematical Association of America.

Coffin, C., Curry, M.J., Goodman, S., Hewings, A., Lillis, T. and Swann, J. (2003) *Teaching Academic Writing: A Toolkit for Higher Education*. London: Routledge.

Collier, A. (1994) *Critical Realism: An Introduction to Roy Bhaskar's Philosophy*. New York: Verso.

Colligan, S. (2001) The Ethnographer's Body as Text and Context: Revisiting and Revisioning Through Anthropology and Disability Studies. *Disability Studies Quarterly*, 21(3): 113–24.

Collins, H.M. (2001) Tacit Knowledge, Trust, and the Q of Sapphire. *Social Studies of Science*, 31(1): 71–85.

Collins, K. (1999) *Participatory Research: A Primer*. Cape Town, South Africa: Prentice-Hall.

Collins, R. (1979) *The Credential Society: A Historical Sociology of Education and Stratification*. New York: Academic Press.

Cooke, B. and Kothari, U. (2001) *Participation: The New Tyranny*. London: Zed Books.

Corder, S.P. (1973) *Introducing Applied Linguistics*. Harmondsworth: Penguin.

Corey, G. (1996) *Theory and Practice of Counselling and Psychotherapy*. Pacific Grove, CA: Brooks/Cole.

Cornwall, A. and Jewkes, R. (1995) What is Participatory Research? *Social Science and Medicine*, 41(12): 1667–76.

Creswell, J.W. (1998) *Qualitative Inquiry and Research Design: Choosing Among Five Traditions*. Thousand Oaks, CA: Sage.

Creswell, J.W. (2005) *Educational Research: Planning, Conducting, and Evaluating Quantitative and Qualitative Research* (2nd edn). Upper Saddle River, NJ: Merrill-Prentice Hall.

Crooks, T.J. (1988) *Assessing Student Performance* (HERDA Green Guide no. 8) Sydney, Australia: Higher Education Research and Development Society of Australasia.

Dallal, G.E. (1990) Statistical Computing Packages: Dare We Abandon Their Teaching to Others? *The American Statistician*, 44(4): 265–6.

Daniel, R.S., Dunham, P.J. and Morris, C.J. Jr. (1965) Undergraduate Courses in Psychology: 14 Years Later. *The Psychological Record*, 15: 25–31.

Davison, J. (2004) Dilemmas in Research: Issues of Vulnerability and Disempowerment for the Social Worker/Researcher. *Journal of Social Work Practice*, 18(3): 379–93.

Delamont, S. and Atkinson, P. (2001) Doctoring Uncertainty: Mastering Craft Knowledge. *Social Studies of Science*, 31: 87–107.

Dell'Orso, F. (2006) *Bibliography Formatting Software: An Evaluation Template*. Retrieved 20 February 2006 (available online at http://www.burioni.it/forum/ors-bfs/text/index.html).

Deng, Z. (2004) The Role of Theory in Teacher Preparation: An Analysis of the Concept of Theory Application. *Asia-Pacific Journal of Teacher Education*, 32(2): 143–57.

Denson, P. (1992) Preparing Posters Promotes Learning. *The Mathematics Teacher*, 85(9): 723–4.

Denzin, N.K. and Lincoln, Y.S. (2000) *The Handbook of Qualitative Research* (2nd edn). Thousand Oaks, CA: Sage Publications Ltd.

Denzin, N.K. and Lincoln, Y.S. (2005) *The Sage Handbook of Qualitative Research* (3rd edn). Thousand Oaks, CA: Sage.

Dewey, J. (1939) Experience, Knowledge, and Value: A Rejoinder. In J.A. Boydston (ed.) *The Later Works (1925–1953): 1939–1941/Essays, and Miscellany*, vol. 14. Carbondale IL: Southern Illinois University Press, pp. 3–90.

Dick, A.L. (1997) Mainstreaming the Alternative: Reflections on a Lost Opportunity in Library and Information Science. In J. Mouton and J. Muller (eds) *Knowledge, Method and the Public Good*, pp. 493–510. Pretoria: Human Sciences Research Council.

Eagle, G., Hayes, G. and Sibanda, T. (2006) Standpoint Methodologies: Marxist, Feminist and Black Scholarship Perspectives. In M. Terre Blanche, K. Durrheim and D. Painter (eds) *Research in Practice: Applied Methods for the Social Sciences*, pp. 499–522. Cape Town: University of Cape Town Press.

Ebel, J.E. (no date) *Applying to Graduate School*. Retrieved 3 January 2006 (available online at www.bc.edu/offices/careers/meta-elements/pdf/gradschool.pdf).

Edwards, D.F. and Thatcher, J. (2004) A Student-Centred Tutor-Led Approach to Teaching Research Methods. *Journal of Further and Higher Education*, 28(2).

Eisen, A. and Berry, R. (2002) The Absent Professor: Why We Don't Teach Research Ethics and What To Do About It. *The American Journal of Bioethics*, 2(4): 38–49.

Eisenhart, M. and DeHaan, R.L. (2005) Doctoral Preparation of Scientifically Based Education Researchers. *Educational Researcher*, 34(4): 3–13.

Engeström, Y. (1987) *Learning By Expanding: An Activity-Theoretical Approach to Developmental Research*. Helsinki, Finland: Orienta-Konsultit.

Erber, R. and Gilmour, R. (eds) (1994) *Theoretical Frameworks for Personal Relationships*. Hillsdale, NJ: Lawrence Erlbaum.

Erickson, F. (1986) Qualitative Methods in Research on Teaching. In M.C. Wittrock (ed.) *Handbook of Research on Teaching*, pp. 119–61. New York: Collier-Macmillan.

Evans, L. (2002) *Reflective Practice in Educational Research*. New York: Continuum.

Feigin, J.R., Orum, A.M. and Sjoberg, G. (1991) *A Case for Case Study*. Chapel Hill, NC: The University of North Carolina Press.

Fishman, D.B. (1999) *The Case for Pragmatic Psychology*. New York: New York University Press.

Fiske, A.P. (1992) The Four Elementary Forms of Sociality: Framework for a Unified Theory of Social Relations. *Psychological Review*, 99(4): 689–723.

Fixico, D.L. (1996) Ethics and Responsibilities in Writing American Indian History (Special Issue: Writing about American Indians). *American Indian Quarterly*, 20(1): 29–39.

Flores Farfán, J.A. (2006) Intervention in Indigenous Education: Culturally-Sensitive Materials for Bilingual Nahuatl Speakers. In M. Hidalgo (ed.) *Mexican Indigenous Languages at the Dawn of the Twenty-First Century*, pp. 301–23. Berlin/New York: Mouton de Gruyter.

Fook, J. (ed.) (1996) *The Reflective Researcher: Social Workers' Theories of Practice Research*. St. Leonards, NSW, Australia: Allen and Unwin.

Fraser, S.W. and Greenhalgh, T. (2001) Coping With Complexity: Educating for Capability. *BMJ*, 323: 799–803.

Freire, P. (1972) *Pedagogy of the Oppressed*. Harmondsworth and London: Penguin.

Gal, I. and Garfield, J.B. (eds) (1997) *The Assessment Challenge in Statistics Education*. Amsterdam, Netherlands: IOS Press.

Garfield, J.B. (1993) Teaching Statistics Using Small Group Cooperative Learning. *Journal of Statistics Education*, 1(1). Retrieved 1 February 2006 (available online at www.amstat.org/publications/jse/v1n1/Garfield.html).

Garfield, J.B. (1995) How Students Learn Statistics. *International Statistical Review*, 63(1): 25–34.

Garner, M., Clerehan, R. and Channock, K. (eds) (1995) *Academic Skills Advising: Towards a Discipline*. Melbourne: VLLN.

Garner, M., Raschka, C. and Sercombe, P. (2006) Sociolinguistic Minorities, Research, and Social Relationships (Special Issue: Sociolinguistic Research – Who Wins? Research on, with or for Speakers of Minority Languages). *Journal of Multilingual and Multicultural Development*, 27(1): 1–3.

Giancoli, D.C. (1988) *Physics for Scientists and Engineers* (2nd edn). Englewood Cliffs, NJ: Prentice Hall.

Gibelman, M. and Gelman, S. (2001) Learning From the Mistakes of Others: A Look at Scientific Misconduct in Research. *Journal of Social Work Education*, 37(2): 241.

Giddens, A. (1997) *Sociology*. London: Polity Press.

Glaser, B.G. (1992) *Basics of Grounded Theory Analysis: Emergence versus Forcing*. Mill Valley: Sociology Press.

Glaser, B.G. and Strauss, A. (1967) *The Discovery of Grounded Theory: Strategies for Qualitative Research*. Chicago: Aldine.

Glesne, C. and Peshkin, A. (1992) *Becoming Qualitative Researchers: An Introduction*. New York: Longman.

Golde, C.M. and Dore, T.M. (2001) *At Cross Purposes: What the Experiences of Today's Doctoral Students Reveal About Doctoral Education*. Unpublished manuscript, University of Wisconsin.

Goldstein, H. (1992) If Social Work Hasn't Been Making Progress as a Science, Might it be an Art? *Families in Society*, 73: 48–55.

Gorard, S., Taylor, C. and Moore, L. (2004) *Combining Methods in Educational Research*. Buckingham: Open University Press.

Grant, L., Preissle, J., Beoku-Betts, J., Finlay, W. and Fine, G.A. (1999) Fieldwork in Familiar Places: The UGA Workshop in Fieldwork Methods. *Anthropology and Education Quarterly*, 30(2): 238–48.

Greenhalgh, T., Toon, P., Russell, J., Wong, G., Plumb, L. and Macfarlane, F. (2003) Transferability of Principles of Evidence-Based Medicine to Improve Educational Quality: Systematic Review and Case Study of an Online Course in Primary Health Care. *BMJ*, 326: 142–5.

Greggory, I. (2003) *Ethics in Research*. London: Continuum.

Grundy, A.L. (2004) *Learning Experiences and Identity Development as a Research Assistant*. Unpublished Master's Thesis, Brock University, Ontario, Canada.

Grundy, A.L., McGinn, M.K. and Pollon, D.E. (2005) Striving Toward Inclusive Research Practices: The Evolution of the Participant-As-Transcriptionist Method. *Disability and Society*, 20(4): 453–68.

Grundy, A.L., Pollon, D.E. and McGinn, M.K. (2003) The Participant as Transcriptionist: Methodological Advantages of a Collaborative and Inclusive Research Practice. *International Journal of Qualitative Methods*, 2(2): Article 3. Retrieved 12 June 2006 (available online at http://www.ualberta.ca/~iiqm/backissues/2_2/pdf/grundyetal.pdf).

Guba, E.G. and Lincoln, Y.S. (1981) *Effective Evaluation*. San Francisco, CA: Jossey-Bass.

Guba, E.G. and Lincoln, Y.S. (2005) Paradigmatic Controversies, Contradictions, and Emerging Confluences. In N.K. Denzin and Y.S. Lincoln (eds) *The Sage Handbook of Qualitative Research* (3rd edn) pp. 191–216. Thousand Oaks: Sage.

Habermas, J. (1971) *Knowledge and Human Interests* (J.J. Shapiro, trans.) Original work published 1968. Boston: Beacon Press.

Hall, B. (2005) *In From The Cold? Reflections on Participatory Research*. Paper presented at the meeting of the CUExpo, Winnipeg, Canada.

Halonen, J.S., Appleby, D.C., Brewer, C.L., Buskist, W., Gillem, A.R., Halpern, D., Hill, G.W. IV, Lloyd, M.A., Rudmann, J.L., Whitlow, V.M., Beins, B. and Braswell, M. (2002) *Undergraduate Psychology Major Learning Goals and Outcomes: A Report*. Retrieved 9 June 2006 (available online at http://www.apa.org/ed/pcue/reports.html).

Hammersley, M. (1989) *The Dilemma of Qualitative Method: Herbert Blumer and the Chicago Tradition*. London: Routledge.

Hammersley, M. (2004) Teaching Qualitative Method: Craft, Profession, or Bricolage? In C. Seale, G. Gobo, J. Gubrium and D. Silverman (eds) *Qualitative Research Practice*, pp. 549–60. London: Sage.

Hanfling, O. (1981) *Logical Positivism*. Oxford, UK: Basil Blackwell.

Haralambos, M. and Holborn, H. (1995) *Sociology: Themes and Perspectives*. London: Collins Educational.

Harris, M. (2001) *Cultural Materialism: The Struggle for a Science of Culture* (review edn). Walnut Creek, CA: AltaMira Press.

Heiman, G.W. (1998) *Understanding Research Methods and Statistics: An Integrated Introduction for Psychology*. Boston, MA: Houghton Mifflin.

Hempel, C.G. (1965) *Aspects of Scientific Explanation and Other Essays in the Philosophy of Science*. New York: Free Press.

Henry, E.R. (1938) A Survey of Courses in Psychology Offered by Undergraduate Colleges of Liberal Arts. *Psychological Bulletin*, 35: 430–35.

Hepler, J.W. (1959) On the Teaching of Experimental Psychology. *American Psychologist*, 14: 638–41.

Hickey, S. and Mohan, G. (eds) (2004) *Participation: From Tyranny to Transformation?* London: Zed Books.

Hinkle, D.E., Wiersma, W. and Jurs, S.G. (1998) *Applied Statistics for the Behavioral Sciences* (4th edn). Boston: Houghton Mifflin.

Holder, W.B., Leavitt, G.S. and McKenna, F.S. (1958) Undergraduate Training for Psychologists. *American Psychologist*, 13: 585–8.

Holland, D. and Lave, J. (eds) (2001) *History in Person: Enduring Struggles, Contentious Practice, Intimate Identities*. Santa Fe, NM: School of American Research Press.

Howat, P., Maycock, B., Jackson, L., et al. (2000) Development of Competency Based University Health Promotion Courses. *Promotion and Education*, 7(1): 7–33.

Jackson, K. (2003) Blending Technology and Methodology: A Shift Toward Creative Instruction of Qualitative Methods With NVivo (Special Issue). *Qualitative Research Journal*, 3, 96–110. Retrieved 28 January 2008 (available online at http://www.latrobe.edu.au/aqr/journal/special_AQR2003.pdf).

Jackson, S.L. (2003) *Research Methods and Statistics: A Critical Thinking Approach*. Belmont, CA: Wadsworth.

Jackson, S.L., Lugo, S.M. and Griggs, R.A. (2001) Research Methods Textbooks: An Objective Analysis. *Teaching of Psychology*, 28: 282–8.

James, E.L., Graham, M., Snow, P. and Ward, B. (2006) Teaching Research and Epidemiology to Undergraduate Students in the Health Sciences. *ANZJPH*, 30: 575–8.

James, R., McInnis, C. and Devlin, M. (2002) *Assessing Learning in Australian Universities*. Centre for the Study of Higher Education, University of Melbourne and Australian Universities Teaching Committee, Canberra, Australia. Retrieved on 28 January 2008 (available online at http://www.cshe. unimelb.edu.au/assessinglearning/docs/AssessingLearning.pdf).

Janesick, V.J. (1998) The Dance of Qualitative Research Design: Metaphor, Methodolotry and Meaning. In N. Denzin and Y.S. Lincoln (eds) *Strategies of Qualitative Inquiry*, pp. 35–55. Thousand Oaks: Sage.

Jay, J.K. and Johnson, K.L. (2002) Capturing Complexity: A Typology of Reflective Practice for Teacher Education. *Teaching and Teacher Education*, 18: 73–85.

Johnson, B. and Christensen, L.B. (2003) *Educational Research: Quantitative, Qualitative, and Mixed Approaches* (2nd edn) Boston: Allyn and Bacon.

Jones, C., Turner, J. and Street, B. (eds) (1999) *Students Writing in the University: Cultural and Epistemological Issues*. Amsterdam: John Benjamins.

Kawulich, B.B. (1998) *Muscogee (Creek) Women's Perceptions of Work*. Doctoral Dissertation, Georgia State University. Dissertation Abstracts International, AAT 9903268.

Kawulich, B.B. (2004) Muscogee Women's Identity Development. In M. Hutter (ed.) *The Family Experience: A Reader in Cultural Diversity* (4th edn) pp. 83–93. Boston: Allyn and Bacon.

Keller, J.M. (1983) Motivational Design of Instruction. In C.M. Reigeluth (ed.) *An Instructional-Design Theories and Models: An Overview of Their Current Status*, pp. 386–434. Hillsdale, NJ: Lawrence-Erlbaum Associates.

Kincheloe, J.L. and Mclaren, P. (2000) Rethinking Critical Theory and Qualitative Research. In N.K. Denzin and Y.S. Lincoln (eds) *Handbook of Qualitative Research* (2nd edn) pp. 279–313. Thousand Oaks: Sage.

Kitchin, R. (2000) The Researched Opinions on Research: Disabled People and Disability Research. *Disability and Society*, 15(1): 25–47.

Klein, W.C. and Bloom, M. (1995) Practice Wisdom. *Social Work*, 37(6): 799–807.

Knight, P. (2002) *Being A Teacher In Higher Education*. Buckingham, UK: Society for Research into Higher Education and Open University Press.

Kraft, N.P. (2002) Teacher Research as a Way to Engage in Critical Reflection: A Case Study. *Reflective Practice*, 3: 175–89.

Kreber, C. (2004) An Analysis of Two Models of Reflection and Their Implications for Educational Development. *International Journal for Academic Development*, 9: 29–49.

Kulik, J.A. (1973) *Undergraduate Education in Psychology*. Washington, DC: American Psychological Association.

Kurtines, W.M. and Silverman, W.K. (1999) Emerging Views of the Role of Theory. *Journal of Clinical Child Psychology*, 28(4): 558–62.

Lalonde, R.N. and Gardner, R.C. (1993) Statistics A Second Language? A model for predicting performance in psychology students. *Canadian Journal of Behavioural Science*, 25(1): 108–25.

Laroche, L. and Roth, W.M. (in press) Teaching and Learning Qualitative Research: Educational Space as Fluid. In S. Kouritzin, N. Piquemal and R. Norman (eds) *Qualitative Research: Challenging The Orthodoxies*. Mahwah, NJ: Lawrence Erlbaum Associates.

Lather, P. (2004) Critical Inquiry in Qualitative Research: Feminist and Poststructural Perspectives: Science 'After Truth'. In K. DeMarrais and S.D. Lapan (eds) *Foundations For Research: Methods of Inquiry in Education and the Social Science*, pp. 203–16. Mahwah, NJ: Lawrence Erlbaum Associates.

Laudan, L. (1996) *Beyond Positivism and Relativism. Theory, Method, and Evidence*. New York: Westview Press.

Lave, J. (1993) The Practice of Learning. In S. Chaiklin and J. Lave (eds) *Understanding Practice: Perspectives on Activity and Context*, pp. 3–32. Cambridge: Cambridge University Press.

Lave, J. and Wenger, E. (1991) *Situated Learning: Legitimate Peripheral Participation*. Cambridge, UK: Cambridge University Press.

Lea, M.R. and Stierer, B. (eds) (2000) *Student Writing in Higher Education: New Contexts*. Milton Keynes: The Society for Research into Higher Education and Open University Press.

LeCompte, M.D. and Preissle, J. (1993) *Ethnography and Qualitative Design in Educational Research* (2nd edn). San Diego: Academic Press.

Lee, W.S. (2006) *Software Evaluation Research: Case Study Methodology Designed Research*. University of North Carolina at Charlotte, Department of Software and Information Systems. Retrieved 16 June 2006 (available online at www.sis.uncc.edu/~seoklee/Projects/CSM.htm).

Lesser, A. (2004) Franz Boas. In S. Silverman (ed.) *Totems and Teachers: Key Figures in the History of Anthropology*, pp. 1–26. Walnut Creek, CA: AltaMira Press.

Light, G. and Cox, R. (2001) *Learning and Teaching in Higher Education: The Reflective Professional*. London: Paul Chapman Ltd (Sage Publications).

Lillis, T.M. (2001) *Student Writing: Access, Regulation, Desire*. London: Routledge.

Lincoln, Y.S. (1990) The Making of a Constructivist. A Remembrance of Transformations Past. In E.G. Guba (ed.) *The Paradigm Dialog*, pp. 67–87. Newbury Park: Sage.

Lincoln, Y.S. (1995) Emerging Criteria for Quality in Qualitative and Interpretive Inquiry. *Qualitative Inquiry*, 1: 275–89.

Lincoln, Y.S. and Guba, E.G. (1985) *Naturalistic Inquiry*. Newbury Park, CA: Sage.

Lloyd, M.A. and Brewer, C.L. (1992) National Conferences on Undergraduate Psychology. In A.R. Puente, J.R. Mathews and C.L. Brewer (eds) *Teaching Psychology in America: A History*, pp. 263–84. Washington, DC: American Psychological Association.

Lopez, J. and Potter, G. (2005) *After Postmodernism: An Introduction to Critical Realism*. New York: Continuum.

Lowman, J. (1995) *Mastering the Techniques of Teaching* (2nd edn). San Francisco, CA: Jossey-Bass.

Lux, D.F. and Daniel, R.S. (1978) Which Courses Are Most Frequently Listed By Psychology Departments? *Teaching of Psychology*, 5: 13–16.

Mahoney, J. (2004) Revisiting General Theory in Historical Sociology. *Social Forces*, 83(2): 459–89.

Malinowski, B. (1935) *Soil Tilling and Agricultural Rites in the Trobriand Islands*. London: Allen and Unwin.

Mariano, C. (2000) Case Study: The Method. In P. Munhall and C. Oiler Boyd (eds) *Nursing Research: A Qualitative Perspective* (2nd edn). pp. 311–37. Sudbury, MA: Jones and Bartlett.

Marlow, C.R. (2005) *Research Methods for Generalist Social Work*. Belmont, CA: Brooks/Cole.

Marshall, A. and Batten, S. (2004) Researching Across Cultures: Issues of Ethics and Power. *Forum Qualitative Sozialforschung/Forum: Qualitative Social Research*, 5(3): Article 39. Retrieved 5 April 2005 (available online at http://www.qualitative-research.net/fqs-texte/3-04/04-3-39-e.htm).

Maslow, A.H. (1954) *Motivation and Personality*. New York: Harper and Row.

Maxwell, J. (2005) *Qualitative Research Design: An Interactive Approach* (2nd edn). Thousand Oaks, CA: Sage.

McAuliffe, D. and Coleman, A. (1999) Damned If We Do And Damned If We Don't: Exposing Ethical Tensions In Field Research. *Australian Social Work*, 52(4): 25–31.

McDonough, S.H. (2002) *Applied Linguistics in Language Education*. London: Arnold.

McGovern, T. (ed.) (1993) *Handbook for Enhancing Undergraduate Education in Psychology*. Washington, DC: American Psychological Association.

McGovern, T.V., Furumoto, L., Halpern, D.F., Kimble, G.A. and McKeachie, W.J. (1991) Liberal Education, Study In-Depth, and the Arts and Sciences Major – Psychology. *American Psychologist*, 46: 598–605.

McGuigan, F.J. (1960) *Experimental Psychology: A Methodological Approach.* Englewood Cliffs, NJ: Prentice-Hall.

McKeachie, W.J. (ed.) (2002) *Teaching Tips: Strategies, Research, and Theory for College and University Teachers* (11th edn). Boston, MA: Houghton Mifflin.

McKeachie, W.J. and Milholland, J.E. (1961) *Undergraduate Curricula in Psychology.* Fair Lawn, NJ: Scott Foresman.

McTavish, D.G. and Loether, H.J. (2002) *Social Research: An Evolving Process* (2nd edn). Boston: Allyn and Bacon.

Melville, R. (2005) Human Research Ethics Committees and Ethical Review: The Changing Research Culture for Social Workers. *Australian Social Work*, 58(4): 370–83.

Merriam, S.B. (1998) *Qualitative Research and Case Study Applications in Education.* San Francisco: Jossey-Bass.

Merriam, S.B. (2006) Transformational Learning and HIV-Positive Young Adults. In V.A. Anfara Jr. and N.T. Mertz (eds) *Theoretical Frameworks in Qualitative Research*, pp. 23–38. Thousand Oaks, CA: Sage.

Merrill, L.L. (2000) Frank Joseph McGuigan (1924–1998). *American Psychologist*, 55: 676–7.

Mertens, D.M. (1998) *Research Methods in Education and Psychology: Integrating Diversity With Quantitative and Qualitative Approaches.* Thousand Oaks: Sage.

Michell, J. (1997) Quantitative Science and the Definition of Measurement in Psychology. *British Journal of Psychology*, 88: 355–85.

Michell, J. (1999) *Measurement in Psychology: Critical History of a Methodological Concept.* New York: Cambridge University Press.

Michell, J. (2003) The Quantitative Imperative: Positivism, Naïve Realism and the Place of Qualitative Methods in Psychology. *Theory and Psychology*, 13(1): 5–31.

Mikkelson, B. (2005) *Methods for Development Work and Research: A New Guide for Practitioners.* New Delhi: Sage.

Miles, A.B. and Huberman, M. (1994) *Qualitative Data Analysis: A Sourcebook of New Methods.* Beverly Hills. Sage.

Mill, D., Gray, T. and Mandel, D.R. (1994) Influence of Research Methods and Statistics Courses on Everyday Reasoning, Critical Abilities and Belief in Unsustained Phenomena. *Canadian Journal of Behavioural Science*, 26(2): 246–58.

Miller, J.F. (1992) *Coping With Chronic Illness: Overcoming Powerlessness* (2nd edn). Philadelphia: F.A. Davis.

Mills, J. and Clark, M.S. (1994) Communal and Exchange Relationships: Controversies and Research. In R. Erber and R. Gilmour (eds) *Theoretical Frameworks for Personal Relationships*. Chapter 2. New York: Psychology Press.

Milroy, L. (1987) *Observing and Analysing Natural Language*. Oxford: Blackwell.

Mitchell-Kernan, C. (2005) Doctoral Education: Reform on a Weakened Foundation. *Communicator*, 38(10): 1–3.

Moon, J.A. (2004) *A Handbook of Reflective and Experiential Learning*. London: Routledge Falmer.

Mooney, R.L. (1957) The Researcher Himself. In *Research for Curriculum Improvement: 1957 Yearbook*, pp. 154–86. Washington, DC: Association for Supervision and Curriculum Development.

Mouton, J. and Muller, J. (1997) Knowledge and Method in a Postmodern Age. In J. Mouton and J. Muller (eds) *Knowledge, Method and the Public Good*, pp. 1–18. Pretoria, South Africa: Human Sciences Research Council.

Mullaly, R. (2002) *Challenging Oppression: A Critical Social Work Approach*. Ontario, Canada: Oxford University Press.

Mullen, E.J. (1983) Personal Practice Models. In A. Rosenblatt and D. Waldgogel (eds) *Handbook of Clinical Social Work*, pp. 623–649. San Francisco: Jossey-Bass.

Mutua, K. and Swadener, B.B. (eds) (2004) *Decolonizing Research in Cross-Cultural Contexts*. Albany, NY: State University of New York Press.

NASW (National Association of Social Workers) (2005) *Social Work Student Profile*. Washington, DC: NASW.

Neuman, W.L. (2000) *Social Research Methods. Qualitative and Quantitative Approaches* (4th edn). Boston: Allyn and Bacon.

NHMRC (National Health and Medical Research Council) (2003) *Guidelines for Ethical Conduct in Aboriginal and Torres Strait Islander Health Research*. Retrieved 4 March 2008 (available online at http://www.nhmrc.gov.au/ethics/human/ahec/history/_files/e11.pdf).

Noddings, N. (1998) *Philosophy of Education*. Boulder, CO: Westview Press.

NRC (National Research Council) (2005) *Advancing Scientific Research in Education*. L. Towne, L.L. Wise and T.M. Winters (eds) Committee on Research in Education, Center for Education, Division of the Behavioral and Social Sciences and Education. Washington, DC: The National Academies Press.

NSECHR (National Statement on Ethical Conduct in Human Research) (2007) Retrieved 1 April 2008 (available online at http://www.nhmrc.gov.au/ethics/human/ahec/guidelines/ntnl_stat_guide/index.htm).

Nunes, J.B.C. (2006) Mediação da tecnologia na produção do saber: análise da pesquisa em educação. In R. Lima (ed.) *Educação, Ciência e Desenvolvimento Social*, pp. 351–80. Belém, Brazil: Universidade Federal do Pará.

O'Connell, A.A. (2002) Student Perceptions of Assessment Strategies in a Multivariate Statistics Course. *Journal of Statistics Education*, 10(1). Retrieved 8 January 2006 (available online at www.amstat.org/publications/jse/v10n1/oconnell.html).

Ohuche, R.O. and Anyanwu, M. (eds) (1990) *Perspectives in Educational and National Development*. Onitsha, Nigeria: Summer Educational.

Okeke, C.O. (2003) *The Gendered Perception of Schooling Amongst Secondary School Students: A Qualitative Approach.* Unpublished doctoral dissertation, University of Nigeria – Nsukka.

Oliver, M. (1992) Changing the Social Relations of Research Production? *Disability, Handicap and Society*, 7(2): 101–14.

Onwuegbuzie, A.J. (1997) Writing a Research Proposal: The Role of Library Anxiety, Statistics Anxiety, and Compositional Anxiety. *Library and Information Science Research*, 19: 5–33.

Onwuegbuzie, A.J. (1998) Role of Hope in Predicting Anxiety About Statistics. *Psychological Reports*, 82: 1315–20.

Outhwaite, W. (1998) Realism and Social Science. In M. Archer, R. Bhaskar, A. Collier, T. Lawson and A. Norrie (eds) *Critical Realism: Essential Readings*, pp. 282–96. London: Routledge.

Palmer, P.J. (1998) *The Courage to Teach: Exploring the Inner Landscape of a Teacher's Life.* San Francisco: Jossey-Bass.

Parker, G. and Baldwin, S. (1992) Confessions of a Jobbing Researcher. *Disability, Handicap and Society*, 7(2): 197–203.

Pascarella, E.T. and Terenzini, P.T. (2005) *How College Affects Students: A Third Decade of Research* (vol 2). San Francisco: Jossey-Bass.

Patton, M.Q. (1996) Preface: A Look at the Mosaic of Qualitative Family Research. In M.B. Sussman and J.F. Gilgun (eds) *The Methods and Methodologies of Qualitative Family Research*, pp. xvii–xxiii. New York: Haworth Press.

Perlman, B. and McCann, L.I. (1999) The Most Frequently Listed Courses in the Undergraduate Psychology Curriculum. *Teaching of Psychology*, 26: 177–82.

Perry, F.L. (2005) *Research in Applied Linguistics: Becoming a Discerning Consumer.* Hillsdale, NJ: Lawrence Erlbaum.

Pettit, J. (2006) A Case Study About the Design of Experiential Learning: Creating a New MA Curriculum. In L. Stackpool-Moore, P. Taylor, J. Pettit and J. Millican, *Currents of Change: Exploring Relationships Between Teaching, Learning and Transformation. Conversations From the Learning and Teaching for Transformation Workshop*, pp. 23–6. Falmer: IDS.

Pietersen, C. (2002) Research as a Learning Experience: A Phenomenological Explication. *The Qualitative Report*, 7(2). Retrieved 6 March 2006 (available online at http://www.nova.edu/ssss/QR/QR7-2/pietersen.html).

Pike K.L. (1967) *Language in Relation to a Unified Theory of the Structure of Human Behavior.* The Hague: Mouton.

Plutchik, R. (1968) *Foundations of Experimental Psychology.* New York: Harper and Row.

Polanyi, M. (1966) *The Tacit Dimension.* New York: Doubleday.

Polkinghorne, D.E. (1992) Research Methodology in Humanistic Psychology. *The Humanistic Psychologist*, 20(1): 218–42.

Postman, L. and Egan, J.P. (1949) *Experimental Psychology: An Introduction.* New York: Harper.

Preissle, J. (1999) An Educational Ethnographer Comes of Age. *Journal of Contemporary Ethnography*, 28(6): 650–59.

Prosser, M. and Trigwell, K. (1999) *Understanding Learning and Teaching: The Experience in Higher Education*. Buckingham, UK: The Society for Research into Higher Education and Open University Press.

Punch, K.F. (1998) *Introduction to Social Research: Quantitative and Qualitative Approaches*. London: Sage.

QAA (Quality Assurance Agency for Higher Education, UK) (2004) Code of practice for the assurance of academic quality and standards in higher education, Section 1: Postgraduate Research programmes (2nd edn). Mansfield: QAA.

Ramsden, P. (2003) *Learning to Teach in Higher Education*. London: Routledge Falmer.

Reamer, F.G. (2005) Research Ethics. In R.M. Grinnell and Y.A. Unrau (eds) *Social Work Research and Evaluation: Quantitative and Qualitative Approaches*, pp. 33–44. New York: Oxford University Press.

Reason, P. and Bradbury, H. (2001) *Handbook of Action Research*. Participative inquiry and practice. London: Sage.

Reigeluth, C.M. (ed.) (1999) *Instructional-Design Theories and Models: A New Paradigm of Instructional Theories*. Mahwah, NJ: Lawrence-Erlbaum.

Rein, M. and White, S. (1981) Knowledge For Practice. *Social Service Review*, 55: 1–41.

Richards, L. (2002) *Introducing N6: A Workshop Handbook*. Victoria, Australia: QSR International.

Richardson, V. (2006) Stewards of a Field, Stewards of an Enterprise: The Doctorate in Education. In C.M. Golde and G.E. Walker (eds) *Envisioning the Future of Doctoral Education: Preparing Stewards of the Discipline*, pp. 251–67. San Francisco: Jossey Bass.

Ritzer, G. (2000) *Modern Sociological Theory* (5th edn). Boston: McGraw-Hill.

Roberts, A. (2002) A Principled Complementarity of Method: In Defence of Methodological Eclecticism and the Quantitative–Qualitative Debate. *The Qualitative Report*, 7(3). Retrieved 31 October 2003 (available online at http://www.nova.edu/ssss/QR/QR7-3/roberts.html).

Roberts, P. (2000) *Education, Literacy and Humanization: An Introduction to the Work of Paulo Freire*. Westport, CT: Greenwood.

Roth, W.M. (2005a) *Doing Qualitative Research: Praxis of Method*. Rotterdam, Netherlands: Sense.

Roth, W.M. (2005b) Textbooks on Qualitative Research and Method/Methodology: Toward a Praxis of Method. *FQS: Forum Qualitative Sozialforschung/Forum Qualitative Social Research*, 7(1). Retrieved 25 August 2006 (available online at http://www.qualitative-research.net/fqs/fqs-eng.htm).

Roth, W.M. and Bowen, G.M. (2001) Of Disciplined Minds and Disciplined Bodies. *Qualitative Sociology*, 24(4): 459–81.

Roth, W.M., Riecken, J., Pozzer, L.L., McMillan, R., Storr, B., Tait, D., Bradshaw, G. and Pauluth Penner, T. (2004) Those Who Get Hurt Aren't Always Being Heard: Scientist–Resident Interactions Over Community Water. *Science, Technology, and Human Values*, 29(2): 153–83.

Roulston, K., deMarrais, K. and Lewis, J. (2003) Learning to Interview in the Social Sciences. *Qualitative Inquiry*, 9(4): 643–68.

Roulston, K., Legette, R., DeLoach, M., Buckhalter Pittman, C., Cory, L. and Grenier, R. (2005) Developing a Teacher–Research Group in Music Education: Mentoring and Community Through Research. *Research Studies in Music Education*, 25(1): 1–22.

Rowntree, D. (1987) *Assessing Students: How Shall We Know Them?* (2nd edn). London: Kogan Page.

Royse, D. (2004) *Research Methods in Social Work*. Pacific Grove, CA: Brooks/ Cole.

Ruane, J.M. (2005) *Essentials of Research Methods: A Guide to Social Science Research*. Malden, MA: Blackwell.

Rubin, A. and Babbie, E.R. (2007) *Research Methods for Social Work*. Belmont, CA: Brooks/Cole.

Sanford, F.H. and Fleishman, E.A. (1950) A Survey of Undergraduate Psychology Courses in American Colleges and Universities. *American Psychologist*, 5: 33–7.

Sar, B., Yankeelov, P., Holt, T., Bledsoe, L., Faul, A. and Frey, A. (2002) Ethics and the Practice of Social Work Research. In P. Black, E. Congress and K. Strom-Gottfried (eds) *Teaching Social Work Values and Ethics: A Curriculum Resource*, pp. 102–106. Alexandria, VA: Council on Social Work Education.

Sarantakos, S. (2005) *Social Research*. Basingstoke, UK: Palgrave.

Schatzman, L. and Strauss, A.L. (1973) *Field Research: Strategies for a Natural Sociology*. Upper Saddle River, NJ: Prentice-Hall.

Schoenfeld, A. (1985) *Mathematical Problem Solving*. Orlando, FL: Academic Press.

Schön, D.A. (1983) *The Reflective Practitioner: How Professionals Think in Action*. New York: Basic Books.

Schön, D.A. (1987) *Educating the Reflective Practitioner*. Presentation given at the Annual Meeting of the American Educational Research Association, Washington, DC. Retrieved 28 January 2008 (available online at http://educ. queensu.ca/~russellt/howteach/schon87.htm).

Schwandt, T.A. (1994) Constructivist, Interpretivist Approaches to Human Inquiry. In N.K. Denzin and Y.S. Lincoln (eds) *Handbook of Qualitative Research*, pp. 118–37. Newbury Park, CA: Sage.

Schweigert, W.A. (1994) *Research Methods and Statistics for Psychology*. Pacific Grove, CA: Brooks/Cole.

Scollon, R. and Scollon, S.W. (1995) *Intercultural Communication*. Oxford: Blackwell.

Scott, D. (2005) An interview with David K. Scott. *Spirituality in Higher Education*, 2(2). Retrieved 25 February 2006 (available online at http://spirituality.ucla. edu/newsletter/past/Volume%202/6/1.html).

Scott, S.S., McGuire, J.M. and Foley, T.E. (2003) Universal Design for Instruction: A Framework for Anticipating and Responding to Disability and Other Diverse Learning Needs in the College Classroom. *Equity and Excellence in Education*, 36(1): 40–49.

Searle, S.R. (1989) Statistical Computing Packages: Some Words of Concern. *The American Statistician*, 43(4): 190–98.

Secret, M., Ford, J. and Rompf, E.L. (2003) Undergraduate Research Courses: A Closer Look Reveals Complex Social Work Student Attitudes. *Journal of Social Work Education*, 39(3): 411–23.

Seel, H.G. (2000) The future prospects for (qualitative) psychology. *Forum: Qualitative Social Research*. Retrieved 27 June 2000 (available online at http://qualitative-research.net/fqs/fqs-e/2-00inhalt-e.htm).

Sercombe, P.G. and Garner, M. (2005) *Perceptions of Identity Among International Students in Newcastle*. Paper presented at Conference on 'Investigating Third Spaces', School of Education, University of Leicester, UK.

Sewell, W.H. (1992) A Theory of Structure: Duality, Agency and Transformation. *American Journal of Sociology*, 98(1): 1–29.

Shaughnessy, J.J., Zechmeister, E.B. and Zechmeister, J.S. (2003) *Research Methods in Psychology*. New York: McGraw-Hill.

Shepard, J. (1990) *Sociology*. New York: West.

Shepard, L.A. (2000) The Role of Assessment in a Learning Culture. *Educational Researcher*, 2(7): 4–14.

Sherraden, M. (2000) *Asking Questions Well: The Role of Theory in Applied Social Research*. Keynote address at the Twelfth National Symposium on Doctoral Research in Social Work, Ohio State University.

Shilton, T., Howat, P., James, R. and Lower, T. (2002) *Review of Competencies for Australian Health Promotion*. Report no. 97. Perth: Western Australian Centre for Health Promotion, Curtin University and the National Heart Foundation of Australia (WA Division).

Silver, P. (1983) *Educational Administration: Theoretical Perspectives on Practice and Research*. New York: Harper and Row.

Silverman, D. (2001) *Interpreting Qualitative Data: Methods for Analysing Talk, Text, and Interaction* (2nd edn). London: Sage.

Sin, C.H. (2005) Seeking Informed Consent: Reflections on Research Practice. *Sociology*, 39(2): 277–94.

Smallwood, S. (2005) Doctoral Degrees Rose 3.4% in 2004, Survey Finds. *Chronicle of Higher Education*, p. A10.

Smith, L.T. (1999) *Decolonizing Methodologies: Research and Indigenous Peoples*. London: Zed Books.

Smith, L.T. (2005) On Tricky Ground: Researching the Native in the Age of Uncertainty. In N.K. Denzin and Y.S. Lincoln (eds) *The Sage Handbook of Qualitative Research* (3rd edn) pp. 85–108. Thousand Oaks: Sage.

Smith, M.K. (2001) David A. Kolb on experiential learning. *The Encyclopedia of Informal Education*. Retrieved 31 August 2006 (available online at http://www.infed.org/b-explrn.htm).

Stackpool-Moore, L., Taylor, P., Pettit, J. and Millican, J. (2005) *Currents of Change: Exploring Relationships Between Teaching, Learning and Transformation*. Conversations from the learning and teaching for transformation workshop, pp. 23–6. Falmer: IDS.

Stake, R.E. (1978) The Case Study Method in Social Inquiry. *Educational Researcher*, 7(2): 5–8.

Stake, R.E. (1995) *The Art of Case Study Research*. Thousand Oaks, CA: Sage.

Stanley, B.H., Seiber, J.E. and Melton, G.B. (eds) (1996) *Research Ethics: A Psychological Approach*. Lincoln: University of Nebraska Press.

Stanovich, K.E. (2004) *How to Think Straight About Psychology* (7th edn). Boston: Allyn and Bacon.

Steinberg, D.M. (2004) *Social Work Student's Research Handbook*. New York: Haworth Press.

Stewart, P. and O'Neill, N. (1999) Critical Literacy: A Qualitative Investigation of Some Conceptualizations, Practices and Implications for English Teaching. *Education Research and Perspectives*, 26(2): 73–84.

Stoecker, R. (2005) *Research Methods for Community Change. A Project-Based Approach*. Thousand Oaks: Sage.

Strauss, A. and Corbin, J. (1998) *Basics of Qualitative Research: Techniques and Procedures for Developing Grounded Theory* (2nd edn). Thousand Oaks: SAGE.

Strauss, A., Corbin, J., Fagerhaugh, S., Glaser, B., Maines, D., Suczek, B. and Weiner, C. (1984) *Chronic Illness and Quality of Life*. St. Louis: C.V. Mosby.

Strayhorn, T.L. (2005) More Than Money Matters: An Integrated Model of Graduate Student Persistence. *Dissertation Abstracts International*, A66 (2): 519.

Swearingen, K., Lyman, P. and Varian, H.R. (2003) *How Much Information?* Berkeley: University of California at Berkeley. Retrieved 10 January 2005 (available online at http://www.sims.berkeley.edu/research/projects/how-much-info-2003).

Talbot, L., Graham, M. and James, E.L. (2007) *A Role for Workplace Competencies in Evidence Based Health Promotion Education*. Manuscript submitted for publication.

Tashakkori, A. and Teddlie, C. (1998) *Mixed Methodology: Combining Qualitative and Quantitative Approaches*. Thousand Oaks: Sage.

Tashakkori, A. and Teddlie, C. (2003) Issues and Dilemmas in Teaching Research Methods Courses in Social and Behavioural Sciences: US Perspective. *International Journal of Social Research Methodology*, 6(1): 61–77.

Terre Blanche, M. and Durrheim, K. (2006) Histories of the Present: Social Science Research in Context. In M. Terre Blanche, K. Durrheim and D. Painter (eds) *Research in Practice: Applied Methods for the Social Sciences*, pp. 1–17. Cape Town: University of Cape Town Press.

The Evolution of Experimental Psychology (1999) *APA Monitor Online*, 30(11). Retrieved 7 March 2006 (available online at http://www.apa.org/monitor/ dec99/ss5.html).

Thyer, B.A. (2001) What is the Role of Theory in Research on Social Work Practice? *Journal of Social Work Education*, 37(1): 9–25.

Tobin, K. and McRobbie, C. (1997) Beliefs About the Nature of Science and the Enacted Science Curriculum. *Science and Education*, 6(4): 355–71.

Veneklasen, L. and Miller, V. (2006) *A New Weave of Power, People, and Politics: The Action Guide for Advocacy and Citizen Participation*. Rugby: Practical Action.

Vygotsky, L.S. (1989) *A Formação Social da Mente*. São Paulo, Brazil: Martins Fontes.

Wagner, C. (2003) *Placing Psychology: A Critical Exploration of Research Methodology Curricula in the Social Sciences*. Unpublished Doctoral Thesis, University of Pretoria.

Wagner, C. and Maree, D.J.F. (2005) The (Non)Effect of the Knowledge Era on Undergraduate Research Methodology Curricula in the Social Sciences. *SA Journal of Industrial Psychology*, 31(1): 39–46.

Wainwright, D. (1997) Can Sociological Research be Qualitative, Critical and Valid? The *Qualitative Report*, 3(2). Retrieved 8 December 2001 (available online at http://www.nova.edu/sss/QR/QR3-2/wain.html).

Waldrop, D. (2004) Ethical Issues in Qualitative Research with High-Risk Populations. In D.K. Padgett (ed.) *The Qualitative Research Experience*. Belmont, CA: Brooks/Cole.

Ward, B., Dickson-Swift, V., James, E., Snow, P., Spark, J. and Verrinder, A. (2008) Incorporating Research Training Into Undergraduate Pharmacy Courses: A Case Study From Australia. *Pharmacy Education*, 8(1): 1–6.

Ward, B., James, E., Graham, M. and Snow, P. (in press) Assessing Epidemiological Learning Amongst Undergraduate Students. *Focus on Health Professional Education*.

Wenger, E. (1998) *Communities of Practice: Learning, Meaning, and Identity*. Cambridge, UK: Cambridge University Press.

Wild, C., Triggs, C. and Pfannkuch, M. (1997) Assessment on a Budget: Using Traditional Methods Imaginatively. In I. Gal and J.B. Garfield (eds) *The Assessment Challenge in Statistics Education*, pp. 205–20. Amsterdam, Netherlands: IOS Press.

Wildy, H. (1999) Statuses, Lenses and Crystals: Looking at Qualitative Research. *Education Research and Perspectives*, 26(2): 61–72.

Wilensky, U. (1997) What is Normal Anyway? Therapy for epistemological anxiety. *Educational Studies in Mathematics*, 33: 171–202.

Willer, D. (1992) A Comment on Developed Theory and Theory Development. *Sociological Theory*, 10(1): 106–10.

Williams, M. (2000) Social Research – The Emergence of a Discipline? *International Journal of Social Research Methodology*, 3(2): 157–66.

Wright, B.D. and Linacre, J.M. (1989) Observations are Always Ordinal; Measurements, However, Must be Interval. *Archives of Physical Medicine and Rehabilitation*, 70: 857–60.

Yates, S.J. (2004) *Doing Social Science Research*. London: Sage.

Yin, R.K. (1984) *Case Study Research: Design and Methods*. Beverly Hills, CA: Sage.

Yin, R.K. (1993) *Applications of Case Study Research*. Newbury Park, CA: Sage.

Yin, R.K. (1994) *Case Study Research: Design and Methods* (2nd edn). Newbury Park, CA: Sage.

Zarb, G. (1992) On the Road to Damascus: First Steps Towards Changing the Relations of Disability Research Production. *Disability, Handicap and Society*, 7(2): 125–38.

Zuber-Skerritt, O. (1992) *Professional Development in Higher Education*. London: Kogan Page.

Zucker, D.M. (2001) Using Case Study Methodology in Nursing Research. *The Qualitative Report*, 6(2). Retrieved 21 June 2006 (available online at http://www.nova.edu/ssss/QR/QR6-2/zucker.html).

Index